Leach Library
276 Mammoth Road
Londonderry, NH 03053
Adult Services 432-1132
Children's Services 432-1127

POWER YOUR PROFITS

POWER YOUR PROFITS

How to Take Your Business from $10,000 to $10,000,000

SUSIE CARDER

ATRIA BOOKS
New York   London   Toronto   Sydney   New Delhi

An Imprint of Simon & Schuster, Inc.
1230 Avenue of the Americas
New York, NY 10020

Copyright © 2020 by Susie Carder

Several client names have been changed to
protect their identities, but their situations are real.

First Atria Books hardcover edition May 2020

ATRIA BOOKS and colophon are trademarks of Simon & Schuster, Inc.

For information about special discounts for bulk purchases,
please contact Simon & Schuster Special Sales at
1-866-506-1949 or business@simonandschuster.com.

The Simon & Schuster Speakers Bureau can bring authors to your live event.
For more information, or to book an event, contact the Simon & Schuster Speakers
Bureau at 1-866-248-3049 or visit our website at www.simonspeakers.com.

Interior design by Jill Putorti

Manufactured in the United States of America

1 3 5 7 9 10 8 6 4 2

Library of Congress Cataloging-in-Publication Data has been applied for.

ISBN 978-1-9821-3768-7
ISBN 978-1-9821-3770-0 (ebook)

CONTENTS

Foreword by Lisa Nichols   vii

Introduction: Putting on Your Big Girl Panties   1

Chapter One: Mastering Your Mindset   9

Chapter Two: Leading Your Business with Power   43

Chapter Three: Planning Your Profitable Business   67

Chapter Four: Selecting and Building Your Team   119

Chapter Five: Operations Infrastructure   143

Chapter Six: Selling Your Products and Services   173

Chapter Seven: Marketing and Sharing Your Message   215

Chapter Eight: Math Is Money and Money Is Fun   243

Chapter Nine: You Got This!   285

Acknowledgments   301

Appendices   305

Notes   313

Index   315

FOREWORD

I feel like through this book I'm sharing my very personal, precious God-appointed gem with the world.

When I first saw Susie, I was attracted to her light and her energy. She was a badass—a woman who made me stop and say "Wow." What endeared me to her that day was that when I asked her to share her knowledge of wealth and prosperity with me, she asked me to be an auntie to her two African American daughters. She told me she could show them what it meant to be a great woman, but not a powerful black woman. So she asked me to be their auntie, and I accepted. I have to tell you that one request literally melted my heart.

Most people who know me or have seen me speak have heard my story about meeting Susie. I knew I had the gift of oration, the gift of connection, and the gift of inspiration, along with the dream of building a business to serve and inspire others to transform their lives. But I did not know how to pull the pieces together. Then Susie walked into my life.

Even then, God was thinking of what we could do together in the world because we were breaking molds in each other's lives. At that time,

I had never been asked to help a white woman. And I had never asked a white woman to mentor or coach me. There was a dividing line in society that I had never crossed. I know others had, but I had not. Then this blond-haired, hazel-eyed woman came into my life and became the catalyst and one of the cornerstones of my business turnaround and the success of my career.

Susie helped me to transform my life and my business into the success it is today. I literally traveled from welfare to Wall Street. I think people would call my journey from bootstrap to big time, where I was able to power my profits, and Susie was the light on my path.

Over the years, Susie became nothing short of oxygen for me. I say that because when I could not find my own strength to continue to see possibility in myself, she lent me hers. She was willing to pardon my limited mindset and repeatedly teach me the skill set and mindset that I needed to build my dream. I was born to be a speaker. But Susie taught me how to be an effective, results-driven, outcome-producing CEO. My gift has made me popular, but my CEO skill set has made me a successful businesswoman.

Susie is the one who taught me how to add systems and infrastructure to my gifts. She taught me how to understand and use numbers in my business, rather than being afraid of them. She helped me heal my relationship with money. If you are willing to trust where she is, instead of being committed to staying where you are, she can take you to the place you say you want to go.

Susie awakens something in you. She is an inspired teacher, trainer, and coach with the ability to fill the gap if you listen, implement, and stay in action on what she's taught you. If you do, your life will transform; it cannot stay the same.

Looking back, the best part about working with Susie, as I hope you discover, was her ability to show me what I wasn't seeing. She lit up my blind spots and showed me how to put the pieces of the puzzle together.

And when that happened, I started getting results. I discovered that I wasn't a victim of my business; I was driving my business. She moved me from the backseat to the driver's seat of my business. That was the most exciting part.

What Susie teaches you is not going to be absorbed overnight. She's not going to give you something that you consume, digest, and wake up knowing all the systems for. You have to walk with it; you have to be with it; and you have to sign up to be her student for a while.

She makes the complex seem easy, and she makes the numbers fun. But the strength of the system she helps you build makes your business sustainable and larger than you. Beware of the hardest part of working with Susie: she holds the bar pretty damn high. Believe me, she had me running. She will stretch you and encourage you to dig down deeper and reach up higher than you ever imagined. But don't you owe it to yourself to build something that can evolve into a legacy versus just a moment?

I was so fortunate to have Susie as my coach. I am a coach today because a coach stepped into my life and disrupted it so beautifully. I never planned to have coaching as a part of my business. It wasn't until Susie became an intricate part of transforming my life that I felt like I owed it to other entrepreneurs to give them the gift I received.

I trust that you will receive this gift of being guided by Susie. What she has in store for you is worth every ounce of your energy, every minute of your time, and every bit of your attention. And you are worth it.

—Lisa Nichols,
bestselling author,
CEO of Motivating the Masses Inc.

PUTTING ON YOUR BIG GIRL PANTIES

This book is for all of us who have tried to bootstrap, bubble-gum, and duct-tape our way to figuring out how to run a successful business. It is also for those who want to make money for themselves instead of working for others, but don't know where to begin. It is for those who have grown a business to a certain height, but can't seem to get over the hump and take it to the next level. And it is for every entrepreneur in between.

In this book, I share the journey of how I mapped out building four multimillion-dollar businesses. I started from scratch and bootstrapped my way to powerful profits, but it wasn't always easy. I didn't have money and a plan handed to me with the encouragement to "go out there and have fun." Nobody told me "we've got your back." I didn't have examples to follow because my parents weren't entrepreneurs. And I didn't start with a business degree, or go to a formal business school.

I learned everything about business through trial and a lot of error, books, seminars, audio programs, online programs, and hiring business coaches. I have taken courses in sales, communication, leadership, management, business strategy, diversity, social media, and personal development, to name a few. I basically learned what I needed when I needed it. If I experienced a legal issue, I learned about business law, so I could protect my business and its assets. If I had issues with employees, I took a course on human resource management so I could grow as a manager and leader.

BE HUNGRY

Looking back on my childhood, I didn't know what an entrepreneur was, but I knew I had to be one. I was hungry, both figuratively and literally, because I grew up with eight brothers and sisters—my small house had nine kids in it, including me. My dad was in the military and my stepmom was a seamstress, so we were a blue-collar family. Finance was not discussed in my house; it was a dirty word. If we ran out of food before our bimonthly shopping trip to the commissary, meals were thin until the next payday. From an early age, I learned not to ask for money because there wasn't any. If I wanted to go to cheer camp or take gym-nastics, I had to figure out a way to make it happen.

I became entrepreneurial without even realizing it. At home, we used to make cookies in three-dozen batches. Each of us kids would have a certain number of cookies. My siblings would gobble their cookies rather quickly, but I would wait until everyone else ate theirs, and use mine for bartering. I would trade my cookies to avoid my chores. Our chore list would rotate each week, but washing dishes for eleven people was a tough one. So I would say, "Wash my dishes and I'll give you a cookie." It worked every time. I did the same thing with my Halloween and Easter candies—hold and trade. That is why I am still not big on sweets!

Back then, I knew that we were lucky to get school clothes; even if they were from thrift stores or yard sales, they were still new to me. Everything in my family was a hand-me-down, and with six girls and three boys, there weren't a lot of extras—even your underwear was a hand-me-down. I knew that I had to make some money so I could buy my own underwear! I didn't want to go to the Goodwill and buy my school clothes; I didn't want to go to my friends' yard sales and buy their used clothes. I wanted my own clothes and I wanted to be able to buy what I wanted when I wanted.

When I was a young girl, my dad shared this with me, "Sue, you can have whatever you want. Just get a job, work hard, and earn it."

GET YOUR PANTIES IN A BUNCH

At twelve years old, you had to be creative to make money. I sold catalog products door-to-door, but I lived in a poor community, so that didn't last long. I cleaned houses, washed windows, did yard work, did laundry, and babysat to start rubbing nickels together. I remember the first time I made money: I went down to the dime store, and they had a bin of panties for a dollar a pair. I bought ten pairs! They had flowers on them and were in different colors. They were beautiful. For the first time, I had something of my own I didn't have to share with anyone else. (I had to hide them from my sisters because when you have a family that big, everything is fair game.)

My mom made all of the school clothes we didn't get secondhand. She was a seamstress in a men's clothing store, so the fabric was cheap. But I wanted store-bought clothes that still had tags on them. I wanted something from a store like Contemporary Fashion, which was trendy, yet inexpensive. I realized that if I wanted nice things, if I wanted anything, I just had to figure out how to make the money to get it. That began my journey into entrepreneurship and my lifelong quest of visualizing, dreaming, and creating my future. I learned that everything you want is at your fingertips, and everything you desire you could create with a vision, a plan, and a strategy.

Growing up in a big family, there were a lot of conversations, but we never discussed college. My dad's rule was that when you turned eighteen, you were supposed to get a job or get married. That was a woman's role: find a good husband. Well, I didn't know what a good husband was. At seventeen, I moved out. I figured it was one less mouth to feed for my parents, and that was a good thing, right? So I wrote a note, packed up my things, and moved in with six roommates: five boys and a girlfriend of mine. We shared a room. Wow, what an eye-opening experience that was. I worked nights at the Kentucky Fried Chicken and went to high school during the day. Needless to say, my parents were a little upset with me leaving a note and just leaving, but I thought I was doing them a favor.

FINDING MY GROOVE

My life forever changed when I went to cosmetology school after graduating from high school. I always loved making people beautiful; it was fun, glamorous, and exciting. It was beautiful. Everybody dressed up, and it felt very "Hollywood." It was something that I really wanted to be a part of, and I was really good at it. I was great at making friends with clients and they gave amazing tips! I was blown away by how generous people could be when they felt served. The benefit of growing up in a big family is it that it came natural to me to take care of people.

The challenge as a hairdresser was you had to build a clientele, you had to market yourself, you had to upsell, and you had to work as fast as your mouth could talk to make any money. I won't lie; for those first several years I was on the struggle bus. I was always working another job just to make ends meet. But I knew if I could figure the business part out, I could make a lot of money. So over the next few years (and really, every year since), I studied. I went to the library, to bookstores, and business seminars. I started to understand the process of building a business.

The biggest learning experience came in my twenties, when I hired a coach who charged me more than a thousand dollars to help me with my business. As a single mom raising two kids, I was scared to death to invest that money in myself, but I knew I didn't know how to grow a business. I have always been willing to bet on me! I believed if I just knew what to do, I could make it happen.

I will share a little more about what my coach helped me to do in the next chapter, but I know that was the *best* investment I ever made. It made me realize that I could pay experts to guide me and shorten my learning curve. I also realized that when I had a business plan and accountability, I could excel. That year I went from making $25,000 to more than $75,000! The following year my sales doubled again, and the year after, they doubled again. I started to see that this business thing was *fun*!

TIME TO HAVE SERIOUS FUN

Eventually I was making $250,000 a year as a hairdresser and only working three days per week. The next step was to be an owner. I didn't understand what it took to be a salon owner, but hindsight is 20/20. The investment I needed to buy the salon was $30,000, so I created a business contract to borrow the money from my father-in-law, and I agreed to pay him back with interest.

It was a beautiful salon. The seller had sunk $150,000 into it, but she couldn't make it work. My business partner and I knew we could do better. We created a business plan and did all the financial projections. We knew that we could make it a one-million-dollar salon. It took us two years with only six styling stations, but we hit our mark by changing the business from a booth rental scenario with independent contractors to a commission salon. For context, at the time, the average salon that produced a million dollars had thirty technicians and/or stations. Switching up the model, we could increase that significantly. In our salon, we decided that stylists would get a commission on everything that they made instead of paying for their spot or their booth. Previously, as a landlord, you could only earn about $7,200 a week by renting out each chair for about $300 a week. Using the commission method, we increased our profits dramatically! In San Diego at that time, 80 percent of the salons and spas were staffed by independent contractors. So what we were doing was definitely against the grain at the time, but it worked out in the long run.

As is true with each business I have created since then, I started that business with the idea that I would sell it. (I had no idea who would ever buy it, but I built it with a buyer in mind.) I would teach the technicians what it took me years to learn how to do! Each business brought me one step closer to financial freedom. Each business taught me the skills I needed to go to the next level. I went on to build the largest training and development company in the beauty industry by teaching others how to run a salon effectively. I also built the largest online platform for the beauty industry and won the Microsoft Innovative Business Award. Since then I have sold businesses for millions of dollars and helped others to grow theirs by millions. That's how I became *the* profit coach!

My clients would come to me with any number of problems. Many were not generating the money they felt they could be, others were making lots of money but had nothing to show for it, and others just had no idea how their businesses were doing. When I helped them create systems that allowed them to make more money, keep more money, and track their money, they started calling me their profit coach. It really rang true for me. I not only help my clients to create more money in their businesses, I also help them to grow their financial wealth, overall prosperity, and business profitability.

WHAT'S NEXT FOR YOU

This book will help you to develop your plan, as I hold your hand through the journey of building your own empire! Through these pages you will realize that wealth is your birthright, something I've turned into a slogan because I believe it so deeply. Everyone is born with the capacity for greatness. Yet it is something that we build; no one hands it to you, and no one knights you! *You* choose it, you cultivate it, and you generate it.

In the very first chapter, you will realize that in order to create something new, you must let go of the old you. The old beliefs, the old patterns, and your old self-sabotage have to go. I want to take out what's hard and put the *fun* into business. Let me tell you, nothing is more fun than making the money you dreamed of making. Nothing is better than hitting the goals you put on your dream board and your goal board. Nothing is more satisfying than looking all those haters in the eye and saying, "I DID IT!"

This can go either way: it can be a good read, or it can be the life-changing experience you have been looking for. In each chapter, I will share "client spotlights" that show by example how some of the strategies I discuss were implemented by my clients and the impact that they had. (Several client names have been changed to protect their identities, but their situations are real.) This means they worked through an issue by applying what they learned, and you can, too!

I encourage you to keep a pencil at your side as you read. Make notes, answer questions, and do the assessments in each chapter. The "Step into the Big Time" sections of each chapter will help you to be honest about where you are so you can move to where you would rather be as a successful entrepreneur. If you do the work throughout this book, you will get the dynamic results that many of my clients have achieved.

I have worked with thousands of clients all over the world, and it's the same everywhere. Business is business is business! We just have a few formulas and projections we need to create, and a few systems to put in place, and you can be on your way to a profitable business. This is freeing. You deserve it. I know that if you follow the plan, your world will change forever! Mine did.

Chapter One

MASTERING YOUR MINDSET

Back in 2005, I received an offer to buy my business for millions of dollars. I had started as a hairdresser making twenty-five thousand dollars per year, and I created a beauty industry giant that sold for millions! Can you imagine? I always built my businesses as if they would one day be sold and now that time had finally come. When I started, I had no idea who would buy it, but putting a plan in place and building business systems helped me to live that American dream. All of the envisioning, goal setting, hard work, commitment, and dedication had come to fruition.

Do you have a business idea that you want to get off the ground? Do you have an existing business and a dream without a clear path to how you will make it come true? Are you working hard in your business without backup and support from others? I know what that's like. Why would a beauty school graduate who grew up poor ever have hope of growing million-dollar businesses? That is exactly what I did. And now you can, too. This book will help you to map that out for yourself. This book is the journey; it leaves the bread crumbs on the path to powerful profitability.

It took me twenty years to build three multimillion-dollar businesses of my own while creating millions for others. This single mom with two little girls who was once afraid to invest in her business is now helping others—helping you—to unpack the journey so you won't have to wait so long to achieve the same results. I am going to share with you the lessons I had to learn the hard way. I am going to challenge you to take the actions that I know will lead you to business success.

You may still have obstacles to overcome or issues to work through. Still, I know that though we may have limiting beliefs that threaten to block our paths, we can knock them down. We can let go of the hurts, mental blocks, and bonds that hold us back. We can drop the baggage and have the business of our wildest dreams. It all starts in our minds.

WHERE OUR MINDSETS COME FROM

When I was six years old, my mom dropped me and my sisters off at my dad's house and said, "Oh, I'll be back."

It was Easter. I had a little basket, and I wore a pretty dress. My mom said she would be back for me, so I sat on the front porch in my cute little dress and waited for her. I really thought she would be back.

After a few hours, my dad came out on the porch and told me that I should come inside because she wasn't coming back.

"No, she'll be back," I insisted. "I'll wait here."

"Honey, she's not coming back for you. Come inside."

"No, she said she's coming back, so she's coming back."

After a while, I finally went into the house. "Okay," I conceded, "we're spending the night, but tomorrow, she'll be back."

The next day I went out outside and sat on the porch. My dad came outside and said, "She's not coming back."

"No, she's coming back."

He said, "Honey, she's not coming back. She left you and your sisters; she's not coming back."

For years, I just remembered sitting on that porch. I quit saying "she's coming back," and I quit waiting for her to. She really did leave me. That experience made me believe that if I were better, if I were good enough, if I were the perfect child, then she wouldn't have left me.

Beliefs like that can work for you and they can work against you. On the one hand, they will make you beat yourself up. Can you relate? Were you ever told that you didn't matter or you were not enough? On the other hand, beliefs like that can make you fight to be better than the best. You don't want to feel bad about yourself, so you work harder than anyone else to stay on top. It becomes the classic double-edged sword.

GRABBING YOUR BAGGAGE

Many of us pick up and carry baggage, hurts, and limiting beliefs from our childhoods that impact our current success. If you feel that you are not worthy, you may unconsciously block your own success at every opportunity. If you don't choose to let go of what no longer serves you, it can keep you from your destiny, your greatness. It may also blind you to the opportunities that are all around you. I often say that your net worth will only go as high as your self-worth. If you are feeling down on yourself, you might not grow as far as you are able. That baggage may hold you down. For example, if you don't believe you are worthy of your hourly rate or your salary, you may lack confidence in a conversation with a potential client, and instead of showing them your value and asking them to pay it, you just tell them about your services and hope they will decide to buy. You won't ask them to buy; you just hope they will and wonder why they don't. Lots of money will slip through your fingers that way.

As that little girl abandoned on the front porch, I grabbed the baggage of not being worthy. I wasn't enough to make my mother come back. As I grew up, not being enough became a theme, and my behaviors and actions reflected that, even though I did not realize it at first. My double-edged sword came out as always striving to be better. I would say, "I'll show you."

"I'll prove to my family. I'll prove to my dad. I am somebody." On the flip side of the sword, life kicked me in the face when I chose unhealthy relationships. My marriage was not healthy—I just patterned what my parents did, which was a mess.

That baggage kept me from trusting friends or people in general, and I was slow to let people into my circle. When people did enter my life, I was generous to a fault because I didn't want people to leave. I wanted them to stay and love me. I didn't want to be left again. I also began to believe that if I could make enough money, then I would be good enough. If I had the right job or business, then I would be good enough. If I had the right car, then I would be good enough. If I had the right house in the right neighborhood—you fill in the rest.

It was all the material things you think are going to make you good enough, but that's just an empty shell game until you get to the root cause. I just kept trying to fill this void. This was true in both my personal and business life. Instead of letting poor-performing employees go, I would work harder and take up their slack so I didn't have to fire them. I wanted them to like me, so I didn't do what was best for the business; I did what fed my limiting beliefs about myself. Actions like that cost me in both time and money.

If that little girl didn't learn to release her baggage by digging to the root cause, she could have allowed the feeling of not being enough to keep her from her greatness. She might have played small and decided she couldn't strive to make lots of money in business because no one would love her enough to pay her—she didn't have enough value. But instead, over time, and through personal development coaching, she chose to use those limiting beliefs as fuel to fight to be better than the best.

I am not that little girl anymore. But having worked through and released that baggage doesn't mean that my mind chatter doesn't get loud on occasion, trying to tell me that I am not enough. Now I know how to turn it off. Now I can thank it for sharing, but send it away so that it doesn't negatively impact me. I now recognize when that negative mind chatter arises, and I know that I am the cause of it. When I take responsibility for that chatter, I can do something to change it. I have control.

That ability to shift my mindset in a way that serves me didn't come naturally. I have been working on it since the early nineties. Since then, I have been learning how to transform my thoughts. I've learned how to drive those thoughts that become my actions, and to watch those actions lead to my results. Personal development is not something you "do" once and then forget. It is a continuous learning opportunity that allows you to walk on a path of success. If I am not involved in some form of personal development, I could stay stuck inside of mediocrity. And I don't want to be.

The intention of this book is not to work through all of the personal development tools available, but I encourage you to tap into resources that can help you to release, let go, and open up to growth. This is important because if you bring the wrong mindset to planning your business, you will not be as successful, or you will sabotage that success. You cannot have a mindset of lack and limitation and expect abundance and great opportunity. Alignment of positive thought and action will be required.

#MondayMotivation
"If I am not involved in some form of personal development,
I could stay stuck inside of mediocrity. And I don't want to be."
—SUSIE CARDER

Is there something that happened in your life that you recognize as deadweight? Is there something that has held you back from the success you want and deserve? Whether you feel something was done to you, or you're stuck in a negative behavior you can't break out of, it is time to recognize you are responsible. You may not be to blame, but you are responsible for how it impacts your life. If you continue to see problems arise in your career or in meeting your goals, you must recognize that you are always there. Perhaps the common denominator is you.

That may sound harsh, especially if you feel that you were dealt a bad hand, but the sooner you realize it, the sooner you can understand its truth and then let it go. When you accept responsibility, you then have the power to change it. If it is always someone else's fault, that means you are powerless to make things different. "If only the economy weren't so bad" or "If only he didn't cheat me out of that deal" or "If only my parents had paid for my education" or any other hypothetical situation cannot absorb the blame for where you are in life. The blame game will never give you the power to make a change. Let go of the *if onlys* and complaining to take action to change your situation.

CLIENT SPOTLIGHT:
HOW NICOLE'S BAGGAGE WAS WEIGHING HER DOWN

I had a client named Nicole, who was an interior decorator. She came to me because she didn't believe in herself or her ability to make money from her business. Nicole's husband was a neurosurgeon, and she really didn't need to work, but she loved interior design and had been doing it for several years without making any money. She wanted to take things slow and be methodical as she proved to her husband, who thought of her business as a hobby, that she could generate enough money to take her family on a European vacation.

When I began working with Nicole, it became clear that her lack of confidence in herself made it difficult for her to charge what she needed to make any money. That was her mindset. She wasn't feeling valued and she didn't command value for her work. So our work started with some personal development. For example, I had her put a "badass list" together; it's a list of all the things that she'd accomplished, from her education to her awards to personal achievements. This helped Nicole to start owning her expertise. People weren't just hiring her, the person; they were paying for her skill set and her talent. Shifting that is one of the biggest and hardest parts we entrepreneurs face. We make it about us, and if we don't feel worthy, we don't command the fees we deserve.

After addressing this, step one is always the business plan. In the plan, we addressed questions like, what's your big why? You need something that is going to make you get out of bed in the morning. For Nicole, that was making her husband proud and her funding the European vacation.

Who's your ideal client? Nicole was serving friends, but not feeling comfortable charging them. The solution? Stop serving friends and join a networking group to meet those ideal clients who will see your value and be willing to pay for it. Nicole had to get comfortable asking them for money for what she was doing.

Through the planning, we did financial projections and figured out, based on her overhead, what we needed to charge. We determined her products and offerings, developed a marketing plan to spread the word, drew up a financial plan to pay for it and get paid, and then created the systems (like accounting and client management) to support her step-by-step growth. This written plan became her road map.

By Nicole sticking to her plan, going into networking groups and meeting more of her ideal clients, and being more comfortable asking for money, I helped her to grow her business to $50,000 in the first year, $150,000 in the second year, $300,000 in the third year, and to a European vacation in the fourth year! The right mindset, coupled with a plan, made all the difference.

BELIEF VERSUS ACTION IN CREATING
YOUR BUSINESS REALITY (E + R = O)

Think about this concept of responsibility for a moment: if there are others out there who were dealt the same bad hand as you, how come some of them are very successful, and you are not? They all experienced the same thing. Why aren't all businesses suffering in a down economy? Why do others have great strategic partnerships? How do some people find a way to work through school or win scholarships? How do some succeed without the degree? It was their response to life events that allowed them to have a different outcome.

In other words, what happens to you in life (E) generates your response (R), which determines your outcome (O). So, if your business isn't as successful as you want it to be, choose a different response to change the outcome. If you are not happy in the relationship you are in, and you normally just complain to your girlfriends, choose another response. If you don't want the same lackluster results (outcomes), change your response.

If you just stay in your present moment, believing this is all there is, you will not take the action required to produce a different result. And even more important, if you don't believe you can achieve different results, you probably won't. You bear more fruit from what you believe than from what you think. For example, if you think you want to make an extra six figures of business income, but you believe that you aren't good enough to make more than $100,000 per year, you may never reach those extra six figures. Or you might make the extra money, then sabotage yourself and squander it to get you back to your financial comfort zone. Your underlying beliefs are very strong and will determine your rate of success. Beliefs can propel you forward, but they can also hold you back.

Think of this formula whenever you get stuck in the mindset that you can't make something work: E + R = O. Events plus your response to them determines your outcome. Choose to think and do something different to reach a different result. Challenge your existing belief that has gotten you to where you are, and decide to change that belief so you can get to the next level. If, as you think about it, you recognize that you are holding on to a belief that does not serve you and won't help you to grow (like "I'll never find enough clients to make another thousand this month"), write that belief down. As you read it to yourself, ask if that is a true statement. If it is false, choose to release it and let it go. In this example, many people have been able to make an extra thousand dollars in a month, so it is possible. So that belief is false. Next, write down a new empowering statement to replace it. For example, "I easily attract all the clients I desire to reach my revenue goals."

OPEN YOUR MIND TO NEW POSSIBILITIES

Given that you are responsible for your life and your business's results (as author Joe Vitale says, "It's not your fault, but it is your responsibility"), you can now choose to allow yourself to grow a business with ease and joy. Sounds crazy, but it's true.

You might say, "I worked hard to get my business where it is. It's not all roses and unicorn farts, you know."

I know. I get it. I worked hard to create my first ten million—only to lose it and get it back again. I know that it is not always easy; I have the skinned knees to prove it.

But it is fun to know that I am responsible for my own results. When you finally get that and can say, "I really am the designer of my own future," it is powerful. I can say, "I have a high school education, and I am a multimillionaire." How does that happen? I could just have a minimum wage job. As the designer of my own future, who is not limited by my environment or my beliefs, I can ask, "What do I want to design? What do I want to create?" And then I can take action and do that!

That reminds me of something else that happened when I was a kid. I was in seventh grade. I remember going to my friend Joanie Ring's house. I grew up with nine brothers and sisters, so there were eleven people in our three-bedroom home. That was just normal for me. My other friends were in a similar situation but without as many kids.

Joanie was having a pool party. We went to her house. Everything was immaculate and pristine white. They had five bedrooms, and there were only two daughters living there with their parents! They had this big, beautiful pool. That day, to me, was the first time I saw possibilities. It was the first time I opened up to the thought, *What could life be like?* Thinking of my friend Joanie I said, "If she can do it, I can do it." (Never mind that her parents were the ones doing it!) In that moment, I embraced another possibility. It was vision boarding before it was a thing. I said, "Here's what I see," and I held on to that. I didn't want to live in my current circumstances; I wanted that new possibility.

So I set my life up from a very early age to say "What are the things that I like, and how do I get those?" There was no "I'm not going to get it." It was always "How do I get it? How much money do I need to make? What kind of job do I need to have?" And I set my mind to doing what it took to create the experience I wanted to have. I took responsibility, and I took action. I decided that I wasn't going to let my current situation affect my future realization.

STIRRING UP YOUR REBEL CHILD

Think back to a time in your youth where you had a spark of imagination or a dream so big that it bubbled up and made you smile. When we were kids, we had all these great dreams and aspirations. Then our influencers (parents, teachers, families, friends, and authority figures) chimed in and told us that it was not possible, that it's never been done before, or to stop dreaming and face "reality." What they didn't tell us is that we create our own reality. We bring about what we want to see in our lives or what we *expect* to see in our lives. So, as a child, if you expected that all you would see were the same struggles, the same poverty, and same disappointment as those around you, that might be where you ended up. But since you are reading this book, you obviously decided to see beyond that. You knew somewhere inside that you were destined for more. And you know what? You are. You can have it all.

You don't need my permission to do anything, but I want to give it to you anyway. You have the right to want whatever you want. You have the right to create an awesome business that you love and that your clients love working with. You have the ability to create success, abundance, and wealth beyond measure.

Stir up that rebel child who is not willing to settle, who loves dreaming of possibilities, and who has the desire, belief, and courage to stand up for what she believes in. I encourage you to stir up that rebel child when someone tells you that your business won't survive. Stir her up when someone doubts the value of your company. Stir that rebel child up when doubters try to tell you that you can't grow to the next level. Don't allow someone else's doubts to become beliefs for you. You can power your profits. And I am here to help you to do just that.

"Wealth is your birthright!"
—SUSIE CARDER

VISUALIZE YOUR BEST BUSINESS NOW

Take a moment to think of your business (your current one or a new one). If failure were not an option, and resources were infinite, what would your ideal business look like? Go ahead, close your eyes for a minute, and think about it. If you had all the resources in the world and the perfect team members and the ideal location and the perfect strategy, what would your business look like? What level of sales are you reaching? What kind of clients are you serving? What stages are you appearing on? What systems do you have in place that allow you to work on your business and not in it? Also, look ahead and visualize how many team members you have, what they say about working with your business, how many products or units you are selling, what vision of the business you are fulfilling, and how your customers say they feel when they experience your product.

Take some time to think about those questions, and write down your answers. Have fun with it and make it whatever you want to see.

_____

_____

_____

_____

_____

_____

_____

_____

_____

Writing these down will help you gain clarity and aid you in refining your mission statement in the planning chapter. If you can see your ideal business in your mind's eye, then you can start building the road map to having that ideal business.

#MondayMotivation

"The future you see is the future you get."

—ROBERT G. ALLEN

One great thing about visualizing your business at its peak (and writing it down) is that you can hold that vision and then ask yourself, "How did I get here?"

If you act with the end in mind, you will do what is necessary to create the vision you imagined at the outset. As Neville Goddard, a mid-twentieth-century thinker, said, "There is a wide difference between thinking *of* what you want in this world and thinking *from* what you want."[1] If you start with the end in mind, you are at your destination looking back to your present moment. You are thinking *from* what you want to create. Then you can follow the path that leads you there.

One of the primary reasons a business fails is lack of clear, concise goals and a plan to get there. If you have a clear vision of what you want to create in your business, and you establish a plan to take you there, you have every right to expect success. As you will learn in this book, I believe that having a detailed, written plan is critical to your success. And whether you are starting from scratch or you are starting anew, using what you learn herein will change that plan for the better.

Start that planning now by taking the time to see yourself and your business at its pinnacle. Use the exercise below as a thought starter and write down what that vision looks like and how you will feel when you reach it. Keep that written vision handy as you work through this book.

YOUR IDEAL BUSINESS—EXERCISE

Fill in the blanks below using your ideal business concept.

I am so grateful that one year from now (you can stretch this out if you want), my ideal business generates $_____ in annual revenue. My personal, annual salary from my business is $_____. I can make contributions (giving and tithing) of $_____ each year because of my success.

My "Big Why" for creating this awesome business was to:

_____

_____

My ideal clients are those who:

_____

_____

My clients love the products/services we provide, which include:

_____

_____

It feels so good to know that we are known in our community/across the nation/around the world for:

_____

_____

I love that this business allows me to have and feel:

_____

_____

_____

_____

Say to yourself, "Who could have known that this business would be so fun and exciting to be a part of while being so successful? I love the impact I am making in the world!" If you need more space to write about your fabulous business that brings you joy while you serve others, grab a journal or notebook that you can use as you work through this book. That way, you can keep all of your thoughts, ideas, and information together.

REPRESENTING YOUR VISION OF SUCCESS

It is not enough to have a goal of bootstrapping to the big time in your business. You have to be truly committed to achieving the results that you say you want. If you cannot see yourself becoming who you have to be to achieve your goals, you may never get there. Passion fuels the persistence required to persevere.

When I think about what matters to me and why I want to achieve my goals, I have three priorities: faith, family, and then my business/ career. I am not here just to work and have successful businesses. The beautiful thing for me is that my life purpose and my business are in alignment: they are one. That is not always true for everyone. When I took Barbara De Angelis's course, one of the things that really hit home with me was that sometimes your job allows you to live your purpose and sometimes your job is your purpose. During that time, my salon was my job or my investor; it funded my dream business, which was a training business.

A job is not a purpose for a lot of people. Some people get out of work every day and think, *I've got to go find something else*. Well, if your life's passion is working with youth at risk, or helping battered women, or saving the dolphins, your purpose may not be your job, but your job may allow you the financial ability to go live your purpose. And that's okay. As long as your purpose is incorporated in your everyday life, it need not be what you do for a living to pay the bills. You may even have to work two jobs to build your dream. I just happen to be lucky that my life purpose is now my job, and I designed it that way.

When I designed it, I didn't know how to pay for it or how to make it pay me. I didn't know the business side of empowering people. When I looked at what I loved doing, I just knew that I loved empowering people. Then I thought, *Well, how do you make money at that?* I had to learn about the education I needed now that I understood what my passion and my purpose was; I took courses in sales, leadership, communication, entrepreneurship, personality profiles, and strategic development. I learned all I could from business experts and library books to help me to live with passion and purpose, and yet I realized it didn't have to be my job.

In the marketplace right now, there's this pressure that your job has to make a profound difference. Well, does it? Can't you just volunteer at a shelter? What's that thing you love doing? Find it. Take a moment right now to center yourself and find a place of peace. Don't let an inner conflict distract your thoughts. In that quiet moment, ask yourself this: "What was I put on the earth for? How can I fulfill this purpose in my daily life?" Then be still and let the answers flow to you—listen. I believe that God's gift to me was my life and my gift back to God is what I do with my life. I do that with my job, with my community, with my children, and with my grandchildren. For some people, their work is not the vehicle of their purpose, and that's perfectly okay. There's holistic success that encompasses more than just our businesses. A holistic approach includes areas like emotional life, intellectual life, your spiritual side, your career, your financial health, parenting, and your love relationships. There is more to life than running a business, so be sure to look at what you want in all areas of your life.

If you are not sure that you are living your purpose, I encourage you to tap into personal development resources. Some of those that were helpful for me along the way are described below.

* *What Color Is Your Parachute?*[2] (http://www.parachutebook .com/)—A perennial bestselling book by Richard Bolles. As *Time* magazine has said, it "is about job-hunting and career-changing, but it's also about figuring out who you are as a person and what you want out of life."
* *The Passion Test*[3] (https://thepassiontest.com/)—The *New York Times* bestselling book by Janet and Chris Atwood. It is "[a] clear, simple, and effective method to help you identify your core passions so you can create the fulfilling life you deserve" (John Gray, Ph.D.).

You can find these books in your local library, on their websites, or at book retailers. These resources, along with other personal development work, can help you to identify your passion and purpose. I know that when I read the *Parachute* book, it really helped me to look at my skills from another perspective. It asks questions and says, "Don't worry about your education," as relates to potential skill sets. This gave me the freedom to say, "Oh, okay. If I could be anything . . ." And it opened me to seeing that I could be a speaker, even though I was a hairdresser at that time. I was making a ton of money as a hairdresser, but I was bored, and I didn't know what else I could do because I didn't have a formal education. That book opened my eyes to new possibilities.

I loved talking to people and loved making people feel great about themselves, so being a speaker was a good fit for me. It fired me up. When I considered being a speaker, my first question was "What would I even speak on? I'm a hairdresser." So I decided to start speaking about beauty in the workplace to build my hairdressing business. The *Parachute* book encouraged me to just get out there and speak.

Then, I started thinking, *Where do my clients hang out?* And I realized that most of my ideal clients who were paying good money for their hair were working at corporations. So I said, "I need to get into some conference rooms." I had to figure out how to talk to these women while they were at work. That's when I thought of "lunch and learns." I would contact a business, offer a free lunchtime session on how your professional presence helps you earn at least 15 percent more income, and the rooms would fill up. That way, I could talk to fifty women at a time and get five clients out of it. The average earnings per client were $175 each once they came into the salon, so even though the lunch-and-learns were free, I still made money.

I constantly challenged myself to win more and more clients at each session. I would say "That was great; how can I do better?" Then I would list three things I liked about the experience and one thing I could improve upon. In the beginning, the three good things were:

1. I showed up
2. I didn't vomit
3. I got clients

The one thing I could improve upon was my speaking ability, because I sucked! I needed to be more prepared and I wanted to be in front of more people, faster.

That's how I started speaking. It wasn't a big and glamorous beginning, but it turned on something in me that led to personal fulfillment and business success. It was also the catalyst to my becoming a profit coach who created six-, seven-, and eight-figure businesses. Had I not taken that step to explore speaking, from right where I was at that time, I may not have come to fulfill my purpose. I found that I loved speaking and sharing and educating others, and it has led me on an exciting journey that allows me to help awesome entrepreneurs like you.

But what if you discover your purpose, and it has nothing to do with this business that you started reading this book to take to the next level? Where do you go with that? Be open to change. Nothing has to be written in stone, and it is never too late to get in alignment with your purpose. Check out the next client spotlight, and allow it to give you courage to make a change.

CLIENT SPOTLIGHT: DAVID IS CHANGING LANES

"David" (not his real name) is a client I met at a retreat. He was an eye doctor—an ophthalmologist. He had just signed up for coaching, and we did a lot of personal development in the retreat. He said he listened to his inner voice, and it told him, "You're not happy at this job. You need to sell your business."

He had a million-dollar practice! He had hired me to build it to the next level. He later wrote and said, "I sold my practice. I got out of the relationship I was in for eight years. I sold all my property, and I'm now I'm just traveling the world to figure out what's next for me."

He learned what he did not want and was willing to look inside and make changes so he could find what he did want. Now, that is courageous!

Tapping into your purpose doesn't have to be so dramatic, but the joy you will experience aligning your purpose and passion will be well worth any transition you have to make to get there. If each step you take in your life and in your business taps into what brings you joy and fulfillment, you will be successful. That great feeling you carry with you will overflow into other areas of your life and create that holistic success you deserve.

In contrast, if all you do is go through life living by the "should" on your shoulders, you may never experience the joy and success that you seek. "You should do this," or "You should do that" because of the business you have or the family you have or because of the place that you live. Let go of the *shoulds* and jump into your desires, your passion, and your purpose. Let those positive aspects drive you instead of being forced down a path of shoulds. You have the permission to be, do, or have whatever you want, so go for it.

LOOK BEFORE YOU LEAP

What if you discover, like David in the spotlight above, that you are not working in a business that fulfills your passion or purpose, but you want to be? Remember, sometimes what you do at your job will influence how you express your purpose, so you don't have to immediately jump ship and create a business to make them one and the same. Many people love cooking and want to make sure everyone has food in their belly, but it doesn't mean they will be successful in running a restaurant. You have to look before you leap.

One way to do that is by doing a mini-business plan with your business idea. It is actually more of a feasibility study. You look at all the strengths and weaknesses of the business concept before you invest a lot of time and money into it. It is like testing the waters before you jump in the pool. Once you determine that the idea looks good enough to pursue, then you do the full business plan that I discuss in Chapter 3—"Planning Your Profitable Business." If it does not look like a viable idea, this is still good news because you didn't put tons of money and effort into it only to have it fail.

Much like in a business plan, some of the items you will evaluate in your feasibility study include:

* Defining your business concept
* Identifying the business mission, goals, and objectives
* Deciding what your business management needs (solo, team, external support)
* Best business structure (sole proprietorship, LLC, corporation)
* Figuring out the products and services your customers want and are willing to buy, along with their sourcing, benefits, and proprietary status
* Determining production and operation needs, including suppliers and distribution
* Finding a space to work or house equipment, etc.
* Defining your target market and identifying market trends

* Researching your competitors and market appeal
* Evaluating your pricing strategies, production and sales volumes, and payment policies
* Figuring out start-up costs and what it will take to break even

After you have looked at each of these areas, you can then reflect over your research and assess the strengths of the business concept, its weaknesses, improvements to the concept, worst-case scenarios, and finally, its chance of success or failure. Don't be afraid to say it is a "no-go." You don't want to turn your passion into drudgery with no chance of survival. If this concept is a "no-go," brainstorm other ways you can tap into your passion. There is more than one way to do most things.

If your feasibility study shows you have a great chance of success, get fired up and read through the rest of this book so you can plan your successful venture and put the systems in place that will allow it to be most successful.

LISTEN TO YOUR DISSATISFACTION

If you are a natural pessimist like me (surprised?), you may know what you don't want before you learn what you do want. If you listen to your dissatisfaction, it will show you what you don't want so you can flip it to what you do want.

For example, the Contrast to Clarity[4] exercise in the *Live Your Best Life Now* course helps you to catalog what you don't want in a particular category, say "Your Ideal Business," and then turn it around to expose what you do want. See below for a sample of the handout.

**Contrast to
Clarity Worksheet**

My Ideal _____

Contrast (*what I don't like*)	Clarity (*what I do like*)
1.	1.
2.	2.
3.	3.
4.	4.
5.	5.
6.	6.
7.	7.
8.	8.
9.	9.
10.	10.

© 2017 Sue Ascioti-Plange and Tanya Brockett

On the left side of the handout, you list all the things you don't want or like in your business. Complete this list, item by item, until you have exhausted what you don't want to see in your ideal business. As an example, you might write down some of the following contrasts about your ideal business:

* I don't like working with clients who can't afford my services.
* I don't want to borrow money for new equipment purchases.
* I don't like not knowing where I stand financially every month.
* I don't like being the technician *and* the rainmaker for the business.

Then, on the other side of the handout, opposite each item of contrast, you write down the opposite. You will write what you want to see instead of the contrast. For example:

* I love working with clients who see my value and are willing to pay for it.
* I create sufficient cash flow to self-finance equipment purchases.
* I have an accounting system that allows me to review financial reports each month with ease.
* I attract qualified, motivated team members to provide excellent service to my clients.

These are just examples, but you get the picture. You want to write your Clarity statements in the positive, instead of negating the negative. For example, instead of "I won't work with deadbeat clients," you could say what we used above, "I love working with clients who see my value and are willing to pay for it." It shares what you want to experience as if it were already so. Using the financial clarity statement above, if you don't have the accounting system in place, one of your milestones for the business can be to select, install, and maintain an accounting system in your business, and create the operating procedures to produce meaningful financial reports each month. The work to do so in the short term will pay off for you in the long term.

The same approach can be taken for each area of your life: your family, your spiritual life, your passions, and more. If you naturally tend to point out the things you don't like in your life, this exercise can help you to turn those around to expose what you do want. Once you know that, you can take action toward your newly defined purpose or goals.

ANOTHER WAY TO SEE SUCCESS ALL AROUND YOU

We are all more than just what we do. Life is not all about working, so it is important to look at several areas around you when visualizing your success. When I was running my salon, I wrote down my vision. I wrote down what I wanted to see in my life. That included what kind of clients I would have, what kind of house I would live in, what kind of money I wanted to make, and I set my goals around that vision.

I shared earlier that my priorities were to my faith first, my family second, and my career third. Those are (still) my priorities. But then I also looked at my education, my health and well-being, and my finances and used those six areas to set goals that allowed me to move forward in my business and life.

To do this, I used those six areas and I wrote down my big why—why was it important for me to have success in these areas? Then the second piece was to ask, "What are all the goals in this area?" Then, from the goal, I broke it down into milestones and actions—what were the things that I needed to do to make those happen? Thinking with the end in mind, what does it look like when I've succeeded in these areas? Use the following form to do the same. (First, you might want to copy it for each of the six areas in your life.)

Priority Area: _____

My Big Why: _____

Goals in This Area:

_____

_____

_____

_____

_____

Milestones and Actions for These Goals:

_____

_____

_____

_____

_____

_____

_____

_____

_____

The goals change for me all the time. I evaluate every year in every area. I started way back in my twenties, but still, to this day, I go through this process. Though I now have twelve areas that I look at, for probably up until the last ten years it was just those six areas. When you do an exercise like this, most of us can say "I want this, and I want that," but the hard part is figuring out the how. How do I get that? This is where I ask, "What actions do I need to put in place to hit my goals?"

Here you want to look at the baby steps so you don't get overwhelmed with the "bigness" of your goals. Break it down into goals and milestones. For example, on these pages I want to write a book that will make a big impact on people's lives. But there is so much I want to share. Instead of being overwhelmed by all the information and advice I have to offer from my twenty-plus years of experience, I'm just taking it a chapter at a time. I don't have to look at the whole thing. Milestone number one is to write chapter number one; milestone number two is to write chapter number two, and so on. I can have my completion date in mind and take a small chunk at a time.

To keep my book-publishing goal in front of me every day, I created a visual representation of it I could check in with on a regular basis. I took a book off of my shelf, covered it with my mock-up cover that says it is a *New York Times* bestseller, and set it on my desk. I look at it every single day, so that I am reminded of my goal and the steps I need to take to make it happen.

You can do the same thing. You can write your goals out and post them in a place where you will see them every day. You can put them into visualizations—whether that's a digital visual board that you can see on your computer or a physical vision board on your wall—and create a representation of what it is that you're trying to achieve. You need to look at it every day and not just shove it in the drawer and never see it again. Don't write it on scraps of paper that you're going to lose. Keep your goals in your sight so you are reminded of them frequently.

BRIDGING THE GAP ON YOUR ROAD MAP

After you Step into the Big Time at the end of this chapter, you will come to know where you are, and where you want to be, and begin to recognize the gap between the two. This is not a scary thing! This is juicy, because then you will know what you need to do to move forward. This information is so valuable. You have eliminated a blind spot, so you can now do something about it. Working with a coach is critical here.

As I first shared with you in the Introduction, when I was in my twenties, I went from $75,000 to $250,000 as a hairdresser because I invested in a coach. I was a single mom at the time and my kids were my "big why." There was no back door for me. What I find is that a lot of entrepreneurs have a back door. They have a spouse, they have a job, they have this back door that says, "Oh, if this thing doesn't work, I could still pay my bills cause I have this job or I have a husband or I have a wife." So when I look at what makes some entrepreneurs succeed and some fail, the ones who don't give themselves a back door, like me, don't have a choice. They just have to succeed. Right? I had to succeed. I refused to be in poverty just because I grew up that way. I had to figure this out.

I wanted to step it up a notch, I had no back door, I had a why that was big enough, and I loved what I did. Yet there was always another ladder to climb—another mountain to reach—that made me say "Oh, I want to do that next. Oh, I want to have that." You are always growing then because in order to take the next steps to reach the next level, there is something more you have to do or more you have to bring out of yourself in order to achieve that. That is where the coach came in for me.

At that time, I think my coach's fee was around $1,000 a month. That was a lot of money for me. I was a single mom, raising two kids with no child support, so $1,000 a month was the difference between having day care or not. It was the difference between having groceries or not. But I knew I either had to change careers or change the way I did business because I couldn't live off $75,000 a year in Southern California with two little kids.

The first thing my coach had me do was to write a business plan. We nailed down who my ideal client was and who my current client was, and we found a gap. The clients that I wanted had money to burn, and my current clients were coupon clippers. They were always looking for a deal. So we created what we now call our client avatar. For me, that was a woman who was in a two-income household with children. She worked, she was a professional, and she had to look good. She colored her hair, she was really into her image, and she was maintaining her hair on a regular basis. Identifying my ideal client really gave me clarity between what I had and what I needed.

Then she put together a financial spreadsheet of what it would look like month over month and broke it down to how many salon clients I needed to see. Then we started projecting. If I wanted to make $100,000 (my first goal), how many clients did I need to see each week and month and how much income did I need to earn per client to make that happen?

That simple step got me really clear. She also recommended that I move locations, from Vista to Carlsbad, California, but I was too scared to do that because I didn't have the resources. I would've made more money if I had moved to Carlsbad, but I was too afraid because of the financial responsibility I had. My fear stopped me from really playing big, and I didn't have any friends or family in my corner saying "You can do it," and I wasn't getting child support or alimony or anything like that. I was the only breadwinner, and I was barely making enough to get by.

Thankfully, though, my coach helped me clarify what I wanted. When I think back to that experience, I realize I was hungry, and I was willing to pay a lot of money to this stranger to get a different result. At first, I wasn't making the kind of money I wanted to make. But having a coach flipped it for me.

#MondayMotivation

"A coach is someone who tells you what you don't want to hear, who has you see what you don't want to see, so you can be who you have always known you could be."

—TOM LANDRY

Sometimes it is hard to hear what you need to fix to get where you said you wanted to go. With that first coach, I had to ask myself, "Do I struggle or do I listen?" I decided to be uncomfortable in the short run to get the payoff in the long run. I more than tripled my income working with a coach, so I can say that it was worth it.

Now that I have been branded *the profit coach,* I help others to find the money that is all around them and help them to reach financial freedom in their businesses. I now set Tom Landry's quote as a premise and tell you, "I'm going to say things you're not going to like. I'm going to show you things that are uncomfortable so that you can get the intended outcome you said you wanted. There's no maliciousness. Everything I'm doing is for the good of what you say you want. When it gets hard and uncomfortable, I'm just going to remind you, you said you wanted this. I'm not being a bitch. I'm not being mean. I'm being a stand for you when you can't stand for yourself."

That's what coaches do.

Step into the Big Time: **Self-Assessment—Where Am I? (Accepting and Releasing the Baggage)**

Believe it or not, I'm naturally pessimistic. I grew up in a "No" environment.

"No, you can't have this," "No, you can't do that," "No, no, no, no."

Maybe you can relate. That was just my upbringing. There was always drama. Actually, I learned how to have a relationship from soap operas. I watched soap operas like *Days of Our Lives, General Hospital,* and *As the World Turns* every day; watching them daily after school is how I learned about love. I came to believe that if there wasn't drama and trauma, it must not be love. If it was real, women were supposed to make dramatic facial expressions and storm out of the room. I was all drama, trauma, and victim because that's what I saw.

In my household, I saw that my parents didn't talk to each other; they just shut each other out. And I knew I didn't want that, but I also absorbed that this is what love looked like. Storming out if you're in a fight, being loud, and playing the victim. Later in my marriage, it was always his fault. Right? I just played into the drama. My husband was dramatic, too. So we were both two traumatizing drama queens with no idea how to be in a healthy relationship. If I was angry, I stormed out and slammed doors.

Later, I thought, *Wait, you're supposed to chase me right now and show your undying love and say you would do anything for me.* Sigh.

Oh dear, my dramatic youth.

Eventually, in my mid-twenties, my mindset expanded, and I started to dream about what I wanted out of life. But I didn't have the road map for how to get there. I had to find that along the way.

The mind is so powerful. My mind has enabled me to achieve great wealth, feel amazing love, and become a connected mom because I worked on the ten areas that I share in the assessment on page 40. It is still an ongoing process. I'm not finished. Right now, I'm working on my unconscious limiting beliefs, the ones that I don't even know are present. I'm working with a clarity coach who is helping me clear my blind spots, so that I can reach the next level as a *New York Times* bestselling author. You can't go to another level until you accept your present one. Open your eyes to your current level; don't shut yourself off from it just because it doesn't look great. Accept it, do a meditation around it, and allow it to be there. Doing this inner work is not always a logical, linear progression. You need to work on the unconscious behavior that you're living inside of and not just settle in your conscious mind.

So for me, I had to dig deep and let go of loving the struggle. If love meant chaos and drama, I had to shift what love meant, so I could feel and express it differently. I couldn't just do that on a logical, conscious level. I had to do it on a subconscious level.

The same was true for me in the area of money. When I shifted my mindset around money, I learned I could attract it, but my unconscious mind would sabotage all I'd earned. I couldn't keep it. To declare, "I have money," wasn't enough. Somehow, I would find a way to lose it. That was a huge source of stress because I was a single mom raising two girls, and I was losing money. Literally! I would lose checks that I had received. Back in my salon days, I would receive $400 checks and not deposit them and then not be able to find them! It may sound crazy, but so many of the systems I am sharing with you in this book were those that I needed to give me structure, so I wouldn't sabotage myself. I needed predictable results. So while I was working on the inside, I created systems on the outside to support me.

So, when you are setting a goal for yourself, you just can't say, "I wanna make a million dollars," because that leaves room for your subconscious self-sabotage to come in. If you subconsciously don't believe you will make a dollar, let alone a million, you may not reach that level. Clear the path internally to clear the road ahead. Know where you are, so you can then move forward. This process is so liberating. You can get out of your head and see the reality on paper and realize it is not as bad as all the mind chatter in your head. Even better is that now you can look at that and say, "Oh. Here is where I am and here is where I want to go. Now I can see a pathway." That's why assessments are so powerful. That's why I rely on them so much throughout this book.

Now it is time to do an assessment on mindset to take a look at where you are and where you want to go. This will help you to determine what gaps (if any) you need to close to commit to the changes necessary to grow your business. When you look at the Mindset Assessment, be honest with yourself in your responses. This is all about and for you. No one else will benefit from your honesty like you will.

As you look through each of the ten items below, rate yourself on a scale of one to ten, with one being the farthest from the truth, and ten being "I got this!" Grab a pencil and write it down right here on this page. After you finish rating yourself in each area, add all of your points (there can be no more than 100 points) and write that number down in the "Grand total."

Mindset Assessment

Rate your mental readiness from 1 to 10, with 10 meaning that you rock this and are ready to grow.

I am . . .

1. Committed to letting "the struggle" go   _____
2. Clear on my life purpose   _____
3. Managing ups and downs   _____
4. Comfortable with change   _____
5. Free from the past   _____
6. Conscious of my limiting beliefs   _____
7. Aware of what stops my success   _____
8. Engaged in ongoing personal development   _____
9. Maintaining healthy boundaries   _____
10. Coachable (not committed to being a lone ranger)   _____

Grand total = _____

As you look at these statements, what comes up for you? Do you find yourself reveling in chaos? Do you look for the fight or the struggle? Does everything have to be hard for you to have pride in accomplishment? If this is true for you, your number for item #1 might be less than a five. That's okay; write it down. Then continue through the remaining questions and acknowledge your truth in each area.

Did you find that you had several low numbers? If you did, you are in good company. Most of my clients score in the 20–30 point range (out of 100; max is 10 points per question for 10 questions). No one has ever scored a 100. So if you came in around the 10–30 point range, it might be a good time to do an online search and plan to:

1. Read and apply more personal development resources like books on limiting beliefs. Visit the self-help section of the library or bookstore.
2. Learn releasing and belief-busting techniques like the Sedona Method, Emotional Freedom Technique (Tapping), and Ho'oponopono. Do an internet search to find and learn about each of these.
3. Create positive mantras or belief statements around mindset (several books by Dr. Wayne Dyer and Louise Hay can help here).
4. Work with a therapist in your community to help let go of the past. Ask for referrals or look in your local directory.

Don't worry; having a low score on this assessment is great information to have! There are few things more debilitating than having a blind spot. Now you know where gaps are so you can do the personal development work suggested in the steps above to jump the chasm.

If you are in the 31–60 point range, you are more self-aware, so it may be time to invest in yourself so you can take things to the next level. Look at where you are stuck the most. What areas can you improve in? Pick one or two that could stand the most improvement, and of those, focus on the area that is the biggest priority for you. Where could you elevate your mindset with extra support? Read the books I mentioned in this chapter or reach out to others who can help you to grow.

If you are in the 60–90 point range, congratulations on where you stand. Improve from here with action plans, especially in your two lowest-scoring areas. Journal your growth so you can replicate it in other areas in your life.

If you are in the top 5 percent, you are clearly ready to move ahead with your intention to create a powerfully profitable business. You recognize that continuous learning will benefit you as you grow. Situations may arise that make you question your capacity to handle things, but you remain aware that your positive mindset will help you to work through it. When challenges arise, you can revisit this tool; your score may change and begin to signal a need for attention, but you will be prepared to handle it. Be open to keeping your pulse on the results of this assessment.

Chapter Two

LEADING YOUR BUSINESS WITH POWER

Who do you have to become to lead a profitable business? Not every entrepreneur is well suited for each stage of growth that a company will travel through to reach the top. The skills that it takes to launch a business are not the same as those needed to grow, leverage, or fine-tune the business. Do you have all the other skill sets it takes beyond just the skills of the technician? Fifteen percent of your financial success is that technical ability—the ability to do hair, do the accounting, or do the coaching. The other 85 percent is the sales, the marketing, the operations, the finance, the communication, the hiring, and the leading. So when you look at the percentage of success by what it is you do, that's a small piece. My business didn't turn around until I really got that—my being just a technician and having a technician mindset wasn't enough—when I realized that, *Oh I have to do all these other things . . .* that's when things changed. You have to become the leader of the business. And you not only need leadership skills yourself, but you will need to be able to recruit, hire, and manage other leaders on your team.

GUIDANCE FOR AND ATTRIBUTES
OF AN AUTHENTIC LEADER

When I was young in business, I used to think that being the boss meant that I was a leader. Bosses aren't automatically leaders! Leaders enroll others to take the necessary actions when they are not around. They empower their team and give them the authority to do more. They don't just boss people around to inflate their own ego.

As a young leader, I had a team member I will call Jill. She was a nice gal, around twenty-two years old. She gave the best head massages on the planet. Everyone at work loved her, but I started to notice she was always in the bathroom. I thought, *This girl must have irritable bowel syndrome. What is going on with her?*

I didn't realize at the time that she was shooting heroin in our fancy salon restroom when she disappeared for long stretches. She was tripping when she was shampooing our clients' hair. (She gave the best shampoos!) As a young leader, I wasn't sure what to do. (I mean, how do you address that?)

She was also constantly late; she had demerits up the wazoo. I had a long-held need to be liked (and to be loved), so of course people walked all over me. If I held you accountable, you wouldn't like me. And if you didn't like me, I wouldn't like coming to work. So I said nothing.

One day, she came to a meeting thirty minutes late. As she casually stepped into the room, she said, "I was here, I promise. I just fell asleep in my car."

All these little things just weren't making sense, but I was just trying to be nice, to be a good leader, to have empathy, to have all the things you're supposed to have as a leader. But I was really missing the bigger picture. I wasn't listening. Eventually we had to call her parents to put her into treatment for her addiction.

Sometimes you can't see that the writing is on the wall. It's right in front of you, but are you willing to look at it and take action?

I have enjoyed business and financial success through the years, but I had to learn a lot of business skills the hard way. Over the years, I have gleaned a few nuggets of wisdom that have served me (and my clients) well, and I'd like to share them with you.

THE THIRTEEN SKILLS IT TAKES TO BE A GREAT LEADER

1. Continuous Improvement—Leaders continue to learn. If you do just a little research about leaders, you will learn that they are avid readers. They constantly search for knowledge so they can be better. Some executives read several books per month. I am continually improving upon my leadership abilities. Once I reach one level, I am challenged to go to the next level. For example, when I first started managing people, I wanted everyone to be like me. My philosophy was, "I can do this, and I am showing you how to do it, so just do it." I became irritated and frustrated when they didn't measure up, and I just didn't want to manage them anymore. What I learned to do was share the company's vision and guiding principles, and hold people accountable to their results. I invite you to do the same. Recognize that you will always be learning and discovering new and better ways to lead and inspire your team.

2. Self-Control—It is all about discipline: to follow the schedule, to follow the systems, and to model how you want your team to behave. If you, like me, are passionate about your work and your business, it can be great when your passion is fun and exciting and benefits the team. But if the flip side of that passion is bursting into anger when someone doesn't respond to a situation the way you would, that can be damaging. Believe me, I have had to repair a relationship or two for this very reason. You will need to be mindful of how your behaviors, responses, and reactions will impact your team.

3. Discernment—As a leader, you will need to be able to recognize and understand the differences between your company's values and the actions of you and your employees. You will be looked to for insight and being the one "to grasp and comprehend what is obscure," according to *Merriam-Webster's Collegiate Dictionary's* entry for *discernment.* When you are clear and confident, you will be at your best. For example, as the leader in my own company, I had to show discernment when deciding whether to continue working with a client who didn't honor agreements. Integrity and respect are high values for me, so when they are compromised by someone I work with—even a paying client—my values guide my decisions. As a leader, you may be forced to make tough decisions and will need to show discernment.

4. Organization—Good organization will make your life and your company much more efficient and easier to manage. Organization is about creating systems in your business that allow the completion of tasks in the most effective manner. The more organized you and your teams are, the more time you can spend on a critical function of any business: building strong relationships. As a leader, strive to use new technologies to enhance, track, and create efficiencies in business systems. Make your work and that of your employees effortless.

5. Relationship-Building—You will build your base of business faster with the help of your team and people around you. The truth is that great businesses have great relationships with their vendors, suppliers, shareholders, and customers. Understanding how communication in the workplace impacts everyone in the company is critical to an organization's success. It is imperative, even in this digital age, to focus on the human side of the business and to remember to add a personal touch. When we create a culture that embraces and supports each team member to be fully self-expressed, we can have amazing results in business. And remember, everyone is responsible for communicating and maintaining effective relationships.

6. Active Listening—Effective listening demands active participation. Surveys indicate that we hear about half of what is said because we are preoccupied with other thoughts (such as preparing our response). "We have two ears and one mouth for a reason." We are meant to listen twice as much as we speak. If you live by this, it will serve you well. Unfortunately, some people are so impressed by the sound of their own voice that they never stop talking long enough to listen to what is being said by the other person who is supposed to be a part of the conversation. In social conversation, you may miss something very important if you aren't listening attentively; in sales, you can lose orders. The businessperson who actively listens for a prospect's needs and wants, and who looks for ways to satisfy these needs and wants, winds up on top. Fortunately, listening skills can be improved with practice. (This is such an important topic that I have included a handout, "How to Improve Listening Skills," in the Appendices.)

7. Emotional Empathy—Empathy is being aware of and understanding the thoughts, feelings, and experiences of another without having them yourself. Many believe that business leaders of past generations were encouraged to focus on left-brain thinking while empathy is a right-brain emotion; thus, leaders were detached and unconcerned about what their employees were experiencing. Current leadership theory acknowledges the need for leaders to understand their team's perspective, even if they disagree. I used to confuse empathy with sympathy, but leadership consultant and author Steve Rush, in his book *Leadership Cake*,[1] has a great example to explain the difference: "*Sympathy* is about when you see a team member in a hole and you jump in with them. Now you are part of the problem. *Empathy* is about throwing them a ladder and helping them out. Now you are part of the solution."

8. Accountability—"Spare the rod, spoil the child," said authority figures of yesteryear. It sounds harsh nowadays, but there's some wisdom there. I had an experience as a young leader that taught me the importance of this. Back then, I was afraid to make decisions because I worried my team would quit or stop producing when I held them accountable and responsible. I became suppressed and fearful, not wanting to upset the applecart. When I didn't say what needed to be said, and didn't hold them accountable, just like a spoiled child, they were worse with each incident. I learned that no matter what I said or how I said it, people would interpret what they wanted to hear both positive and negative. I also learned that if you come from a place of contribution with no malicious intent, you couldn't go wrong.

9. Holistic Learning—Are you willing to be uncomfortable in your shoes to be a great leader? Are you willing to look in the crevices of your own self to truly become a great leader? What are you willing to explore to understand you? As a leader, you must recognize that there is not just one side to you. There is so much more to you than just your business skills and knowledge. You want to be aware of the whole of you from a variety of perspectives. Only allow us to focus on areas of improvement. But as I share below, my go-to assessment of choice is the Harrison Assessment. It provides a well-rounded perspective of an individual.

10. Results-Based Management—Ultimately, it is not just you, the leader, who has to focus on creating results; it's the whole team. As the leader, however, you are looking at what actions your team members need to take in order to reach their goals and objectives. If they don't deliver the outcome on time or at all, and all they offer are excuses, it's an indicator that the project is above their skill set or they aren't great with time management. When you know what results to track, you can begin to manage the results instead of the story about why results weren't produced. Take a close look at your business. What kinds of results do you expect your team to achieve each day? Each month? Which actions must they take to achieve these results? (Some of these numbers will be created in the planning and sales chapters of this book.) Look for the indicators and signals that results are not being achieved and address them immediately.

11. Financial Literacy—Numbers tell a story of your business, both positive and negative. There is no emotion tied to it; it is just a logical perspective of what is happening in your business. (This doesn't mean that you are not mindful of the people charged with creating the numbers.) Numbers reveal the health of your business, and being able to analyze and interpret these numbers gives you power. Armed with this power, you can take action to fix any problems, address any challenges, and grow to new heights.

Fortunately, you don't need an MBA in finance to be a good financial manager. I believe you can effectively manage your company's financial performance by focusing on five specific activities:

1. Ensure that the company has timely and accurate accounting and reporting systems.
2. Identify the right numbers/key indicators to watch.
3. Know how to read the key financial documents: balance sheet, income statement, and cash flow statement.
4. Manage cash flow.
5. Use financial information to forecast the future.

Perhaps the biggest mistake entrepreneurs make (aside from running out of cash) is thinking that financial management involves looking only at the past. Your job as the business leader is to use the financial information to look into the future and generate action plans to improve the business's cash flow and strategy. That's a role you can't delegate to anyone else! The key is to develop financial "intelligence," the ability to scan the horizon at the thirty-thousand-foot level, develop a big-picture perspective, and take appropriate action to improve the business's financial performance and productivity.

12. Quantifiable Expectations—As a leader and business owner you have to step up and take responsibility before anyone else will. I used to want my team to take on new approaches before I was willing to. I figured I was the boss, why don't they just do what I say? It doesn't work that way. Just because you pay people doesn't mean that they will do exactly what you say. They are watching you and looking for you to take lead. When you hold yourself to a higher level of accountability, they hold themselves to a higher standard as well.

You can hardly be surprised that your team hasn't met your expectations when they have no idea what those expectations are. Many business failures stem from not setting clear expectations. If expectations are unclear, the consequences for missing the mark are not likely to be known. And without consequences, the team has no motivation to exceed or meet the expectations set by the leader. How can we manage our business and teams if we don't have a standard for measuring progress and capabilities? If we haven't created criteria, how can we expect our team, managers, and leaders to achieve them? We can't. Our team is craving accountability—a measuring stick for a job well done. We have to teach our teams how to perform and give them measurable and quantitative objectives (many of these measures will be addressed in later chapters).

There are several benefits to setting clear expectations and holding your team (and yourself) accountable for them. When you set expectations in line with your company's values, 1) it allows team members to decide if they can operate in alignment with those values; 2) it allows you to focus on the activity, performance, and the metric, and not on the individual's character when correction is needed; and 3) it creates less drama and allows for better coaching opportunities for the team.

13. Genuine Acknowledgment—The flip side of consequences and accountability is acknowledgment and praise. Your team needs to know what they do well and that you appreciate their efforts. It is human nature to be quick to find what's wrong with each other and to seek correction, but so often if we simply acknowledge behaviors that are helpful when we see them, our team will strive to deliver more.

My favorite kind of acknowledgment is verbal. I have seen miracles time and time again, simply because I stopped to acknowledge someone. Sometimes our team members work hard and don't have anyone who will give them acknowledgment. I believe that I created a team of committed individuals because I cared above and beyond the paycheck. I looked for opportunities to give acknowledgment or do something special for each person. The world is hungry for acknowledgment. People are hungry for bosses, associates, and loved ones to say that they matter.

In my business, we make it a habit to start every meeting with acknowledgment for all the ways the team met or exceeded expectations. We then focus on the positive outcome we want to see, and cheer, acknowledge, and praise along the way! When you stop and recognize the difference other people make, it absolutely makes a difference in the lives of the people around you.

To fully celebrate the success of your team, you need to keep your ego in check. This is a balancing act. You have to have confidence to play big in the world and promise great outcomes as a leader, but you also have to stay humble enough to praise others for a job well done and encourage them to rise to the next level. This is one area where having a coach can be beneficial. Your coach can help you to evaluate the impact of your success and ego on your team and your business in an unbiased way. If left unchecked, you can become so full of yourself that you don't notice your team dropping off like flies and your revenues dripping down the tubes. It goes back to that Tom Landry quote about coaches showing you what you need to see to become the person you knew you could be. Stay open to acknowledging yourself with the support of a sharp business coach.

WHOM DO YOU HAVE TO BECOME TO LEAD YOUR BUSINESS WITH POWER?

Many of us entrepreneurs start our businesses as technicians. This means we have a skill, specialty, or trade that we apply to serve our clients. We open our businesses to provide the product or service that stems from that expertise. And some business owners like being the technician. They want to be the one to coach the client one-on-one or do the manicures or review their clients' books. They enjoy it and want to keep doing so. But as some people say, "If you are not growing, you are dying." If you want to grow your business to reach new levels of profitability or reach new markets or serve more clients, you may need to loosen your grip on being the technician and start growing into more management-level positions.

How do you know when it's time to grow? When demand starts creating pressure and you no longer have the time to manage the business because you are too busy "doing" the business. When you spend eight hours working on client projects and then spend the next four hours doing the marketing and business development and finance. This is when you need to step back and ask yourself, "What's the highest income-producing activity only I can do?" So for me, it's teaching, coaching, and selling clients. If you are an accountant, it could be preparing/delivering a financial analysis and presenting an accounting workshop. For speakers, it could be delivering the keynote.

Now look at the other tasks on your job description: Do the other activities have as high a price tag and can they be delegated to someone else? The answer is very likely yes. If you can hire an administrative or virtual assistant to send emails to new prospects you recently met at a chamber event, and pay them a fraction of what you are earning, wouldn't it make sense to do so? If you make $250 per hour providing financial analysis reports, and it only costs you $20 per hour to pay an administrator to process business cards that would take you an hour to do, you are essentially losing $230 per hour doing a task that should be delegated. And your admin may be able to do that task in three minutes instead of the hour that it takes you, so you are now actually losing $240 by doing his/her work. You call yourself saving money, but you are actually wasting money.

So you can see that it may be time to give yourself a promotion in the business, and allow others the opportunity to shine at their level of expertise. Let others come in and do what they enjoy and excel at doing while you go out and make more money so you can pay everyone. Take a look at your job description—are you doing someone else's work at a much higher price tag?

MOVING UP THE RANKS

If we don't launch (or buy into) a business with a team already in place, we are often the one providing that service in the early stages. We service the client, we network for new clients, we enter their business cards in our system, we write the ad copy, we manage the social media, and we empty the trash cans in our office. We often do it all.

The needs of the business change as our business, client base, and reach expand. We are no longer enough! (This is one time where *not* being enough is okay.) We have to wean ourselves from doing all of the client work, so we can grow into the management of an enterprise. This can be tough to do because we are used to doing it all and we want to be the ones to work with our clients. Believe me, I know how this feels.

When I made this transition in my first business, I was so used to being the one producing the results that I only felt valued if I was producing or selling something. When my team was using my work, my products, and my approach to do a great job for our clients, I thought it reduced my value. It took me a while to appreciate the skill of motivating someone *else* to produce the results, and that *their* results enhanced me and my role as a leader. When you're a great leader, you recognize that your team's success is your success! You must put your ego aside with humility and grace.

Leading a business will require different skills and values at differing levels of growth. For years, I have been sharing the following levels of leadership with my clients:

1. Individual Contributor
2. First-Time Manager
3. Manager Managing Others
4. President
5. CEO

These levels, presented in order of growth and significance, each require different skills and a different balance of time, and place value on different elements. When you understand what the role is and the time each person spends in each role, you have more freedom as a leader. To synthesize this, see the table below.

Role/Descriptor	Skills	Time Allocation	Values . . .
Level 1: Works *in* the business. Holds herself accountable.	Technically proficient in all areas of the business.	85%/15% Result-oriented tasks versus admin, planning, etc.	The technical work, results, and goals accomplished.
Level 2: Works in business but also manages contributors.	Planning, hiring, communication, delegation, tracking, coaching, praise, and acknowledgment	50%/50% Technician versus manager	Shift from doing work to delegating to others, responsible for team success, managerial work, displays integrity.
Level 3: Solely support contributors	Selecting, empowering, training, and delegating to managers	100% Strategy and implementation	On the management skill set; displays strong leadership
Level 4: Corrals the entire team	Reviews effectiveness of plans and their execution. Manages profits, communicates with multiple layers of employees; plans three to five years out	Creates room for time to reflect on what worked, becoming more efficient, and maximizing productivity	Trusting and accepting advice from department managers
Level 5: Visionary and long-term thinker (operations and industry perspective); change agent; decision-maker; concise and direct.	Leadership; assembling team of high-achievers; awareness of industry changes; manages and facilitates the board of directors	Holds meetings with managers; talks with industry leaders; travels to industry events	Leading, inspiring, coaching the team; being spokesman for company

As you can see by this table, you will have to grow as your business grows. I learned this in the early days with my salon business. In the salon industry, most owners have to work behind the chair in order for the business to be successful. But I knew I wanted to create a business, not a job. The salon business was also very dysfunctional: we were paying 30 percent commission, and the salon down the street would pay 70 percent commission on products and services. So I had to create a business that was based on more than just a percentage of commission if I wanted to be profitable and attract great stylists. I learned that a lot of stylists were living hand to mouth and didn't have basic benefits, so I started offering things like insurance, education, and advancement opportunities.

That is when I really thought out how to train people so that individual contributors are the worker bees. Then out of the worker bees, there are usually a couple of people whom you want to groom for leadership. For me, I would look at my individual contributors or stylists and identify my rising star. This is the one who loved to manage things and people. Unfortunately, many leaders take our rising stars, who are great technicians, and put them in a managerial role when they suck at managing people projects. They don't like it, and they don't succeed there.

We have to look at who can do both—who is turning in their weekly reporting sheets, who loves doing that stuff, and who loves looking at the numbers. That's that first-time manager.

In the salon I used to own, our salon manager was at leadership level three—the "manager managing others." She took care of the day-to-day staff needs. The president was the doer, the implementer of the vision and business strategies. The CEO was the visionary. So I was CEO/president at my salon; in many companies, those two are combined. As the founder, you craft the vision, and then you get it done. When the organization gets bigger, these two positions are often separated.

When I worked with Lisa Nichols in Motivating the Masses, she was the CEO, the visionary. She would create the vision for the company, which was to be "leaders serving leaders, inspiring success while achieving results," etc. (how she wanted the business to be seen in the industry—you will learn more about visions in the planning chapter). I was the president: I managed the business to help it achieve the vision; I got it all done. I provided leadership to the team, managed operations, ensured quality service, and the like.

It's also important to realize that your leadership style will change, grow, and evolve with your experience. I used to believe that to be a great leader I had to do it all and be it all. Now I realize I need to develop, train, and let people fail through their own process. By allowing them to experience little failures, you enhance their process of owning their own greatness.

Great leaders are exceptional masters of their time, working *on* their business instead of getting *in* their business. In short, leaders get things done through other people, and they don't need all the credit. Leaders master communication and are willing to truly consider others' opinions. If you want to be a good or even great leader, leave your ego at the door. The relevance of that last statement grows as your business and leadership skills grow.

#MondayMotivation
"Good business leaders create a vision, articulate the vision, passionately own the vision, and relentlessly drive it to completion."
—JACK WELCH

Our current business environment is full of examples of failed leadership. We often hear of leaders who focus purely on the dollars they can squeeze out of a company—boosting profits while squeezing expenses to the point of distorted ethics and business failure. The pharmaceutical, insurance, and banking industries come to mind where executives are seen receiving huge bonuses, stock options, and huge salaries, while the company loses billions of dollars for its shareholders or doesn't pay a living wage. On a smaller scale, we see leaders who create a business that cannot sustain itself outside of its founder, and when that founder steps away for a minute, the business falters because the leader did not learn to delegate. Or there is the business leader who cannot step outside of his ego long enough to see what his team needs to operate a successful venture, and then takes all the credit when his team is successful in spite of him. As you might guess, this is not the kind of leader I would encourage you to be.

An effective leader is a person with a passion for a cause that is larger than they are. She or he is someone with a dream and a vision that will better society or at least some portion of it. A leader is someone with great courage and strength to handle adversity and pressure. A leader has a strong sense of their core values. Leading without values is like a captain of a ship going to sea without a map or navigation system.

A leader is creative and pliable, willing to change their stance as required and stand by the decision in the face of disagreement from their troops. Leaders are hungry for knowledge and truth, seeking out the latest technologies and opportunities. A great leader has a strong sense of self and a humble heart. These basics in leadership are like food groups to our physical well-being. Do you already have the essentials to become a strong leader for your company? Are you willing to explore the possibility that more balance is required? Stay open and read on.

SURROUNDING YOURSELF WITH EAGLES (DON'T BE THE BIGGEST FISH!)

As discussed in the levels of leadership earlier, leaders must surround themselves with other leaders as their skill set develops. It is no longer enough to be a solopreneur who never ventures out from behind the computer when you are growing your business. You will need to visualize your business being successful and be able to articulate your vision of success to those you enlist to support you on your journey to reaching it. Note, however, that this does not mean that you have to hire a large group of contributors in order to grow your revenues into the multimillions. It means that you surround yourself with fellow eagles who are soaring at heights you want to reach: they can be coaches, network partners, mentors, strategic partners, mastermind group members, and industry leaders. They do not have to be paid employees or contractors, but they could be.

Make it your intention to read several business books each year for your continued growth and development as a leader. It can help you to soar with the eagles even if you cannot directly connect with them.

THE GOLD STANDARD: THE HARRISON ASSESSMENT

Over the years, I have used many communication and leadership tools and assessments to learn how to manage and support team members. You have probably heard about, and maybe even used, some of the assessment tools that are out there. These include DISC, Myers-Briggs Type Indicator (MBTI), Saville Assessment, Gallup StrengthsFinder, Wealth Dynamics, and 360 Feedback. These other tools show the good news about you, who you are naturally, your personality traits, and how to understand others. Better than that, I now use a tool that has proven itself over the past twenty years to be the DNA of managing a person. It's called the Harrison Assessment. The Harrison Assessment is a proprietary tool, much like the others, but is quite detailed and has to be administered by a qualified distributor, so it isn't something I can just reprint here. But it is still so incredibly important to me and my work with my teams and my clients that I would be doing you a disservice if

I did not mention it to you. I have been using the tool for the past two decades.

This tool helps you evaluate your skill set, your leadership style, your culture fit, and most important, what happens when you're stressed out. The juice of this tool is that it really allows you to see that evil twin that's going to pop up inside of you when things get chaotic. This is the dark side we all have lurking within. It takes a long time for people to recognize it and really own it.

When I took the assessment, I answered all the questions. I found that when I am under stress, I don't talk, I pull away, I am dogmatic (which means "bitchy"), I am defensive, I am harsh, or I bark at you. Then I get dominating and self-sacrificing, which means I will do, do, do, for you and then stop and say, "That's it. I'm done." How do you deal with someone like that?

It was hard for me to see this truth at first. In my heart I don't feel controlling; I am just a love bug. I love people, but I never witnessed how that could flip when I was stressed, and I didn't realize how my harshness affected people. So when things would break down around me, it was like having a big safe with a combination lock that was always one tick off, and I could never open the safe. But with the Harrison Assessment, I could see which ticks were off, and then make the adjustments to click the right ticks. Before, nobody showed me the ticks; they would just back off. Now I am aware and I can manage it. It is still challenging at times, but the freedom this knowledge creates for me is tremendous.

CLIENT SPOTLIGHT: THE VALUE OF ASSESSMENTS

I had a client I helped with her event strategy. In her previous events, she would close around $20,000 to $30,000 in sales. After I worked on her strategy and implemented a new plan over a three-day event, we closed $298,000! In three days. And then, after the event, where we posted nearly $300,000, she said, "I'm really just having a hard time paying you." I literally increased her event revenue ten times over, and she had a hard time seeing the value of my work.

My initial thought was, *Are you kidding me? Did you just forget what we did?* Some people do not have the appropriate money mindset, and they can't see how paying a small percentage of $300,000 is better than having a 100 percent of nothing. When you lead people to their success, they sometimes feel that they have created that success themselves. I get that.

But even after ten years of using the Harrison Assessment, I knew I needed to step back to process her comments. She would not have wanted to hear what I was thinking in that moment. I still have to manage my responses, because what I "flip" to under stress can ruin relationships if I don't act responsibly.

After I had time to pull back and reflect (instead of reacting instinctively), I was able to recognize that this person was not my ideal client and that I do not have to constantly prove my worth. I will not be on the chopping block each month because of someone else's negative money mindset and desire for free Google downloads. I was able to gracefully let that client go. Before I knew my response to negative situations and stress, I might not have been so gracious.

"But with the best leaders, when the work is done, the task accomplished, the people will say 'We have done this ourselves.'"
—LAO TZU, *TAO TE CHING*

When I start working with clients, I do the Harrison Assessment with them immediately because it allows me to show them the bad news that they've already told me. I'm not saying this is how they are. They've told me this is how they are.

I have a client right now who lives in *defensive* in her communication quadrant (this part will make more sense when you do the assessment with me). She had a couple of clients who weren't happy with her services, and she just defends, defends, and defends.

I said, "Listen, Janet" (not her real name), "let's go back to your Harrison Assessment. You live in defensiveness, and if we don't fix this, you're going to lose your business. You can defend everything, or we can figure out how to fix this together."

Immediately she said, "You're right."

"I'm not right. You told me you get defensive under stress or duress" (through the assessment).

I believe that understanding who you are is one of the most brilliant tools a leader can have. To be able to say, "Here's the good news about me, and here's the bad news about me," is very powerful.

As I have shared, I know that when I'm stressed I can be very blunt, dogmatic, and dominating. I manage my stress really well, so it takes a lot to get there, but now I truly notice these things about myself. It's not what somebody thinks about me. It's not my husband's opinion about my behavior. It's not an upset employee's opinion about me. It is me. If I know that about me, I can now see it when it starts to come up, and instead of responding in the moment, I can check myself and say, "I really want to chew on this. Give me some time to think about it, and then I'll respond." Before the assessment, I didn't realize the impact my "flipping" had on others.

Let me share a quick story of how you can apply this tool. Before Lisa Nichols and I have a meeting, we both go over our Harrison Assessments. We acknowledge, "Here's what's going to happen for you. Here's what's going to happen for me." It makes both of us aware that it's not personal: we can say, "If I start getting quiet and snippy, you know that

I am feeling stressed and I need support to deescalate that before I become harsh and dominating." It just is a great tool to allow us to be able to work together synergistically with clients and come from a place of leadership.

To tap into this tool so that you can learn invaluable information that will help you communicate like a leader, get in touch with me (www.SusieCarder.com). It can be your guide to a greater understanding of yourself that will help you to rise as a leader.

Step into the Big Time: Leadership Skills Assessment

How good a leader are you? How capable is someone on your team of taking on a leadership role? Sometimes, when we're hiring, we're looking for the messiah, the answer, the sprinkle of fairy dust, a magical person who is going to change everything. When I was working with Lisa, we hired someone to help us raise money for the company. Lisa and I had both successfully raised millions, so we thought we could trust someone else who seemed like an expert, too.

The person we hired turned out to be a wolf in sheep's clothing, and he misled us into losing a lot of money. There were Securities and Exchange Commission (SEC) requirements that we weren't familiar with, but instead of focusing on learning them and building our skill set, we looked for a sprinkle of fairy dust. We were looking for a person to fix our issue, when, at the end of the day, as she and I discussed after we fired him, it would've been easier, smarter, and more profitable for us to roll up our sleeves and just do it ourselves.

One person will never solve all of your issues. As a coach, I'm not going to be your be-all, do-all. My job is to consult with you through your process. Unless someone working with you is a full-time employee, they are not going to own your business's goals in the same manner. As a leader, you need to bring your team members in, but also not be complacent. Lisa and I can't deny the responsibility of what that guy did to us. I can't throw him under the bus, because it was our choice to hire him.

Lisa and I learned that we knew how to write a pitch and raise money, and we just forgot who we were. We were growing and expanding so fast that we had to bring in other team members, but we didn't have a clear eye on what they were doing for us. I believe it's important to hire consultants and others to help you grow, but you also have to be sure that they're the right fit for your team.

Now it is time to take a look at where you are and where you want to go. This will help you to identify areas of opportunity as a leader of your business. When you do the Leadership Assessment, be honest with yourself in your responses. As you look through each of the ten items below, rate yourself on a scale of one to ten, with one being the farthest from the truth, and ten being "Wow, I am a true leader." If you want to take this assessment a little deeper, you can also write a sentence that explains why you rated yourself as you did. This could be an example of a leadership trait you recently exhibited, or a situation that caused you concern.

After you finish rating yourself in each area, add all of your points (there can be no more than 100 points).

Leadership Assessment

Rate your leadership effectiveness from 1 to 10, with 10 meaning that you are a great leader.

Leaders . . .	Your Rating
1. Create the vision	_____
2. Are organized	_____
3. Manage by the numbers	_____
4. Excel at goal setting	_____
5. Are great listeners	_____

6. Display emotional empathy   _____

7. Plan and review   _____

8. Engage in ongoing personal development   _____

9. Manage from results   _____

10. Expect high accountability   _____

Grand total = _____

If you don't have any business goals and you have no idea what numbers you would manage the business by, we need to talk. The work that I do with my clients helps them to use assessments like this one to identify opportunities for growth. I then help them to move the needle as leaders of successful businesses that they can be proud of. Having a coach to guide you through the leadership growth process in your business is essential to rapid success. Your learning curve will be reduced tremendously.

If you scored 0–30, you are in good company. Many business owners start low because they haven't had much opportunity to practice their leadership skills within their own ventures. Take your lowest two scores and set an intention to develop them. Know that it may take a year or more to grow in some of these areas. Becoming a leader is not an overnight process.

For example, look at your score for item #2, organization. Most creatives are not in love with organization. And by that I mean organized in their notes, organized in their checkbooks, organized in their car, organized in their closet, or organized at their desks. They are freer flowing and constantly staying in action.

But if they don't pause, chaos creates clutter. A cluttered mind can't sell. A cluttered mind can't focus. The freedom my clients experience just by getting organized opens up so much possibility for them. If I get unorganized, I've got to stop, organize my desk, and put everything away so I can breathe again. If I just get lazy and just let piles stack up,

I can't focus. So the value of organization allows your mind to be free and more creative. If you need help, find someone like a professional organizer who can help you. You'll have to invest money, but it will truly change your life. On the other hand, you could ask for that as a birthday or Christmas present instead of asking for shoes or perfume. Ask for the things that you need to help you develop as a person or as a business leader.

If you scored 31–60, you might take a closer look at item #9—managing results. Some results and numbers show what activities you're focused on or not focused on. The reality of small business is if you don't sell something or make money, you can't be in business. So the result for sales would be how many contacts did you have or how many qualified leads do you have. How many appointments did you set, how many conversations did you have, and how many people did you close? Those are results you can manage. Because if you don't have qualified leads, you're not closing anyone. If you don't have appointments on the books, you're not going to close anyone, so what did you do and not do? What were your results?

If you scored 60 or above, consider your lowest score and set an intention to make a notable improvement over the next ninety days in that area. You are obviously in position to grow and take on new challenges. Step into your next level with confidence.

———

Now that you know what kind of leader you will need to be to grow your business and *Power Your Profits*, let's take a look at how to create a plan that will take you there.

Chapter Three

PLANNING YOUR PROFITABLE BUSINESS

By now I am sure you have heard Benjamin Franklin's famous quote "By failing to prepare, you are preparing to fail." You could use this mantra to succeed in almost any field, but if you want to hit the big time, creating a business plan is not just important, it's essential. Why? Because not knowing where you are going is the quickest route to losing your way. Without a plan, it is so easy to get caught up in the shiny object syndrome. When you haven't written down your business goals and how you intend to achieve them, you will change your mind the first time something exciting comes across your path.

Think about it. Have you ever seen a marketing message by someone you respect and then thought, *Maybe I should use that for my business*? (Never mind that your business is entirely different and you already created a marketing strategy based on where you wanted to take your business this year.) Have you ever picked up the phone and agreed to invest in an ad for your business, even though it was neither in your plans nor your budget to do so? A solid business plan that you implement and follow can help you to avoid these situations.

Your business plan isn't just a road map for your success; it can also be a powerful fund-raiser. When I wrote the business plan for Motivating the Masses Inc., we were able to use it to raise $2.5 million. We would not have done that without a solid plan that showed a clear path to success. We wrote the plan specifically to entice others to invest in the company and where it was headed (not just where it was at that time). It told the story of possibility, the people behind it, and the impact it would make. That is what people invest in, in addition to the potential monetary return on that investment. Writing the plan, then, helps to tell the story about a business that stimulates that interest for someone to say, "I want to be a part of this. I want to see how this grows and I want to be there when it does. Because you told me a story that says this business is going to make a great impact. I want to be a part of that."

Raising money takes a big investment of time and commitment. It is all about relationship building. We were trying to run a multimillion-dollar business and raise money, simultaneously. It was a lot to manage. So we created a target list of potential investors to pitch the plan to and presented them with the opportunity. (Note: when you are seeking equity investment, there are a lot of SEC regulations you have to abide by. You can't just raise money willy-nilly. See the next section for another example on the fund-raising process.) This allowed us to structure an equity deal that raised the money to grow the business to new heights. But it all started with having a plan so others could see the potential and possibility.

Many business owners also miss the opportunity to use their plan to help them hire the right people. If your plan shares the company's vision, mission, values, and strategies, team members can review it, understand it, and design their own contribution to it. If they review your plan and cannot stand behind the business's purpose and its approach to serving its clients, nor their own contribution to it, they can take their name out of the hat before they get involved. On the other hand, those potential team members may get fired up knowing that they have chosen the right place to work. This happens to me all the time. There will be no surprises when they start work if they have had an opportunity to buy into and get excited about the company's business plan.

MELINA AND THE PLAN FOR PUBLISHING POSSIBILITY

My client Melina owns a publishing company, and she's creating an online platform for her business. She wanted to raise $5 million, so she came to me, and we put together the business plan, the pitch deck (explained below), and an investment strategy. (You can't do this on your own. You need an attorney who specializes in the Securities and Exchange Commission investment laws. Raising equity capital is a big legal quagmire that costs a lot of money, but it is one avenue to build your business. You're either going to borrow from yourself or borrow from somebody else; that's the reality of making money in business.)

After the business planning, the first thing Melina and I did was look in her database to see whom she knew who was influential and could possibly invest. We didn't know for sure what their bank account balance was, we just looked at who they were and that she had a relationship with them. By the time we finished that exercise, we had $25 million in investment possibility with the list of people that we put together and the amount of money that we guesstimated they could invest in her company.

That gave us our hit list. Now we had the list, the business plan, and the pitch deck. The pitch deck is a condensed version of the business plan—anywhere between six to seven PowerPoint slides on the business plan—that includes your mission, your target customer, your goal, and the financial return for investors. At the end of the day, the investors care about you, they care about the business, but they also care about how they're going to make money. That's the biggest priority. They want to know how they are going to make their money back and make more money with you than putting it in a savings account. Keep that in mind. At the end of the day, no matter how much they adore you, it's all about their return on investment and the results you produce.

So once we had the hit list, the business plan, and the pitch deck done, Melina's job was to go have coffee or lunch with each one of those people and go over the opportunity. If they were interested, we would send a nondisclosure agreement and the business plan. Then we would follow up, and follow up, and follow up! If somebody is giving you ten thousand to a hundred thousand dollars, there's a lot of follow-up. It's a sale, just like any other thing you're trying to sell inside of your business. It usually doesn't happen in one meeting. I think that's where people get disillusioned; they think, *Oh, I'm just going to meet somebody and they're just going to write me a check for $10,000.* Nope, not unless they really, really know you, or if it's a referral from somebody else.

(I did have one investor in our company who invested $200,000 and I never met him. He was brought in by our attorney and we received a check by overnight mail. Wow! Now, that happened once, and it was a very rare occurrence. That was a onetime deal.)

I can only hope that Melina will have this happen, but we will have to wait and see how her investment story ends. One thing we do know: she has a plan for where the business is going, for the investment it will require, and for how she will provide a return for her investors.

PLANNING VERSUS FAILING

There are people who literally build businesses on a hope and a prayer. Let's say it all together: hope and prayers are not the foundation for growing a business effectively. They are the formula for bankruptcy. Yes, you can be inspired to create the business of your dreams, but back up that inspiration with planning, so you can achieve your highest and best result.

Most studies say that 80 percent of small businesses go out of business in the first five years. It is probably even higher now, because in the digital era, many businesses start up from people's living rooms. That stat is for people with physical locations who had to sign a lease. It could actually be less than five years, but five years is often when the lease is up. *The lease is up, so I'm out of business,* you think. Right?

With so many people starting online and coaching businesses, there's no automatic need for a physical location. That makes the stats harder to quantify. So I would say that the 80 percent statistic is actually on the low side. People get an idea, launch online, and then say, "I don't know how to make money at this." It's easier to close those doors.

I have also had clients say, "I've been doing this for twelve years, but there's no revenue." There's no revenue because there's no plan. So I tell them, "Let's get a plan in place."

THE SEVEN STAGES OF BUSINESS

Before you begin the planning phase, it might be a good time to look at the Seven Stages of Business. Find your business status in this list—are you moving toward the seventh stage?

Seven Stages of Business
Concept/Establish
Develop/Prepare
Reinforce/Improve
Forecast/Expect
Enrich/Increase
Influence/Capitalize
Engage/Release

Stage 1: Concept/Establish
This is where creation and invention live. Here you define who you are as an entity and what you do in the marketplace.

At this point, you are brainstorming what you want to offer or what solution you will provide that people will pay you for. For example, you can ask: Does the market need another organic shampoo business, and why will mine be any different? What is it about my shampoo product that will make customers switch from what they are already using? With these questions, you are looking to find the competitive advantage: the "what you do differently" that stands out among the crowd. (You can do online research about existing shampoo businesses in your area to find some of your answers.)

Sometimes it is what fires you up that will create the spark for your business concept. It is not always the job or skills that you now have that you turn into a business. Take my client Heidi. She was a gifted and amazing writer. She was a ghostwriter of twenty books for a variety of celebrities, so it seemed natural to launch an online course to teach others how to ghost. But, even though her job was being a ghostwriter, her passion was altogether different.

In our sessions, we discovered that her passion was teaching others how to raise children in diverse cultures and situations while eliminating the hate and adversity they are often faced with. It lit her up. So I said, "Let's figure how to make a business out of that!"

In twenty minutes, we had brainstormed twelve modules of an online course that she could teach on diversity training for families. From that we were able to outline her business plan so she could flesh it out and research further. She created an exciting business concept that made her enthusiastic about writing a plan and creating online courses for it.

Stage 2: Develop/Prepare

Creating the full plan. This is where this chapter comes in handy. You will define your path to make it easier to follow.

Once you have developed a concept that you can put your energy into, it is time to write a business plan for it. Don't worry if you have never written a plan—it doesn't have to be hard!

The beauty of a plan is it has you look at everything so you can see who your competitors are, and see how big the market is, and see who would be a strategic alliance for you, and see whether it is a viable business. I've had clients who put the plan together and say, "I don't want to do this. There's not enough money in it." Perfect! That was a great thing to learn. So, let's spend the time now with planning, and save years of hard work, disappointment, frustration, not enough money, etc. The beauty of putting the plan together is so that you can really see whether it will work for you. Do you really want to do this? Do you want to work that hard?

I remember when Tara came to me for help in creating her business. She was a scientist and professor doing organizational development training for another company. I call her a parallel-preneur because she had a job that was paying her expenses, but she was creating new possibilities through her own venture on the side.

Going through the business planning process was a real eye opener for her because in her job, all she had to do was go out and do the job (the training). When you go into business for yourself, you also have to do the sales, marketing, finances, and more. Developing her business plan helped her to realize all she needed to do to get the business going.

Her first goal in the business was to replace her employment income of $150,000 so she could afford to work in her business full-time. Based on the strategies she created in her business plan, she could do that over a two-year period. She was fine with that because she still had her job to cover her basic needs.

Compare that to me when I started my training and development company. I was making $250,000 at the salon and thought I could just quit the salon, do the training, and still make the same money. Nope!

In my first year in the training business, I think I made about $40,000. Ouch! Big lesson learned: Look before you leap! Don't quit your day job until your business has replaced your income. Otherwise you might put yourself and your family into financial distress. As I learned, I had to create a new strategy.

Another important lesson that can be learned from the planning process is that your business idea may not be able to generate enough money to reach your goals. That is still a great lesson to learn! It is so much easier to learn that before you invest lots of time and money than to feel it later. When you plan and figure out how many of your products or services you have to sell at what price to generate revenue, you quickly learn whether it is enough to make it worth the effort.

Stage 3: Reinforce/Improve

Build on your plan; start hiring support and building infrastructure.

Eighty percent of businesses fail within the first five years. The remaining 20 percent don't pay their owners enough to compensate for what they would make in a job doing that for others. You have to build on your business plan so that you don't short yourself on a long-term basis. Sure, you may have to make sacrifices in salary in the beginning while you get your business off the ground, but don't make that a permanent situation.

Another big issue for many new business owners is whether they have the support they need to make that sacrifice. Many people do not have supportive spouses or family to help them get through the trying first stages. I know I didn't. My "was-band" (ex-husband) used to tell me to "go get a real job." He didn't see entrepreneurship as real, because it wasn't always consistent money coming in in direct proportion to the hours worked. I had a real job. I worked hard for the money, but the inconsistency stressed him out. He had a job working for someone else that issued a paycheck on a regular basis. I didn't. He would have rather I made smaller paychecks as long as they were regular.

And it is hard to stay motivated in an environment where you are constantly told, "Go get a real job." When you hear that every day you start to wonder if you do have a real job. What you need is support to figure this out, not all the doubt. You need to find other unicorns. That is why a community is so important. You need a community of supporters because many people think entrepreneurs are crazy. They want a job with a consistent paycheck and they want someone to tell them what to do so they project that on you and think you are cuckoo.

There also comes a time in your business life that you need to grow to the next level. When your business is young, you can put the systems in place that will make growth possible. Build in systems like standard operating procedures and processes, accounting systems, sales strategies, hiring plans, and the like. When it comes to building a team of people within your business to help you grow (Web designers, virtual assistants, sales people, bookkeepers, and more), just focus on what is "your next." What is the next step your business needs to take and who is the team member that can help you to get there? When I am considering this, I ask myself, "What is the highest income-producing activity that only I can do?" And then figure out how to delegate the rest. It will always be worth it for me to hire someone to process emails or do the accounting when I need to be on calls with clients or networking for new prospects.

Stage 4: Forecast and Expect

Release what isn't working and enhance what is working. This may be boring for entrepreneurs who want to go back to the concept.

What I love about forecasting, which is a secret weapon for my clients, is I put their sales plan together, and then they follow it, and then their sales double. It seems so silly, but it's so true. There's power in creating your financial forecast and strategy. Why leave it to chance? I really take the time and plan the numbers, so if I say I want to make $250,000, then I have to look at my pricing strategy, figure out how many units I need to sell, and see where I am going to find my people.

And once we lay out the plan, then I just hold them accountable to how many conversations did you have? How many speaking events did you go to? There's magic in taking the time, planning that out, and then making sure they take radical action to hit those goals.

It amazes me how many entrepreneurs just sit back and get on the internet, Facebook, and Instagram all day and say, "I don't understand why I'm not making any money." It's because you're not talking to clients! Pick up the phone, go out and meet new people, and get out of the office. Then you can turn your forecast into reality.

Stage 5: Enrich and Increase

Momentum has set in and you are working at maximum capacity. Many businesses can sabotage themselves at this stage.

Let me offer an example from my own business. I have an event that I offer and my goal is to do it once per quarter. In the first event, my goal was to have fifty people in the room. We had thirty-nine people in the room. For the next event, I increased that goal because I was looking at what worked with the last event to fill the room.

This is all about looking at what worked and what didn't work. There were things that just didn't work. If I continue to do those things that didn't work, I'd have the same results. It is almost like those combination locks that we had on our lockers in high school: 26-42-22. As I said earlier, if you get one of those ticks off, it doesn't open the lock. It's the same in business. If I get one of those ticks off, success is not going to open. There are so many different combinations. So our job as entrepreneurs is to ask, "Did I get the results that I wanted?" In this example, my answer was no; I only had thirty-nine out of fifty people attend. So what do I need to do to get fifty people? How much do I need to step out of my comfort zone?

I can't do the same thing or I will get the same result. No, I need a different strategy. Let me try a different strategy until I finally get the combination. Then I can systematically run it using the combination that worked. This is what I do so I don't fall into self-sabotage. Act, document, shift, and move. This is how you get better results.

As entrepreneurs, we often keep moving, but we aren't really documenting and evaluating the change. We are just going back and work the pieces of it that are working to get the thirty-nine people, because pieces of it worked. But what do I do to enhance the pieces that don't work? What I need to do is keep the pieces that work and improve those that don't.

In business, we're always enhancing and refining. We're always looking at what works, and what I can improve upon. I spend a lot of time thinking about my business, not doing my business. I think about *how am I going to meet the right people, how am I going to enhance the service.* I really take reflection time to think on the experience I want for my customer, and what I want for myself. My old belief system was that I can have whatever I want; I just have to work hard. Well, now I don't want to work that hard. I want it to come with ease and grace. I can accomplish the result and not exhaust myself.

Stage 6: Influence and Capitalize

Strategic growth by buying other companies or creating strategic partnerships.

Each person has to decide what their long-term goal is for their business. I have some clients who are perfectly happy replacing their income and making $200,000 per year as speakers. They don't want to have a team of people and large business operations to manage. And that is okay. You have to decide how big you want to play and what you want to do and be okay with that.

If you do want to grow your business, connecting with others of influence or connecting with other people who have like-minded customers will help you build your business faster. You may think it's going to happen online. I say it's going to happen with relationships. The right strategic partnership can propel your business; it can propel it ten times over in the right circumstances.

For me, I want to look at the people who are not competitors to my business. I find strategic coaches who focus on other things besides the financial growth of the business, and then I want to be their partner in being that for their organization. How can I serve your market with my information, and vice versa, how can you serve my market with your information? It has to be win-win; it has to be called collaborative. It can't be the vampires who want to suck the life out of your business and offer nothing in return. If you are going to go into business with a snake, at least recognize it is a snake. But you can't be surprised when it comes back to bite you. Sometimes that is a tough lesson to learn, but often you can use that lesson to help others who come after you.

When I launched my Profit Coach brand, I looked at the people I respected and admired and who had my ideal client (that I can serve) and asked, "How can I meet them?" And then I went about meeting them and building relationships. When I do, I don't say, "Hey, I'm Susie, can I have these clients?" Instead I say, "Hey, here's what I do. How can I support you?" It's coming from a servant's heart first. "What can I do for you?" And the law of reciprocity says it will come back to you. It may not come back from that person, but it will come back from someplace else.

I believe in the law of reciprocity, that if I give, it will come back to me. And then sometimes the blessings don't come back. And that is still a blessing. Have you experienced that? You want something so bad and you're praying for it and you're wishing for it and you've got your goals around it. Well, sometimes man's rejection is God's protection. Sometimes you're not supposed to get it and you don't know why. The answer slowly comes to you. Like me losing all my money in the market crash. That, I would say, is man's rejection. But what I learned from the other side: all the great lessons, all the strategy, and all the things I could see where I blindly trusted. Or where I didn't look at the signs or I was too leveraged. I didn't like those lessons, but they were great lessons that I can now give to other people.

Lisa Nichols always says that sometimes it's like gifts that are wrapped in sandpaper. They're hard and they're crusty and they're scratchy, but there is a gift inside. It took me years to see the lesson and the gift, but I can appreciate it now.

Stage 7: Engage/Release

Now you can walk away from the company or go on vacation! Others are engaged or enrolled to keep business going without you.

My biggest blessing in reaching this stage came when I got in a major car accident, and I ruptured a disc in my neck and my back. I tried for a year to work and heal, but my doctor said, "You have to take time off from work."

I was on ten pain pills a day and a morphine patch to try to manage the pain. I needed neck and back surgery. And using the medication, I realized that I wasn't being of service to people. Although I was scared to take the time off, I knew I had to, so we created a plan of who would take over my clients and trainings. My trainers stepped up and I delegated all the other tasks that were in my job description. And I had to step away from the business for a year.

I didn't go to a business meeting, I didn't look at a P&L; I just took care of me. And in that year the business grew 30 percent! It was such a blessing but it was also humbling for me because my ego wanted to believe "they can't deal without me." I was so self-indulgent and self-important thinking that, but I had always set up my business to survive without me. I knew we had to systematize the business. I went on vacation for weeks at a time so I knew the business could survive. But imagine taking a year off and not being in a meeting. It was hard personally, but also good personally because I really needed that time to heal. I couldn't imagine being on ten pain pills and a morphine patch for the rest of my life.

When you're an entrepreneur, you work all hours, you have no boundaries, and you're just in the grind. And then, for me, all of a sudden my body's failing me—I call it the cosmic boot. It kicked my butt. It kicked me in the face and said, "You will rest." And luckily I had spent years building systems and years prepping people. My philosophy had always been to build a business that you can leave; I just never tried it! That was just a really good theory until then, and it ended up being a blessing. My company grew and thrived with an amazing team of loyal people who held the reins for me.

Understanding the tumultuous nature of business is what I love about the seven stages of business. You can go through these cycles at any time. They can go quickly or they can happen over years; it depends on your momentum in the business. And if you have an understanding of what's coming, you can plan for it.

It helps to know what you can expect. Knowing the seven stages helps you to anticipate what to expect in business before you get there.

When you look at this list, do you see yourself reaching each level? Can you visualize yourself or your business at maximum capacity or rolling along smoothly without you? You can create what you believe, so allow the possibility of these stages applying to you, and see yourself successfully moving to the next level with a solid business plan.

#MondayMotivation

"Our goals can only be reached through a vehicle of a plan,
in which we must fervently believe, and upon which we must
vigorously act. There is no other route to success."
—PABLO PICASSO

SETTING INTENTIONS FOR SUCCESS

When you are creating or expanding your ideal business, you want it to excite you and give you a reason to jump out of bed in the morning. You want your business to be bigger than you. Why create something that doesn't thrill you and impact the world? Your energy, passion, and exuberance are going to shine through and attract your customers and clients. Wouldn't it be great to imagine your best business ever?

Well, if you can see it, you can be it. For example, if you want to become an author, make a mock-up of your book cover with a "bestseller" stamp, wrap it around a book off your shelf, and put it on your desk so you see it everyday. If you want to be on the *Today* show for your events, print out the show logo and post it on the wall near your computer with "Don't miss [Your Name] on the next *Today*." Everything that now exists in our physical world was first a thought. Your thoughts can become things just as easy as for the next person.

What do I mean when I suggest that you set an intention for your business success?

According to Dictionary.com, the definition of *intention* is "an act or instance of determining mentally upon some action or result; the end or object intended; purpose."

I remember when I first started wanting to be a speaker. I really got that vision and I put together a vision board (a poster board on which I pasted pictures and words representing my vision for the future). I visualized being a speaker every day. I saw happy, excited clients running to the back of the room after my speech. I visually saw it and felt the excitement of it until I actually represented or manifested it. What you think about, you talk about, and what you talk about, you bring about. Your words and your thoughts are that powerful.

And I didn't necessarily know how to do that in the beginning, but I just started reading books on mindset and visualization and creating what you want. It sounded hokey to me when I started. But I thought, *Hey, it's better than what I've got. I don't want to be broke all my life.* And it didn't happen overnight. It has been a twenty-five-year journey of consistency. Each step brings you closer, so appreciate where you are now.

I meditate every day. I pray every day. I set my goals every year, I have my plans, and I'm consistent. Are you consistently (consciously and unconsciously) picking up the stick and beating yourself up because you're not good enough? You're not smart enough? You're not making enough money? Your people never get it? Your clients will never get it? You'll never get it? *Whatever it is, put the stick down and start manifesting what you want.*

Manifestation does take action. You can't just think about it. I put my visualization together (vision board), I put my plan together, and then I had to pick up the phone and call people, and network, and find events I wanted to speak at, and do all that work.

As you begin to plan, you want to think of that end result. Where do you see the business being in years to come? One way to do this is to look *from* the end, rather than *to* the end. For example, take out a piece of paper and act like it is a journal entry you are making five years from now (if that is too far ahead, do three years, or one year). In that journal entry from the future, think *back* to all the wonderful things that have taken place to get you where you are. My speaker entry could have been something like:

May 2025: I am so excited about the recent speaking engagement I just had. I was the keynote for an international conference with an audience of 10,000 association members. They had asked me to share my journey as a professional speaker and author. I had almost forgotten all the divine connections that first led me to share the stage with one of the teachers in an international movie sensation and New York Times *best-selling book! It was so fun to inspire others to recognize that they deserve to be wealthy in all areas of their lives: their family life, spiritual life, business life, financial life, and more. I remember how happy I was just to deposit my first $5,000 speaking fee. I giggled all the way to the bank. And this gig paid me five times that. Who knew?*

You get the idea. You write as if you are remembering a past event or series of events that led you to the success you are now (in the future). You can add emotional words, flowery language, fun tidbits, or whatever gets you excited to think about. You want to get into a feeling place of that "future past reality." Now try that with your business. Pretend we are having lunch in the future and you tell me how you came to sell your company for millions of dollars. Or how you positioned your company to go public at a steadily increasing stock price. Or how you created a legacy business for your family.

Once you have established that intention, writing it down can help you to keep it top of mind so you can bring it to pass. That is where business planning comes in. Your written business plan is the physical manifestation of your stated intention and the way you will make it happen. Planning is the way to pull your business from your head and put it on paper so others can help you to achieve your highest intention. One fun aspect of what I do is to help you not only visualize the possibility of a successful, profitable business, but to realize what it will become. So juicy!

CLIENT SPOTLIGHT: NEW BUSINESS, NEW PLAN

Glennae is a participant in one of my coaching programs who wanted to launch a business that coached nurses. She came in at pre-launch and did not have an understanding of how entrepreneurial ventures worked because she had been in a corporate environment. I had her do what I expect most of my clients to do—write a business plan. She did her homework and used LivePlan (see www.LivePlan.com) to develop her initial draft. Now we have something to work with!

I reviewed each area of her plan to help her see the potential her business had. I looked at her sales, marketing, operations, finance, business development, and more. I helped fill in the gaps, and I challenged her to be responsible for the numbers she created. I asked her questions like "Will you only focus on oncology nurses in private practice; what about RNs at the local hospital? How are we going to sell that coaching program: online or through strategy sessions? How are we going to convert people from prospects to paying customers? And how many people do we need to convert in order to reach $250,000 in sales given that your program costs $497?" Together we used the cash calculator and base price tools from Chapter 8 to review each revenue stream. I helped her to own her numbers and her plan so she could see the possibilities.

After one session, she wrote to me: "I'm in tears. I can't believe that I've had one call, and I already feel like I've got the entire value of the whole course. The value of putting together the business plan, I had no idea, would give me such clarity, would give me insight, and have me see the vision that I'm creating for the future." This was exciting! She created the plan, and she did the work. I just helped her to see how she could bring it to pass and how having a plan would help her to be successful doing so. Can you see how fun business planning can be?

Take time now to visualize your business and its success. Seriously, stop reading for a moment, focus on one spot on the ceiling or wall or close your eyes, and visualize how you would like to see your business operating over the next year, three years, five years, or beyond. What's the legacy you want to be known for? For example, when we launched Your Beauty Network's online platform for the beauty industry back in 1998, it was one of the first membership sites in technology. The beauty industry (technology-wise) was already years behind everybody else, the internet was just coming out, and websites were really expensive to make, but we knew that we needed to provide the service. We could see that in our mind's eye. People really needed the systems, the strategy, and the analytics at their fingertips.

So when we sat down in our planning meeting and said, "We're going to launch this thing," we decided we wanted to be the *Good Housekeeping* seal of approval for salons and spas. We wanted people to see the YBN logo on a salon business and know they were certified. We wanted the brand to be huge and well known (in a market that didn't embrace technology).

We had this grand vision that we just kept pushing and pushing, saying, "Here's what we are, here's what we stand for, here's who we're going to be" (the possibility) and we became leaders in the industry and later sold our business for millions. So imagine what is possible, put it into words, and then take action to put it in place. Don't just talk about it; be about it, do it, and implement it.

IDENTIFYING WHAT YOU WANT

In Chapter 1, we talked about identifying the purpose behind what you want to create. Now we'll focus on writing down exactly what you want your business to be and to achieve. Writing it down increases your clarity. You saw how it helped in the business planning process in the spotlight above. Let me share an example of the benefit of clarity from my personal life. I really want you to understand this point.

When I was single, I was tired of dating people who just didn't have the same values I did. My girlfriend told me, "If you are always dating men that are dogs, you must be shopping at the dog pound!" Wow, what a revelation. I was shopping at the dog pound, taking whatever came my way!

Instead, I decided to create a list of everything I wanted in my ideal partner. Writing it down helped me to get clear about what I wanted. My new partner would:

* Have strong character
* Live by his values, including honesty, integrity, love, and communication
* Be a big dreamer!
* Be financially solvent and financially responsible
* Have computer skills (I know this may sound silly, but it was important at the time.)
* Love my kids and treat them as his own
* Cherish my children and me
* Be family-oriented
* Be adventurous
* Love me and adore me
* Be conscious of his physical well-being
* Be a student of the world and a traveler
* Be a good communicator and great listener

Until I put that list together, I was making emotional decisions about my future and that of my children. I can't believe I spent so much of my adult life being unclear about what I wanted. Once I got clear, I met my ideal partner, and he has all those attributes and more! He may not have all these traits 100 percent of the time, but he has them. Now, just like in my personal life, I create all future projects and goals that I can dream *with clarity*.

I want you to do the same for your business.

DEFINING YOUR WHY

It is important to understand why you want to succeed. Uncovering your real motivator for owning and operating your business is so important. Knowing your why can change the course of your business. When you connect emotion to why you want to be successful in business, you become more motivated to achieve your goals. It gives you that additional fuel to keep pressing toward your goal, especially when you run out of steam along the way.

I shared my why with you back in Chapter 1. As a single mom, my two girls, their care, and their education were extremely important to me. I had to be successful because I didn't have a back door to crawl through if I wasn't. There was no backing down from that for me.

I have asked thousands of business owners *why* they want their business and the answer typically is "I want more money, free time, and freedom from nine-to-five." You have to ask yourself, Are you willing to not get paid when the money is tight? Are you willing to make less than some of your team members in the beginning? Are you ready to dedicate yourself to this start-up or expansion? If the answer is no, I ask you to rethink what you are committing to.

Take time to think about the following questions and write down your answers. This will help you gain clarity and serve as the foundation for your mission statement, and more important, your business.

Ask yourself:

* Why do I want to open, have, or expand my own business?
* What are the benefits of having this business?
* What brings me joy about this business? What taps into my passion?
* How does this business use my best skills? What does it contribute to the marketplace?
* When the business is done or is successful, what will it look like?
  * How many team members do I have?
  * How much am I doing in yearly revenue?
  * How many units do I sell?
  * What is the vision of the organization?
  * How are my customers feeling when they experience my company's service?
  * What are my employees or team members saying about working in the business?
  * How much profit do I have?
  * What are our gross sales?

It should be no surprise that it takes more than thinking about having a successful business to bring it into being. Every great project or business must begin with planning. That's why writing down your responses now is important for the work in this chapter.

Each year I do several different plans in order to launch the year successfully—I revise the business plan, financial plan, and strategic plan. The financial plan shows me the dollars and cents that are generated by, being used in, and flowing out of the business. It helps me to stay on track from a financial perspective. The strategic plan I create is my road map to accomplishing all of the business goals and objectives. I spend thirty days creating the next twelve months and then my team and I execute that plan as the year unfolds.

Do you have your plan in place? Whether you answer yes or no, you can use this chapter to assess the existence and readiness of that plan to serve you and your business over the coming year.

NAVIGATING THE STRATEGIC AND BUSINESS PLANNING PROCESS

The planning process is one area of business where I do not recommend delegation. If someone else writes the plan, you are not going to be in alignment with it, and you might not do the work that needs to be done to execute it. I have seen people spend five figures to have a business plan written for them, and then say: "Oh, I don't want to sell that," or "I don't feel like doing what it takes to accomplish that," or "This doesn't make any sense." Why waste the time and money? (We'll present a detailed guide to writing your plan later in this chapter.)

The original business plan has to be conceived and written by you. You can have someone like me poke holes in the plan and edit it, but you need to write it. That doesn't have to be difficult these days. You can use business planning software like LivePlan or BusinessPower-Tool, which asks you questions about your business concept and helps you to capture it into a written document. It has all the templates you need to create a pitch (summary document), the strategy, the written plan, the financials, and more. You can just focus on developing a business that you can commit to, and the software will help you to do the rest.

These programs make it easy to do the writing; they take the "scary" out of it so you can focus on developing the content. You will have to be able to address the questions and find the information to fill the plan, but structuring and preparing it is easy.

When my consulting clients come to me, I ask for their business plan. If they have been in business, and they don't have one, I have them create one. Your first thought might be, *I've been successful making six or seven figures in my business already; why do I need a plan now?*

You need a plan because your existing situation, skills, knowledge, and processes have brought you here, but your well-crafted plan is what will propel you to the next level. If you are not ready, you can keep operating without a plan and without my help. But if you want to increase your business exponentially, you are going to have a working business plan! Check out the next spotlight for a good example.

CLIENT SPOTLIGHT: DOING THE GROUNDWORK

One client, John, was a landscape designer who had a business averaging $58,000 per month in revenue, about $700,000 per year. His goal was to reach $1 million per year, but he just pulled that number out of the air and had no strategy or method to reach it. He presented his plan to me, and I delved into his financials to focus on a working business plan. After doing so, we set a must goal and a stretch goal for his business. The must goal was a target he had to hit to make his business viable (and desirable). His must goal became $1.2 million. His stretch goal was a target that is doable, but will take efficient, positive action to reach. His stretch goal was $2.4 million. Both goals were entirely possible given his financials.

We made several important discoveries after looking closely at his numbers. One was that he was losing about $27,000 per year in overages on labor and parts (this is often a pricing issue). That's money he could put in a retirement plan! It was the equivalent of giving each client several hundred dollars for the pleasure of providing them a service! (If you are losing money, you are giving it away.) Then we found that he was not providing maintenance services, which could generate an additional $150,000. And then we discovered additional design services that could yield $346,000. Both revenue streams were a natural fit for his business but he had not planned for them. He did not have to work any harder to make this additional $496,000; he just had to work more efficiently to realize those gains. That's why people tell me, "I am the money!"

Remember, if you know where you are, you can chart a course for where you want to go. A coach can help you to fill the holes in your plan and help you to create and manage the numbers that will excite you. They will guide you through any fears you have about the planning process and help you to become who you have to be to reach the other side. All you have to do is gather all of your business ideas, strategies, and financial results on paper. Then your coach can show you the money and you can move up from there.

Each business has three core elements in the strategic plan: the strategy, the collective or developmental competence, and the organizational competence. In the plan, you are identifying what the business is going to do, or how it will be successful, what processes and challenges exists within the organization that would help or hinder the achievement of that strategy, and what learning or assistance you or your team need to be successful. Once you have the strategy in place, you can tweak the marketing plan, the financial plan, the sales plan, and the people plan as needed.

You cannot simply write a new strategic plan without considering what it will take to execute that plan, what resources or development are required to make it happen, and how the results will be measured. Do you or your people possess the skills required to pull the business strategy off? Is your organization structured in a way to allow for streamlined action? Identifying what development is required (learning or education both within the organization and its people) is essential for achieving desired results.

#MondayMotivation

"For me, the business plan has to be the dictator for all the decisions in the organization."

—SUSIE CARDER

STRATEGIC PERSPECTIVE

Strategy is the fuel for your business. Strategy is the game plan and the big picture. Too many entrepreneurs can't distinguish the business from their personal wants and needs, so they don't plan their businesses strategically. By looking at the business as an entity, it is easier to create an objective view of the organization.

Every plan must begin with a careful look at where the business is right now. If you called someone to ask for directions to their house, the first thing they would ask is where you are now. One cannot give directions to another destination without a starting point. The same holds true in business: you can't create a plan to get to another level unless you know where you are and what is currently happening. Begin to look at your current state with the questions below.

Strategic Direction

1. Do we have the right products, and if not, what other products do we need?
2. Are we in the right markets, and, if not, what other markets should we enter?
3. Can we leverage what makes us stand out from our competition (competitive advantage)?
4. Are we reaching the right customers? If not, then who are they?

Organization

1. Do we have the right processes for defining our customers' needs? If not, what do we need?
2. Are our prices too high or too low? Why?
3. Are we organized appropriately for the challenges we face, or what is needed?
4. What are our biggest obstacles that lie ahead?

People

1. Are our people innovative enough?
2. Are we skillful in supporting our customers' needs?
3. Do we have a customer mindset? Why or why not?
4. Do we understand where we are versus the competition? If so, what's our position?

By asking yourself key questions about your business and competency, you can uncover the sweet spot in business. You will be able to decide on your next hires, as well as your key expectations of those individuals. I used to be the type of business owner who would just jump into something without thinking; on the way down, I would figure out how to open the parachute. The crazy part is that I was pretty successful doing it that way. But just imagine where I could have been if I had spent the time asking the valuable questions above. Strategic planning is an important task of a business owner and manager. The strategic plan is acted upon with a business plan and performance management (activities for making sure goals are met efficiently and effectively).

DEVELOPING YOUR STRATEGIC PLAN

Once you know where you are and where you want to go, you need a plan to get there. Your strategic plan is like a scaled-down, big-picture version of your business plan. It is more of a snapshot. It will include a high-level overview of where you are going and include sales, marketing strategies, financials, and milestones. (The business plan becomes the "how to" or implementation guide, in a sense.) The plan is to be built by you and your team. The strategic planning team should represent a broad spectrum of segments within the organization, whether that team is a team that works for you or is an advisory team. As you move forward either laying the foundation of your business or renovating it, you need to decide whether there are key members—co-owners, partners, investors, managers, etc.—who should be in on this planning phase. Even if you are the only one in your business, it's imperative that you have outsiders poke holes in the plan and look at it from all angles. (This is a great role for a coach.)

The ideal planning team size is nine to fifteen members, with an outside facilitator. An outside facilitator isn't attached to anyone's ideas or thought processes. You can call your local Chamber of Commerce or SCORE organization (Service Corps of Retired Executives) to find someone to help you create and implement the session. You can call me, too: I can help you create, execute, and implement the strategic plan and get results!

The strategic planning process consists of an orderly sequence of activities, each contributing to the success of the whole. The process should take place off-site, away from telephones and social media, so team members can disengage from day-to-day operations.

The CEO or the owner of the business, which is *you*, must serve as the strategic plan's "spiritual leader." It's so crucial that you plan your role in the business! You decided to be an owner, so step up and take that role seriously. I coach so many business owners who don't want to be mean or stern or hold people accountable. You must lead your people! You must position yourself as the leader or you will never gain their respect.

Here are some best practices/techniques for achieving optimal planning.

* Practice creative thinking. Generate as many ideas as possible during the early, out-of-the-box mode.
* Take a critical, unbiased look at what has worked before and what hasn't worked. Don't be attached to any particular idea or strategy when the process begins.
* Identify your best business practices, and drop others that led to costly mistakes. For example, look at your training programs, sales calls, team development, and meetings. What three things worked well, and what can you improve upon? Don't harp on what didn't work; learn from it. If you take this approach continuously in every area, your business will be in constant improvement.

Based on my experience with my clients and working with a strategic plan in my own business, here is what an organization's strategic plan should entail. It should:

* Be ongoing;
* Be representative of a shared vision of where the business is headed and what is needed for it to get there; and
* Be integrated into a continuous business cycle.

Senior leaders first define the vision; this is the desired future state of the company. Then they agree on two strategies—a business vision and a cultural vision—to work toward the overall vision. Let's look at the business side first.

Usually a three-to-five-year business strategy guides decisions about your organization's markets, products, customers, people, sales, and delivery distribution. Critical success factors are the make-or-break factors your organization must focus on to move toward its vision (for example, improving customer retention or increasing speed to market).

On the other side, the cultural strategy determines how the organization achieves its vision. For example, will product innovation drive the organization, or is customer orientation more important? When senior leaders define values, they describe the organization's fundamental beliefs about how people work with one another to meet goals. Put all these things in place and you have strategic focus. However, to implement the strategies, you still need two integrated systems:

* Business planning
* Performance management

BUSINESS PLANNING

One of the best things the hundreds of people I've worked with share is that this process allows them to see their future. It is the whole road map for the business. Yes, sometimes business planning can be scary, but it doesn't have to be. As you think about your business plan, take note of any resistance you feel. What excuses are you coming up with for not putting your plan together?

"Oh, I've been doing this for years, I don't need a plan."

Or "I know what I am doing, I don't need to plan this out."

Or is it "I don't want to do research that suggests that this isn't a good idea"?

Your excuses are really about accountability. When you create these plans, you're telling the universe, yourself, and your community what you want in life. If you don't take the time to put this together, you will sabotage your bigger vision and your bigger why. I've seen clients spend hundreds of thousands of dollars throwing spaghetti on a wall. They say,

"I'm gonna try this strategy, and I'm gonna try that strategy." If you just put the plan together ahead of time, you save so much potential income. I've had clients spend millions without a plan, only to waste their investment by not executing because they are too busy or lost motivation. What are the excuses you keep telling yourself to stop yourself from doing this?

Business planning identifies short-term plans for achieving specific goals that support the organization's longer-term strategies. In a larger company, each business unit develops plans for its function, division, plant, or department, and then communicates those plans to everyone in the unit. The performance management system takes those plans to the street, so to speak. People set their individual objectives that will contribute to meeting the business unit plans. They also choose competencies and behaviors they'll need to demonstrate to achieve those objectives.

There are brilliant software packages out there that can walk you through the process and guide you through all the elements you need to write a successful plan. They have sample plans on their sites, so I will not try to re-create those here. (Business plans can be thirty or more pages long when finished.) When I first put my business plan together, I rewrote it every month for twenty-four months, changing and refining and enhancing the plan. The plan drove my business in the right direction, and the planning software made it easy for me to make adjustments as I went along.

In general, the plan starts with an executive summary (which is written last), the opportunities, and the execution (which is the sales, the marketing, and the operations). It will identify the milestones and targets, how the company is structured, and then includes the financial plan.

There are seven major sections of a business plan, and each one is a complex document.

1. Business concept. This describes the business, its product, and the market it will serve. It should point out exactly what will be sold, to whom, and why the business will hold a competitive advantage. This is where you tell the unique story of your business and how it will be different than any other business.

My client Sarah had a marketing agency that she didn't want to run anymore. She wanted to start a completely different business. So we looked at what she was passionate about, what she loved doing, what she was good at, and what brought her joy. We discovered that she loved being a TV host, interviewing, speaking, and empowering women. The business concept they came up with is being a speaker doing women empowerment workshops. We decided her keynote topics, created an online course, developed an outline for a book, and created a way to leverage business conferences by interviewing attendees, and playing the videos on the internal TV channel at the conference hotel. She would interview exhibitors to be highlighted on the TV channel as well as others at the hotel event.

2. Financial features. This section highlights the important financial points of the business, including sales, profits, cash flow, and return on investment. This is the financial road map and overview of your goals and objectives. In this section, I have noticed a theme. People want to jump directly from zero to a million. Yes, you can do that with a clear strategy behind you, but most small businesses can't do that in year one. Here I want to see incremental growth in the business, not a jump from zero to sixty. (Most cars can't go zero to sixty very quickly; we're not all Aston Martins!)

For Sarah, we had to figure out how the new business would make money. One of my geniuses is figuring all that out. So we looked at how much money she wanted to make and she determined she wanted $180,000 to replace her income from her previous job (at her own marketing agency). Since her salary is only one thing that the business needs to make money to cover, we *doubled that number to have 50 percent that would stay in the business ($360,000). We then looked at how many speaking engagements, webinars, and coachings she had to do to earn her salary plus business expenses. The TV concept is something that is still is on hold because it was an unknown. It's kind of a future project that we're just putting on hold because we haven't washed it completely out yet. That's her homework.*

3. Financial requirements. This section clearly states how much money (capital) is needed to start the business and to expand. It should detail how the capital will be used, and the equity, if any, that will be provided for funding. Typically, the money to start a business comes from an owner (equity) or other people's money (debt/loans). If the loan for initial capital will be based on security (like the owner's house or business equipment) instead of equity, you should also specify the source of collateral. Note here that 80 percent of businesses fail because they don't clearly know what it is going to cost. They drain their savings. They drain their retirement accounts. They drain their equity in their homes. By putting a plan together ahead of time you can strategically plan your use of funds from a variety of sources.

We looked at Sarah's financial requirements. She is going to be a speaker, so she will need all the assets for that: a speaker one-sheet, online webinar forms, and the webinar back end (payment processors, auto-responders, etc.). What marketing should she use and how much that will cost? (That's her wheelhouse—her expertise—so she won't have to pay that much. I would have to pay somebody to do that.)

The first goal was to break even so that she wasn't borrowing money, or putting her money in, or taking money from the other business.

4. Current business position. This description should furnish relevant information about the company: the who, what, where, when, and why about the business. It contains legal forms of operation, when it was formed, the principal owners, and key personnel, and lists all the players and the roles. In this area, be realistic about how much time and energy it takes to recruit, hire, and train people.

Sarah is the only owner of the business. We have to know what conferences need her expertise and how many there are. We then have to compile a list to start marketing to them, and determine if she needs help. (She already had a virtual assistant in the agency and could use that person in this new venture to reduce her costs.) We will slowly wean Sarah out of her job at the agency so she doesn't have to quit.

5. Major achievements. This is an area where you can toot your own horn. I have to reevaluate the results our business has brought in every year because I forget. When you forget what you've done, self-doubt can creep in. You start to question, am I worth it? Am I good enough? You have to document what is going on, so you can see what your work creates in the world.

A friend of mine who works as a public speaker told me that she felt at one point that she couldn't charge what she was worth because her engagements focused on social justice issues surrounding the death of her daughter. But once she cataloged all of the events and engagements that she participated in on behalf of social justice, she recognized her value. She had made a significant impact in the world. Her plan now includes systems to capture those achievements on a consistent basis.

Share details of any developments within the company that are essential to the success of the business. Share them openly and be proud of what you have accomplished. Major achievements can include items like audience sizes and patents; or intellectual properties like books and recordings, prototypes, locations of a facility; any crucial contracts that need to be in place for product development; or results from any test marketing that has been conducted.

6. How Will I Profit? Now you must think like a capitalist and ask yourself, "How can I turn a buck? And why do I think I can make a profit that way?" Answer that question for yourself, and then convey that answer to others in the business concept section. You don't have to write twenty-five pages on why your business will be profitable. Just explain the factors you think will make it successful, like the following: it's a well-organized business, it will have state-of-the-art equipment, its location is exceptional, the market is ready for it, and it's a dynamite product at a fair price.

If you're using your plan as a document for financial purposes, explain why the added equity or debt capital is going to make your business more profitable. It's important to show how you will expand your business or be able to create something by using that money.

We didn't look at profit for Sarah's business until her second year, because she is still running two businesses and two opportunities.

7. Define Your Market. As you start to look at your market, it is important to really look at your ideal client. The ideal client is a living, paying person whom you want to serve. I find that many people get too general and are not looking at exactly who that person is. Who are they? What are their likes? What are their dislikes? How much money do they make? Remember that client of mine who couldn't pay me after I helped her make $300,000 in a three-day event? Even though she's an amazing person, I must ask if she really is my ideal client. It's exhausting to constantly have to prove your worth and value. It should be exciting to pay me because you know the value I am going to create for you.

A meticulous marketing plan should share a clear strategy for success. A market analysis forces you to become familiar with all aspects of the market. The target market should be defined, and your business will be positioned to capture its share of sales. A market analysis also enables you to establish pricing, distribution channels (how you'll get your product to your clients), and promotional strategies that will allow your company to become profitable within a competitive environment. It also provides an indication of the growth potential within the industry, and this will allow you to develop your own estimates for the future of your business.

Begin your market analysis by defining the market in terms of size, structure, growth prospects, and trends.

For Sarah, her defined market was empowering women, and she got clear on what kind of women, how much money they made, etc. She was her own ideal client so she looked at her lifestyle, what conferences she liked going to, where does she hang out, and how much she was making, etc.

The biggest thing I see in small businesses is they don't really look at the client for what they're proposing. And they end up marketing to a client who can't afford them. Therefore they're always struggling around money or they're afraid to charge what they're worth. So the break-even, the financial component, is imperative. If I can show them they have to charge two thousand dollars for their service in order for them to pay all their expenses, they have a different perspective and the blinders come off. They will see it differently. "Oh, I have to charge this."

So I always want to find that number. It is the minimal, acceptable price we have to charge or you'll go bankrupt or you'll keep taking money from your savings account or your credit card or wherever you're pulling money from. And when they don't get clear on the pricing, that's where they get in trouble.

ESTABLISHING YOUR VISION, MISSION, AND VALUES

Your vision declares the future you are aspiring to that is full of possibility and excitement. It is what you will use as your mission to live and grow into each and every day. It is something that calls you forth to be bigger than you know yourself to be. Decisions for a business should be based on that company's vision statement and the owner's core values.

A catchy phrase or tagline is not enough. Your business vision should be your best business imagined and then condensed into a shorter, pithy statement. It should be visible to your mind's eye as you look to the future, even if it is nowhere in sight today. Vision adds the why to your what (mission). And as we discussed in Chapter 1, on mindset, your vision is the end result. Living your vision is living with the end in mind.

Remember Sarah from the last section? Her vision was *to empower women worldwide.* (Her business is based in the Bahamas, but she wanted to do more global work.)

Though Dictionary.com defines vision as "the act or power of sensing with the eyes; sight," it further defines vision as "the act or power of anticipating that which will or may come to be" and cites as examples "prophetic vision; the vision of an entrepreneur." Perfect! As an entrepreneur, this is the time to imagine your best business and create a vision that propels it far into the future. It can be something that gets you up and out of bed every morning. Vision can keep you committed when you don't feel like being committed; it can give you hope when you feel like quitting. Vision inspires you when you have just had the worst phone call or client visit in memory.

When you run your business based on your vision and values, you can rest easy at night because you know that you have done right by your clients, your shareholders, your employees, and your vendors. Vision becomes the integrity meter of your decision-making process; it helps you to ensure alignment.

VISION STATEMENT EXAMPLES

Susie Carder: Wealth Is Your Birthright!

Cold Stone Creamery: The ultimate ice cream experience

Intuit: To revolutionize the way people do financial work

The vision is the *why* for doing what each of these companies does for those they serve. It is the why to their what and to whom. Notice that the statement may not be true *yet*, but the organization's dream is that it will be one day. What they do within their organization, then, should strive to lead to this vision. They can measure their activities (mission, goals, milestones, and targets) against this vision.

What is your vision? Spend time writing down your vision or re-visiting and revising an already existing one to make sure that it is still viable, dynamic, and powerful. You can start by closing your eyes and imagining your best business ever. Then write down everything you see. After you have exhausted your pen, read over what you wrote and distill it down to its primary essence. That will become your first or next vision statement. Keep in mind that vision statements are not cast in stone and may change and grow with time—especially as you start fleshing it out with your team.

MISSION STATEMENTS

A mission statement describes what an organization does, what markets it serves, and what it seeks to accomplish in the future. A mission statement is an integral part of starting your plan.

* The mission statement describes how the business serves customers so they will underwrite its strategy.
* It serves as a guide for day-to-day operations and as the foundation for future decision-making.
* For employees, a strong mission statement builds commitment, loyalty, and motivation.

Following are some best-practice techniques for writing a mission statement that encapsulates your business's vision and goals.

* Describe the essence of the business in words your employees and customers can understand and remember.
* Focus on specific traits and on target or niche markets.
* When the mission statement is created, post it on conference walls, on promotional materials, and on product packaging.

For example:

Sarah's mission is to strengthen the leadership, power, and voices of all women in our communities and our businesses. Her business creates a world in which all women regardless of race, ethnicity, income, and social status are empowered to their full potential. She believes all women have a voice and can make a difference in the world.

What is your mission? Spend some time writing down your mission or revising an existing one. As BPlans.com says, you want to "capture what your business stands for in a brief and memorable way." While this part of the foundation can be time-consuming, it is time well spent. Remember, the vision, mission, and values are the foundations of your business and are critical to powering your profits.

MISSION STATEMENT EXAMPLES

Google: To organize the world's information and make it universally accessible and useful.

Warby Parker: To offer designer eyewear at a revolutionary price, while leading the way for socially conscious businesses.

Honest Tea: . . . to create and promote great-tasting, healthy, organic beverages.

McDonald's: We are focused on delivering great-tasting, high-quality food to our customers and providing a world-class experience that makes them feel welcome and valued.

VALUE STATEMENTS

The core values of the company can be written into a values statement for all within your organization to read, buy into, and live by. These values are the core beliefs that the company will use to make business decisions, staff decisions, and customer decisions. They are a statement of values you can stand behind and use to provide clarity when making the *right* decisions.

I agree with brand consultant Denise Lee Yohn,[1] who suggested in a *Harvard Business Review* article that there are a few words that you may want to leave out of your value statement. These words are: *ethical, authentic, fun,* and *customer-oriented.* Think about it. If you have to tell yourself or your team that you should act ethically, you may have a problem. Who wants to work with a business that has to remind itself to be ethical? Of course, if you are in business, you should act ethically.

The same is true for the other words on this short list. Saying you are authentic doesn't make you genuine; *be* authentic. Also, all businesses should be customer focused. That's why you are in business, right? Your company solves a need for your customer. If you have to legislate it (organizationally), you might not be it, or you may be trying too hard to look like you are it.

Now, this does not mean that you don't have processes and procedures in place to support the essence of these words. You can still live up to these words internally. You can have a good accounting system and standard operating procedures that hold you accountable. You can have excellent customer service processes in place. But you don't have to express these as external values to those whom you serve.

So what should your value statement be designed to do and what should it include?

For my client Sarah, her values included transparency, empowerment, and financial prosperity.

SWOT ANALYSIS

Draw four quadrants and place the word *strengths* over the word *weaknesses* and *opportunities* over *threats* in the four squares. Reflecting on your business, write down its strengths, weaknesses, opportunities, and threats. When you identify each item, think about how you will use its strengths to overcome your weaknesses and your opportunities to overcome or eliminate your threats. You want to identify potential obstacles and create solutions to mitigate them!

WHAT TO WRITE UNDER

Strengths:

As attorney Suzanne Meehle suggests, answer this question specifically, "How will you use your strengths to address your weaknesses? How will you leverage your opportunities to lessen your threats?[2] Do not overlook this discussion. I want you to really look at each quadrant. Ask yourself, what does your brand do better than your competition?

For example, one of my strengths as a business trainer is that I offer the "it," the specific tools or strategy that will get the client the results they are looking for. I give the tools, the overview of what the tools are, and then the "it"—including how to use it to work like magic in your business. A lot of business trainers simply offer the feeling, hype, or excitement, and it just doesn't work in every market. Business owners need to know how to apply it.

As a company, one of our strengths is being transparent. And we define that as telling you the raw, honest truth. A lot of times that comes down to numbers.

As a leader, you should always share numbers with the team: here are our goals, here's what we want to do. A lot of owners are afraid to share numbers with employees because they fear they may want more money. And in some cases they do. But when you look at all the numbers, if there is no profit, there is no more money to give. If there is, what are things we can put in place: paid vacations, profit sharing, etc.

Transparency and authenticity is being truthful with your team. It is not holding back; it is carefrontation versus confrontation; it is sharing.

An example: At one point, I struggled trying to fill these big-money business summit events. I was suffering alone, I was worried, and wondering if I was doing the right things, or if I was on the right track. I started telling people I was nervous and I started asking for help instead of pretending that I had it all together. I shared my challenge with my marketing person, and they created ideas and offered their assistant to do sales and Facebook Live to help market my event. It was amazing to learn how much people want to help you when you're being honest. We often don't want to show weaknesses and fears. As a leader, I have a business owner's nature, but have to realize whom to trust and share information with. You have to know whom you can be transparent with and how to show your truth so it empowers people.

Weaknesses:

The next step is to chart your weaknesses. What does your business need to improve upon? In all transparency, for my team, it would be to follow up and follow through. How much money are we leaving on the table because we keep running to the next project? Can you relate? What would happen to our business if we could go, "Stop. Let's go deep. Let's make sure everyone is followed up to the degree they need to be followed up with." If you look at sales now, most people will follow up one or two times and give up or forget when the next shiny object comes along. The reality is we need to follow up twenty times or more. Between our schedules and other people's time, it can take many contacts to make the connection. Sometimes our business keeps us from being strategic and putting follow-up systems in place or delegating better.

Opportunities:

A great question to ask in this quadrant is "What market trends could lead to increased sales?" Again, for us, we've been exceptional at seeing the money. We can look at client businesses and say, "Oh, here's money over here. There's more money over here." We are able to see money where a lot of people miss it.

For Sarah, we mapped out the speaking opportunities, the conferences she could attend, and the possibility of charging people a marketing fee for being interviewed on a hotel's streaming service. I knew this service existed because I used it at a conference for ten years. I have paid $5,000 to be interviewed, and my interview would be shown on TVs throughout the hotel while people were getting ready and walking around going to events. It gave me exposure to everyone there while not directly pitching or selling. People would see me there and on the floor, and they would come up to me and say, "Susie, I saw your interview and it was great." That opened the door to closing the client. There really is hidden money everywhere.

To boost her rate of speaking opportunities, we looked at keynotes, one-on-one coaching, speaking fees, and group coaching programs. We created a whole business and found where the money would be based on things she wanted to do. I am a great Xerox machine. If I see a great model, I will replicate it because it works.

There's value in looking at other industries to see what they are doing and how you can adapt their practices to your business. That is why I was able to grow Sarah's business so fast: because I took the systems from my business and applied them to hers. I'm constantly examining best practices in various industries and evaluating how I can incorporate them in another business.

Be aware that even though a strategy worked in one industry, you still have to run the numbers to ensure that it is financially viable in yours. For example, in business, the big trend is to host a membership site, where only members who subscribe can access your content. But a lot of people who pursue this strategy don't think about the numbers. You have to spend a lot of money in marketing to get enough companies to sign up for the membership. For example, if you want to make $100,000 with a nine-dollar-a-month membership, you need 1,111.11 new customers per month. To get a thousand customers, at a closing rate of one in ten, you have to get in front of ten thousand people per month. The average customer stays only three months, so you are likely to lose 30 percent of your membership every month. Does it make good financial sense right now?

Sarah needed to wait to get in front of ten thousand people to make it worthwhile. Online you close only 1 to 3 percent, so you may have to wait even longer. The average person needs an internet marketer to make this strategy work. I created one of the largest membership sites in the beauty industry back in 1998, so I know from personal experience that it *can* work. But the average person would need outside help.

If there is an area in your industry that no longer produces revenue like it once did, how do you reinvent the business to create new revenue streams? What are other industries doing that you can leverage or learn from? Be open to new ideas and approaches.

Threats:

When you look at threats to your business, ask, "What are the advantages that our competitors have over our organization?" For most small businesses, it is cash. Cash is king. Having enough financial cash flow to put all the structures in place is often a challenge. Being a solopreneur, or as I call it, a lonely-preneur, you are there by yourself trying to figure it all out, but it is hard to see outside the silo. This is where coaching becomes incredibly important.

This analysis and questioning is extremely useful. To be able to see what your competitors are doing, what you are doing, what you are leaving on the table, and what external factors could jeopardize the success of your organization is powerful. Are you changing with the times? I think it's important that we address these kinds of questions when we're digging inside the SWOT analysis.

For example, Sarah has the threat of time, being unknown as a speaker, and the possibility of not being able to get on the right stages. She has to make time to confirm proof of concept (when you ask yourself, will this work as a business?). She also has to determine whether she has enough cash from her old company to build this new company.

Pros and Cons:

SWOT analysis helps you with your decision-making process; it creates a visual representation of the various factors, and then it allows you to prioritize how you will address them (instead of running off to the next thing). It allows you to see logically instead of being in the emotion of it. For example, if we just had an event we might say, "Our events are amazing. Yay!" But if we just stay in the "yay," we can't really appreciate the opportunities that might exist. Instead, we do a SWOT analysis for different aspects of the business and the business overall.

For example, after you launch a new product or service, you can do a SWOT analysis on it. What worked? What was your strength? What was your weakness? What was your opportunity? What was your threat?

You can do the same thing for an event or online course. You can ask: What was our strength? What did we do well? What was our area of improvement? Where is an opportunity? And what was threatening us?

"Take a SWOT" at all aspects of your business as you grow along, not just in a formal business plan at the beginning. Use it as a tool to look at your team members; each team member brings strengths and weaknesses, opportunities and threats. Use it to determine where to grow. Ask yourself, "How can I use this tool to help me grow my business and help me to see what changes I need to put in place?"

SWOT analysis is bigger than just putting it in a business plan to never look at again.

You can even do this analysis with a group of your clients. You can gather their feedback about your strengths, weaknesses, opportunities, and threats from their perspective. I was recently involved in reinventing a training program based on the feedback of clients. They shared our opportunities and the weaknesses from their perspective, and gave us a wonderful opportunity to make meaningful changes. Be open to receiving feedback from your customers, a coach or a mentor, a consultant, or peers who are playing as big as you are. (Don't do it with peers who aren't thinking as big as you are because you want to be sure you're also striving in the major leagues.)

Sarah looked at all the information she had pulled together and decided that it was still worth doing the new venture. Now she had a clear idea how to start the business plan. She wanted to make it happen. Walking through it helped her to gain clarity so she can move forward.

GOALS, MILESTONES, AND TARGETS

When working with my clients, we create goals, milestones, and targets. What goal will the business strive to achieve? What milestones will you hit on the way to the goal? What actions will drive the milestone to get it to the goal? I have seen great success over the past twenty years by establishing these three items.

For example, let's say your goal is to increase your social media following to 200,000. The milestone might be a quarterly number. So if you need 200,000 followers, divide that by four, and your milestone is 50,000 followers per quarter. Now you need to figure out what actions you need to take to hit that milestone. Perhaps you will do three Facebook ads, six weekly Facebook Live videos, and three Google ads. Then you have the terms to measure and quantify the results.

Sometimes it helps to break the numbers down to their simplest form because saying "I'm going to aim for 200,000," scares people. Take the 50,000 per quarter and divide it by twelve weeks, and now it's only 4,000 per week. That's more manageable. If I break it down even farther and divide it by five days, it's only 800 people per day.

When your goal numbers are broken down into milestones and targets, you will know immediately that if you do a Facebook ad, and you're not getting 800 people a day, you need to tweak your ad. You need to do something different. But missing your targets doesn't mean you beat yourself up for it. You analyze your stats every week so you know where you stand, but you set out the next day to hit the target instead of trying to make up for previously missed ones.

PLAN YOUR EXIT STRATEGY

When I started Salon Training International, I was already a student of Michael Gerber, who wrote *The E-Myth*.[3] I knew from day one that you build a business to sell it. So, from day one I set the business up to sell. I didn't know whom I was going to sell it to or how much money I was going to sell it for, but from day one, I knew it would sell. I told every new hire that I needed them to build the job out as if they were going to get hit by a bus tomorrow, and somebody else would have to come in and take their place. That sounds morbid, but if you're gone tomorrow, what trail do we need to leave for the next person? Every year we looked at that business and asked, "Is it sellable?"

If the answer was no, we'd work on the primary issues. Whether it was the market position, or it was too heavily dependent on me, we worked on it. I knew I had to get out of the way because my ego self wanted to be important, but my business mind said, "You'll never be able to sell it. You'll never be able to *not* be at work every day."

For example, when I got into the car accident, I had neck and back surgery. For a year, I tried to work and couldn't push past the physical pain and exhaustion. If the business had been just dependent on me, I wouldn't have had a business. I had a team that could keep the business running. If you have no team, you just have a job. It drops when you do. I set up the business, so I could actually take the time to heal. I don't want to build a job. If something happens to you and someone needs to take care of your clients, it's only you. It may take years to get to this position, but it is a process worth doing.

When I was a hairdresser, I was also in a car accident and broke my leg. I was out for two weeks, but I didn't have a plan in place and had to go back to work to make money to support my family. I had to cut hair in a cast and prop my leg up on a vanity. I learned I needed to save money so I had a contingency plan. But it was a big wake-up call. In that moment I learned I owned a job, not a business.

Fifteen years later, when we were approached to sell it, the answer was "Yes, of course, we'll look at it." Now, we had set up the business plan for this day. But I still didn't know if I was going to sell it. I didn't know if it was the right time. I wasn't sure, but the answer was ultimately yes because I wasn't afraid of that conversation. I had been planning it since day one.

If you want to set up the business to truly be successful, the goal is to look for that exit strategy. The exit strategy is either: the business continues to pay you for a lifestyle you want, or it pays you because you sell the business. If the business is all about you, there is nothing to sell. When I sold mine, I had created tremendous value beyond myself. I did that by setting up the business originally to not depend on me. I set up all the systems to put in place. That includes hiring and training people to be leaders. Everything we did we had a system for. Even now, as I am relaunching my brand, I am systematizing every process in my new business. I have an assistant who is creating standard operating procedures (SOPs) for everything that needs to happen in the business. SOPs are road maps for what the previous person did in that role, so when she leaves, I have a road map to follow.

If you, as the business owner, are managing it all and doing it all on a daily basis, there's nothing to sell. You don't want a big, fat job. If you aren't in the day to day, managing every piece of the day to day, you can have a team that would allow you to go away for a month and still have the business run and be efficient. Most business owners can't do that. They can't even go for a week. But this is what you want to create. This is what you want to plan for.

It's just like raising children. You appreciate being needed as a parent, but you don't want your children to rely on you for everything. You want them to grow into responsible young adults who can take care of themselves when you decide to go on vacation with your spouse. You want to know that you have trained them in the way that they should live, so they can continue without you. Eventually they will go on to make their own money, be productive, happy, and prosperous, and you will reap the rewards of your parental investment. That's the role you want to take with your business. You don't want to be the business, you want to be a part of its growth and development, and be able to let it go when it makes sense to do so.

Step into the Big Time: **Business Planning Assessment**

Now it is time to take a look at where you are and where you want to go. This will help you to determine the holes in your business plan, so you can work to close them. When you look at the Business Planning Assessment, be honest with yourself in your responses. Remember, it is not enough to have an *idea* of what you want to do in your business. You have to have a written plan that your team or others can review to see how they can contribute.

As you look through each of the ten items below, rate yourself on a scale of 1 to 10, with 1 being the farthest from the truth, and 10 being "it is written and readable." After you finish rating yourself in each area, add all of your points (there can be no more than 100 points).

Business Planning Assessment

Rate the completeness of your plan from 1 to 10, with 10 meaning that you have a written and complete plan.

1. Vision, Mission, and Guiding Principles   _____
2. Team (or Team Development)   _____
3. SWOT Analysis   _____

4. Marketing

   a. Frequent buyer club   _____

   b. Referral programs   _____

   c. Monthly promotions   _____

   d. Social media strategy   _____

5. Service/Products

   a. What is offered   _____

   b. Service sales and retail sales   _____

6. Finances

   a. Profit and loss   _____

   b. Cash flow   _____

   c. Pricing strategy   _____

7. Ideal Client   _____

8. Compensation   _____

9. Advisors   _____

10. Operational Strategy

   a. Legal compliance   _____

   b. Organizational chart   _____

   c. Job descriptions   _____

Grand total = _____

As you look at these statements, what comes up for you? Did you find that you had several low numbers? If you did, you are in good company. Most of my clients score in the 20–30 point range (out of 100; max is 10 points per question for 10 questions). No one has ever scored a 100. So if you came in around the 10–25 point range, it might be a good time to review material provided by LivePlan or your BusinessPowerTools software, attend webinars, or hire a coach to assist you in your area of need. Check into other resources for further learning. Listen to audio books while you are traveling to and from work. Visit your local Small

Business Development Center or SCORE (Service Corps of Retired Executives) chapter for free counseling.

If you are in the 26–40 point range, it may be time to invest in yourself so you can take things to the next level. What areas can you improve in? Where could you seek assistance to bounce ideas or test assumptions? Connect with your coach or consultant to improve your plan. Welcome their feedback.

If you are in the top 5 percent, you are clearly ready to move ahead with your plan to *Power Your Profits*. If you need ideas, resources, and guidance to enhance your business plan, join us in our community so we can support you.

Chapter Four

SELECTING AND BUILDING YOUR TEAM

Most successful businesses have a team of people who work together to help the organization achieve its mission and goals. Even if you are the only one in your company right now, you likely use a crew of go-to folks to help you to manage your business. Not everyone on your team has to be an employee. Your team can consist of a bookkeeper, a legal adviser, a graphic artist, a social media management person, a salesperson, and other outsourced professionals. Whether the people you work with in your business are internal or external, you need to have a plan for how they can best help the company grow.

GUIDING PRINCIPLES FOR YOUR TEAM

Every business needs to create guiding principles for its team to live by. You create these principles with your team, even if it is just one other person, or you will create them yourself and share them with each new team prospect. To create these principles, you have to look at what is important to the business (which you expressed in the planning phase with your vision and mission), what's the thing that's going to wake you up every morning, and what behaviors you will honor with your clients, whether you feel like it or not. What's the thing that's going to have you be in possibility versus be in identity? We find that when we are in identity, we don't necessarily want to be customer service oriented. You might be cranky or you might be tired. But when you are in possibility, you are focusing on how you can embody the highest expression of your guiding principles each day.

For example, one of my clients, Lisa Nichols, established the following principles for Motivating the Masses Inc.

1. Leaders serving leaders, inspiring success while achieving results
2. World-class service with a servant heart
3. Value: In every conversation, in every interaction
4. Balance with playfulness and creativity
5. Teamwork honoring the dignity of the human spirit
6. Students of the world, through transformation and self-growth

Every week in their team meeting, each person stands and cites one of the guiding principles. Team members read them at the beginning of their meetings, and in their weekly report they choose one that they're going to embody that week. It just gives them another focus versus being in identity, the identity of "I don't want to," "I don't feel like it," or however your identity steps in.

It's a major step to come together as a team to ask, "What are our guiding principles?" Involving your team to create these principles can be a powerful step. In my company, we started by creating a list of words. Then we picked words from the list that inspired us. And then from the words we created sentences, and from the sentences we created the six that became the cornerstone.

If you have a larger organization, each division can create its own guiding principles. Your member services team or your sales team can come together and create their own guiding principles that are aligned at the corporate level. They become the "bold statements" that will hold them to higher standards. This is the juicy part. It's hard to strive for the ordinary when you state principles like "I ignite the dignity of the human spirit with aliveness and genius," isn't it? You want to stand taller when you boldly assert these statements.

Once you create these guiding principles and bold statements, you can post them in your office, in the break room, in the conference room, and in the lobby of your business. Each department or division can have its statements posted that will light them up. If it is just you working in a home office, post your guiding principles on your wall. If you are a solopreneur who works in shared executive space, frame it and put it on your desk.

The intention is to have these inspiring messages in front of you each day as you set out to create magic in your business. Setting the tone for how you serve your clients during your productive and prosperous day will lead you to greater success. When your team acknowledges and adopts these principles, they elevate how they show up on the job. They also know that they will be held accountable to perform as the principles suggest.

When I created bold statements for my businesses, I wanted something that people could really sink their teeth into, but also made you go, "Oh, I have to be something different." We wanted to create it from a place of possibilities. Who am I going to be in the face of no agreement (when a customer's complaining)? Who am I going to be when I don't want to serve them or when I don't feel like it? How do you support that? Your guiding principles lead the way.

BEST PRACTICES FOR NEW HIRES

When you are hiring employees or collaborating with new team members in your business, you want to make sure they can buy in to your guiding principles. In the job interview, read your bold statements. Tell the prospect, "Here's our bold statement for the company. Does that speak to you, or does it not speak to you? Because this is who we are, and this is the game we're going to play." Have them either be involved or not. If they're not involved, then they're not the right person for the organization. If they are involved, then they respond, "Oh my God, I love it." In my experience, most people say, "Oh my gosh, I love it. I love that we're that intentional about who we're going to be every day . . . every day in training . . . every day in the office versus showing up business as usual."

It is fine if the bold statement is not the right fit for a prospective new hire. Don't be offended by it. Just say, "Thanks for sharing. Goodbye." Remember, you don't want everyone to work for you or with you; you just want the right ones. And the right ones can buy into what you know your company to be.

Your guiding principles, then, become a tool in your hiring process. If prospects don't see themselves fitting into your environment, or they don't see themselves thinking positively enough to honor your bold statements, or they don't have enough confidence in their ability to operate in an environment of continuous improvement, then they are not for you. It doesn't matter if you like them and they have a great personality or are a friend of a friend. If they can't align themselves with the company's values, principles, and bold statements, they are not the right fit.

WHAT ABOUT THE AVERAGE BUSINESS?

Many people ask, "Do I need guiding principles if I run a business that provides what clients view as a commodity product or service?" My answer is always "Yes!" It really doesn't matter what the job or business is. We all have to show up as though "I love what I'm doing." Whether you're a plumber, a graphic designer, or a doctor's office, we have to train people how to interact with our clients. Team members have to show your fingerprint for the company. The fingerprint is the DNA of how you want to interact with the client. It says "This is how I want our customers spoken to. This is how I want them to feel when they're done. I want every plumber to be representative of the brand." The customer won't know that you own the brand; they know that whoever knocks on their door is the brand. Right? So each team member needs to represent that brand. Bold statements and guiding principles help this to be true.

For example, I have a client who is a plumber. For him, the statements could be about creating results and happy clients. They could read "unstop what's stopping you" or "serve every single customer I meet, leaving each person with dignity and happiness." If your team is responsible for being the pulse of the company and understands that every customer they touch could lead to three to five more customers, what will that mean for the organization? I think so many companies don't realize that each person could lead to three to five other customers who say, "Oh, I have a great plumber." Or "Oh, I have a great dentist." Or great graphic designer. Or whatever. It is important that your team know this.

We're all interacting in some way, shape, or form with a customer. We're either alleviating pain or causing pleasure. So what's the pain we're solving or the pleasure we're giving? Think of that, and then write your bold statement or your guiding principles around that. What do you want to be known for in the industry when people encounter your team members? I love that when people come into my environment, they ask, "How do I create a team like the one you've created here?" It's very intentional. It's a lot of work. It's a lot of management. But that's how I want the customer to be served. I want them to feel like customers at the Ritz-Carlton who say, "I love it here."

BUSINESS SPOTLIGHT:
RITZ-CARLTON'S SERVICE VALUES

Years ago, I took a class led by the head concierge at the Ritz-Carlton. Their team was given a little card with their gold standard on it. They were told to carry it with them everywhere they went. It reminded each team member of their credo and gave them the responsibility and authority to uphold it. It had statements like: *I am always responsive to the expressed and unexpressed wishes and needs of our guests. . . . I own and immediately resolve guest problems . . .* and *I am proud of my professional appearance, language, and behavior.*

In addition, they carried their three service values:

1. A warm and sincere greeting.
2. Use the guest's name. Anticipation and fulfillment of each guest's needs.
3. Fond farewell. Give a warm goodbye and use the guest's name.

Everyone on the Ritz-Carlton team has these little cards. If you ask someone who works there to pull one out, they have to have it on their person; it has to be in their pocket, in their wallet, or somewhere so they can pull it out at any time. It takes the hotel to the next level of serving. It answers, "How do we want to serve the customer?" And if that doesn't appeal to you, as a prospective team member, then you don't work there.

Wouldn't you rather move people in or out based on your culture?

#*Monday Motivation*
"Let it go to let it grow."
—SUSIE CARDER

LET IT GO TO LET IT GROW

Many clients I work with have created successful companies generating millions of dollars. Others have climbed to the quarter-million mark single-handedly, as the only worker in their business, and now they're ready to move up. Is that true for you? If so, it might be time to recognize whom you need to become to take your business to the next level, and what support you will need to reach it without working yourself to the bone.

As you think about your activities in the business, identify the highest income-producing activity that only you can do. For me, my top three, high-income-producing activities are coaching, selling, and training. For you it could be consultations and paid speaking or client health management and research. Look at your revenue-generating activities and determine what only you can do in your business. Fill in the box below.

> **MY HIGHEST INCOME-PRODUCING ACTIVITIES**
>
> Susie's   Yours
> Coaching
> Selling
> Training

Now, about all that other stuff—delegate it.

This will help you to determine which two team members you will need to hire first. Whom do you need to hire to free you up to do what you do best? The first two people I hired were in operations and finance. That tends to be the case for many of my clients as well. You may need to hire a bookkeeper to help you with accounting and tracking your financial performance. Or you might want to hire an operations person to manage the flow of client interaction, logistics, and business administrivia. (That is my word for handling the minutiae or minor details in the administration of your business.) Sometimes you can find a combination operations/finance person, but in my experience, operations have to talk to customers and finance isn't really good with customers.

Your budget may determine what level of expertise these new hires have. Financials and work volume may also determine whether the new hires are brought in as employees or independent contractors. This is not a decision to be taken lightly. Be sure to review the Internal Revenue Service (IRS) guidelines for businesses in the United States (see IRS Publication 15-A). If you bring someone in as an independent contractor and just pay them for services, and later the IRS determines that they were actually employees, you may be responsible for employment taxes for the individual during the time of employ. Some companies have "outsourced" themselves right out of business because they were unable to come up with the employment penalties. Don't let that be you.

MY FAVORITE TOOL RETURNS—USING THE HARRISON ASSESSMENT FOR NEW HIRES

Remember the tool I used to determine leadership skills in Chapter 2? It's the same one that helps me to determine where my strengths and weaknesses are, and what I "flip" to when I am in stress or duress. For example, when I am in stress or conflict, I flip to being dominating, dogmatic, and harsh. Knowing this, we can be prepared before going into staff meetings and such. This assessment is an excellent tool for new hires in your company. It truly takes the guesswork out of managing someone. It also takes the emotion out of a hiring decision (just because a person interviews well and you like her doesn't make her the right person for the job).

I won't go into the details of the assessment, but suffice it to say that I no longer hire based on résumés and interviews. This is because a résumé can look great, but when that person interacts with an unruly client and flies off the handle, I can't see that propensity in an interview or a résumé. The Harrison Assessment, on the other hand, can tell me if an individual is going to fit into my culture or not. It will do a job match against the top 10 percent of people in that position in the world, whether it's customer service or the CEO or a painter. It evaluates your essential traits, behavior traits, what doesn't work, what traits to avoid, and more. It helps you to see what you are going to have to manage in the future so you are aware of it and won't be surprised when they flip.

I have learned and reinforced my learning with this assessment tool. I made the mistake of not listening to the test and hiring a person anyway. They interviewed well and I thought, "They're great, it'll be fine." No, it was not fine. I felt like I knew her, but it did not work. Feelings have nothing to do with reality.

HIRE WELL AND EXCLUDE YOUR FAMILY

There is no better time to remove emotion from the hiring process than when you are considering employing a family member. I do not encourage hiring family. It can create more headaches than the "favor" is worth. You may think they are doing you a favor by helping you out (and likely saving you money from an experienced new hire), and that you are helping them out (providing employment), but it is rarely worth it in the end. Avoid it. See why below.

CLIENT SPOTLIGHT:
HIRING THE WRONG PERSON

I encourage my clients to find the right person for the skill set they require. I had a client who hired an operations person before we did the Harrison Assessment. So I said, "First of all, never hire another person again without doing the test." And then we had the new hire take the test.

It turned out that he hated change; he didn't want to be organized at all; he didn't want to manage things or people; he was permissive; and he wouldn't say what was on his mind or what was bothering him. I'm reading the assessment, and I'm thinking, *Oh, she has someone who's so wrong for the job, but she's already hired him.* Also, there was extra pressure because he moved his family from out of state to work there.

Of course, a month later she started complaining about him nonstop. All I could say was, "Well, here's how we have to manage it. It would be better to let him go quickly than for you to suffer through keeping him on. It's just not a job match."

And then she plopped the cherry on top.

As I was going through this assessment and observing why this guy was not good for her position, I told her, "We've got to figure out how to weed him out."

Then she dropped the bomb. "Well, you know who he is, right?"

"No, I don't know who he is. I just know his name."

She said, "It's my son-in-law."

"What? You hired your son-in-law without talking to me?" Now she was really walking on eggshells, because if he was not doing his job, he was her son-in-law! What a disaster.

Okay, here's the point. Don't hire without the assessment and don't hire family.

I experienced this myself when I hired my own daughter (who is a Harvard and Wharton grad) to work for me. She's obviously sharp. But that doesn't mean it was a good decision. She came in to work for me off and on through the years, and this time, she was spending precious company time talking smack about me in the break room.

"I'm only getting paid twelve dollars an hour," she said to a coworker (like it was such an injustice).

Someone came into my office and said, "Your daughter's talking smack about you in there."

I walked in there and I said, "Okay, you need to go. You need to get your things and you need to go."

Shocked, she said, "What?"

"I'm not paying you to talk about me. You can go find a job somewhere else."

"But Mom."

I said, "Don't 'But Mom' me. Sorry, no gossip." (That is not in our guiding principles!)

Lesson learned.

My daughter still remembers this incident. She will ask me, "Remember that day you fired me?"

I tell her, "Yeah, and you deserved to be fired. You were gossiping about your mom in the kitchen."

Deciding which position to hire first is not always simple. I encourage you to connect with a distributor of the Harrison Assessment (like me) so you can determine your own strengths and weaknesses. Then you can hire to support your underdeveloped strengths. If you are the only one in your business, perhaps you need an assistant, social media person, or an operations manager. Evaluate where you are first before making that decision. For example, I have a client who used to be an accountant, so she is very linear. She doesn't need an assistant. She is the most detail-oriented personal I know. She needs a salesperson first, to come in and start making sales. She is doing it all, being it all, and the biggest issue for her was "How do I get more bookings," and "How do I close the clients that I'm in front of because I'm stuck doing all this other stuff." So we found a salesperson first. The next person we hired was an operations manager to pull the minutiae off her plate.

INDEPENDENT CONTRACTORS VERSUS EMPLOYEES

When you are still in the start-up phase of your business, it is especially useful and often more cost-effective to bring in independent contractors to do project work, as opposed to hiring an hourly or salaried employee. Many companies grow to millions in sales with independent contractors (ICs). I have one client that does $5 million a year in sales and has no employees—they're all ICs. This is great when you don't want to manage people. Now, that is not to say that you can just assign a task and ignore your IC: they still have to be held accountable to complete your projects according to your specifications. But you can focus on providing your product or service instead of employee management.

When you are hiring ICs, there's still a project description, hiring criteria, a list of expectations, and what you're paying them for. So in the memorandum of understanding (or agreement), you will outline the project they are being hired to work on. For example, for the project an IC is doing called social media, it will include expectations like two posts per day, replying to Facebook messages, responding to Instagram comments, connecting on LinkedIn, etc. You will outline exactly what the criteria are for that role and the fee that you're paying for that.

They will still be held accountable to your bold statements and guiding principles when they are doing your work. You will share with them who you are as an organization, and when they are on the clock for you, they represent your brand. In representing your brand, you tell them what you want, how you want them to answer emails, what should be in the email signature, how you want them to answer the phone, and how you want your posts to look, etc.

So when they put their hat on for you, being an independent contractor, they're stepping into your culture and underneath those bold principles and living in that way even if it's for two hours a day. As I have said, you have to declare what your culture is.

The biggest failure that I've seen with entrepreneurs and independent contractors is the lack of accountability and not having a plan-and-review process. They should be checking in and saying, "Here's how it's going for me; how's it going for you?" It is similar to a plan and review with an employee, but it is just for checking in. I find that most entrepreneurs are frustrated, and they feel like they can't hold ICs accountable. But my position is "Why not? You're paying them. Of course you can hold them accountable." That accountability becomes important in determining what's getting done and what's not getting done. My assistant, for example, sends me an update every week (see a sample below). In it, she notes everything that she's done, what results she has produced, and what items are open or pending. She holds herself accountable to me, and I know where we stand.

Social Media/Admin. Weekly Update: 5/30/18

COMPLETE:

Edits for Email Campaign

Photo shoot support

Signed up for HARO

Created PDF: BIO sheet to be sent with HARO requests

Sent 2 HARO responses

** Shirts ready for drop off—See attached photo in email **

IN ACTION/DAILY:

Social media—scheduled and shared

Social media—checking all platforms, messages, responding, connecting . . .

Blog/weekly

PENDING:

Complete edits for Campaign

Asana for GLP 2.0

NEED CLARITY ON:

Asana for GLP 2.0

STATS: (growth since September)

FB Fan Page: 44,461—Increase of 5,727%

Instagram: 3,385—Increase of 625%

LinkedIn: 8,021—Increase of 264%

Twitter: 2,222—Increase of 37%

Database: 1,449

Budget: –$37.91

Figure 1: Weekly Update

When you put structure and procedures in place that allow your independent contractors to be successful, it creates a win for both of you.

IMPORTANT DIFFERENCES BETWEEN INDEPENDENT CONTRACTORS AND EMPLOYEES

It is important that you understand the tax implications between hiring employees and working with independent contractors. I am not a tax professional, so I encourage you to seek competent counsel regarding such issues, but you should at least know that each of these two relationships has different requirements. Employees who are paid with regularity for acting on your behalf within your organization will expect to be on payroll and receive regular compensation. Each of their paychecks will have federal and state taxes withheld, and potentially other pretax items. The taxes that your company withholds from its employees must be paid to taxing authorities on schedule, so I would recommend keeping a separate payroll account through which those funds will flow. You never want to spend tax dollars by accident because it was in your business checking account. Note: If you are operating your business in the United States, refer to IRS Publication 15-A: Employer's Supplemental Tax Guide.[1] It is a guide specifically addressing employees.

Let me tell you a story to show you how important this is. Gayle* was involved in a business whose owners didn't pay taxes because the accountant said it was being handled. Gayle was operating a family business and the accountant said, "Oh, it's being handled," so she didn't ask any questions.

After six or seven years of not paying taxes, an embezzling charge was handed down. Even though a partner in the business was involved, and Gayle said she didn't know anything about it, the IRS sent her to jail for six months. "I don't know" isn't an answer for the IRS. You cannot plead ignorance if you're choosing to be a businessperson.

And then I have another client who came to her business one day and there were chains on her doors. The IRS had seized her bank account and assets. I want to stress to you that it is no joke to be accountable for the growth and accountable for your success. You must pay taxes (in the United States, anyway).

When I was young, I thought I had a good accountant because

---

* Name has been changed.

I didn't pay taxes. News flash: accountants don't just shield you from taxes. But I didn't know that at the time. The professional was referred by someone else. You have to pay taxes. I'm all about leveraging taxes and leveraging your deductions, but they have to be real and legal. You can't cheat and hide money.

My dad would always say to me, "Sue, you'll always get caught in the end. Make sure whatever you're wanting to do, it's worth the punishment." I want to scare the heck out of people because it is so important. I've had to walk clients through this process with them crying, "Oh, I didn't know." Well, sure you did. You're driving BMWs and Mercedes and you have an amazing house and you're saving $12,000 a year. You knew. Be mindful.

One last reminder about employees versus independent contractors: The level of control you wield over individuals will have an impact on whether they should be treated as an employee or an IC. One client was paying her team member commission as an IC, but the team member was only working for her. The IRS came in and deemed her an employee, and boom, she owed $30,000 in tax liabilities. So before you engage someone on your team, decide if they are an employee or an IC, and make sure the IRS would agree with you. All of your ICs should be business owners in their own right; evidence of this is a business license or federal employer tax identification number shared on a Request for Taxpayer Identification Number and Certification (Form W9) from the IRS. Talk to your accountant about tax implications for your business.

ABOUT INTERNS AND OTHER "FREE" LABOR

Also note that there may be tax liabilities associated with internships and other free labor. Confirm this with your tax professional, but the Small Business vertical on Findlaw.com indicates that for-profit businesses may need to pay minimum wage and applicable overtime for interns if you are not providing educational training, the intern's work benefits you, you are replacing other paid positions with that intern, you are gaining a clear advantage by having the intern, and if you guarantee the intern a job. (See https://smallbusiness.findlaw.com/employment -law-and-human-resources/unpaid-internship-rules.html for more information, or talk to your tax professional.)

You might also speak with your local community college or university internship program. They may provide the internship as coursework and mitigate the educational component, but I can't speak to the other issues.

COMPENSATION STRUCTURES

What you pay your team varies widely. Your industry, your geography, and your budget are all factors in how you compensate your team. One way to get a baseline is to look at the comparable salaries from online sources like CareerOneStop.org, which provides data from the Bureau of Labor Statistics and state occupational wage reports. Many sites claim to have salary data, so do an internet search to find your best source.

What if you just don't have the budget to offer a full salary for your positions? I've been able to hire people under budget because my culture was attractive enough. Money is not the only important consideration. We offered things like flex time, which is a benefit from an employee's standpoint. For salespeople, if they make 100 percent commission, I provide qualified leads for them to follow up on. If I have the budget to offer a base salary plus commission, that is great. But, whatever the budget is, I'm just going to let prospective team members know, "Here's the work I have, and here's the budget I have." I suggest you really look at your budget to determine what you can afford, and then find and hire the best people inside that budget.

In my businesses, we have done well negotiating and finding really great talent for under market value because the culture we have is amazing to work inside of. And, we really take care of our people. We acknowledge them. You can never underestimate the power of the intangibles of acknowledgment and appreciation. They are more valuable than money to a lot of people. Also, if they love the mission and vision of what you're up to and that you're making a global difference, it may make your position more desirable.

Some people will be insulted by your salary and say no, but some people will say yes. If they say no, you say next. You can find great people at any price point. Remember that. Stay within your budget. I'm not saying to lowball people just to lowball people. Offer what you can and seek those who love what you have to offer and can work well within your culture.

Online freelance communities like Fiverr.com can be a great resource for many services. (Just be sure you seek out quality producers.) You can find blog writers, virtual assistants, researchers, social media managers, graphic designers, and more. You can hire them by the project, short or long term, and they can help you to grow without creating employer-employee relationships.

TEAM MEETINGS AND ACCOUNTABILITY

When I sold my company, the new company hired us to stay on as employees. They kept all my team members, including my finance team. In the new company's team meetings, we were in the process of evaluating everyone's accountability, and we noticed some discrepancies in our finances. My partner and I noticed it, and our team also flagged it, but the parent company didn't take note. Our sales numbers were understated. We knew what we sold, but what was showing on the reports wasn't accurate. Where was the missing money?

It turned out that when we sold the company to the larger company, some on the finance team started embezzling money. If a client bought a $5,000 product, he listed it as a $3,000 product and pocketed $2,000. Since the parent company didn't have the same accountability system that we had in place (we kept ours in place and we also added theirs), they were not able to see the discrepancy we saw.

By the time we caught it, he had only taken about $15,000. (It still hurt our bottom line!) The parent company took legal action, and he was immediately fired. It was shocking to me that this person did amazing work for years for us, and then, without accountability, something changed. In the past, he had always had our back. Now he felt like he was working for the man versus working for us, the small business owners. If I didn't have the accountability in place, who knows how much he would have embezzled.

Accountability is important for the livelihood of your business. That story is not uncommon. Once people get in and look at what's inside the business, it can be common for people to embezzle money from you. Watch your money and your profit and loss statements, and don't let improprieties slip by you.

In addition to being diligent with your accountability systems, it is important to be an effective project manager. How are you managing the business's projects and how are you holding your team accountable? I know some people who turn over their bookkeeping and reporting to someone who is not even a CPA, and they wonder why they never have enough money to spend. If they don't manage the project and don't review the statements on a regular basis, they won't even know they're getting milked. Ultimately, they're accountable for that. Having regular (weekly) team meetings is one way to ensure projects are being done properly.

In my team meetings, we start with acknowledgment. We take the time to acknowledge everyone for contributing to our success and for going the extra mile. Then we talk about results: we report on the results created, not the tasks that we are doing. It is not an accounting of all the items you checked off your action items list. It is focused on "what are the results that your actions created?" We can then address open questions or concerns. I ask, "Are there open or pending items that you need from me?" Each meeting has a scribe to take notes and document follow-up that will be required for the next meeting.

I'd like to point out an important aspect of accountability: conditions of fulfillment. This is an area that creates anger and frustration in many environments. Let me illustrate with an old story.

———

A manager tells his employee, "Go get me a rock."

The guy goes outside and brings him a rock.

The manager says, "No, not that rock. I want a bigger rock."

So the guy goes outside and comes back with a bigger rock than the last time.

The manager says, "No, not *that* rock. I want a rock that has jagged edges."

The employee goes back outside, finds a rock with jagged edges, and brings it back in.

The manager says, "Oh, not a rock like that. I want it like this," and proceeds to show him the rock he wants to see.

———

The moral of the story is to be clear in the very beginning. The manager could say, "This is how big I want the rock; this is the color I want the rock; this is the shape I want the rock; and these are the dimensions of the rock." Then the person can go get the right rock the first time. What we find in management and managing people, however, is that we give fuzzy guidance that doesn't allow our team to perform as expected. We say, "Go do my social media" or "Go create a flyer," and then don't give direction. We don't give the conditions of fulfillment to make it happen effectively and efficiently. And so then the boss is frustrated and the person going to get the rock is frustrated. If only the boss had asked, "What are all the things that you need to fulfill on this request?" I encourage you not to be lazy in your requests, but to offer conditions of fulfillment. It will make working with your teams much more enjoyable.

PLAN AND REVIEW

One tool that I use in my own business and with my clients is the Plan and Review Form (see Appendices for the full form). This form is given to team members and is reviewed with them by their team leader each month. It gives team members an opportunity to express what is going well and what they feel they could improve upon. Nine times out of ten, the issue they point out as an area of improvement is something you have been frustrated with them about. It allows the individual to tell on himself so you don't have to be the bad guy. (I don't like being the bad guy. I used to tell my kids, "Don't make me have this conversation.")

So the form asks team members to be specific and list:

* Three things that you like about working here
* One thing that you would like to see improved upon at the company
* Three things that you feel you are doing well
* One thing that you are going to work on improving in the next month

There are no surprises when you commit to having your plan-and-review meetings. If someone is not performing well enough to stay on the team, his or her reviews will bear witness. They will know what is coming because they have had discussions about performance each month. This form eliminates at least 90 percent of blind spots.

EXTERNAL SUPPORT SYSTEMS

Most high-performance people have external support systems in place to hold them accountable to achieving at their highest and best level. Business leaders are no exception. I have a coach for several areas of my life—business and personal. I shared my story with you earlier about how one of my coaches helped me multiply my business income. I also work with fitness coaches to keep my body in peak physical shape, and financial coaches to stay fiscally fit. Consider having a coach on your team to hold you accountable to having the best business possible. (Feel free to contact me at SusieCarder.com.)

In addition to a business coach, you may also want to have a certified public accountant (CPA) on your team to help you stay in line with taxes and financial issues. A corporate lawyer is also valuable, especially if your business requires contracts and legal agreements on a regular basis. Aligning yourself with service professionals will help you to gain strategic advice, wise counsel, and objective feedback on ideas at critical junctures in your business.

Step into the Big Time: Team Assessment

Now it is time to take a look at where you stand with your team. This tool will help you to determine what systems you need to put in place to create a solid team and management process. When you look at the Team Assessment, be honest with yourself in your responses. This is all about and for you. No one else will benefit from your honesty like you will.

As you look through each of the ten items below, rate yourself on a scale of 1 to 10, with 1 being "I don't even know what that is nor do I have it in place," and 10 being "I am on it." After you finish rating yourself in each area, add all of your points (there can be no more than 100 points).

Team Assessment

Rate your team effectiveness from 1 to 10, with 10 meaning that you have the essential elements in place to hire, manage, and transition your team.

I have . . .
1. A written vision statement   _____
2. Written goals and objectives for: six months,
   one year, and/or three to five years   _____
3. Clearly defined project/job descriptions   _____
4. Team meetings once per month or more   _____
5. Measurements for success (accountability)   _____
6. Team leaders (accountability partners)   _____
7. Incentives/rewards   _____
8. Conditions for fulfillment   _____
9. Plan-and-review sessions with my team   _____
10. An exit strategy   _____

Grand total =_____

As you look at these statements, what comes up for you? Did you find that you had several low numbers? Do you have what you need to lead a team to success? Are you ready to move to the next level with your team? Putting the right instruments in place is one of the activities that I help my clients to do. If you are in the 26–40 point range, it may be time to invest in yourself so you can take things to the next level. What areas can you improve in? What could you implement to help your team to be more successful in meeting their goals?

Remember, if you scored less than 25 points, don't worry; this is great information to have. Your blind spot has been diminished. Now you know where gaps are so you can put systems in place to grow and manage your team effectively.

Start with your two lowest scores. If all are low, start with the one that will make the biggest impact in your business. For example, I would address item #3 to write clearly defined job descriptions and then item #5 to define my measurements for success. What is your next?

If you are in the top 5 percent, congratulations; you are poised to grow and take massive action.

If you need ideas, support, and guidance to enhance your team management, seek out your coach to help you turn this information into action.

Chapter Five

OPERATIONS INFRASTRUCTURE

If you were to die or run off into the sunset tomorrow, would someone be able to come in and run your business? For many who start out and operate as the sole employee of the company during the first few years, that answer would likely be no. This is because when you are the only one doing the work, you don't always stop to document what you are doing. Developing systems may not be a priority. You continue to be the technician, serving the client without taking the time to create and employ systems that would make the business run smoothly with or without you.

When I stepped in as a consultant to Motivating the Masses Inc., a company led by internationally known transformational speaker Lisa Nichols, it had plenty of potential, but it was standing on shaky ground. The business relied on her to survive, so she couldn't take a break if she wanted to. The business was fragmented, almost entirely virtual, and had growing sales that were not hitting the bottom line. I came in and established systems, order, and standards, and within a year the company had grown 254 percent. A year later, that growth skyrocketed to 3,000 percent. And year-over-year growth has been between 30 and

75 percent since then. These quantifiable results came from having the right systems in place.

This chapter will help you to determine the organizational systems you can put in place to make your business productive and scalable. We will review a systems checklist and determine what systems you've established, what you need to build, and what those systems entail, so that you can finally take that well-deserved vacation, leaving the business running smoothly with or without you. These systems will help you and your team to manage the day-to-day functions of the business, regardless of who is present.

#MondayMotivation
"It doesn't matter what the widget is, you still have to have business infrastructure."
—SUSIE CARDER

CREATING THE FERTILE GROUND FOR GROWTH

When I launch a new business, I create a Management Tools Binder, where I store all of the procedures, documentation, processes, and tools that the business uses to achieve positive results. If there is an action I have to take, say, in a sales conversation, I will document how that conversation is supposed to flow, a script of what is said, a checklist of follow-up procedures, and the like. All of this then goes into the binder to provide guidance to someone else who will manage that process someday. For a start-up, this binder can grow slowly. Start by creating documentable actions today that someone is likely to have to replicate later. Then file those instructions in the binder so they are easy to find and use when needed. When you find systems that work in your business, you want to document them so you can "rinse and repeat."

This approach to developing systems is fine when a business is in the

$50,000 to six-figure range of revenue. But as you continue to grow, you may have to create more complex systems. The more money you make, the more complicated it can become. (But don't let that stop you from growing!) Your Management Tools Binder will grow as your business does, and eventually it will become the precursor to automated systems and documentation managed by others in your company.

> *"Susie's brilliance is in helping me get out of my own way and expediting the process so that I get the results better, quicker, faster. . . . I'm on track to see about 20% revenue growth this year. I am grateful for Susie for helping me achieve that with her vibrant, real-talk, care-frontational energy that truly puts the sexy in systems."*
> —BELLA S.

By the time clients come to me, they know they need something. For example, Nora was a speaker with a new training company. By the time I met her, she had launched her business, but she wasn't really getting any traction or making any money. This was challenging for her because she left a $250,000 job to start this dream business. She was frustrated.

She had heard me speak at a women's business summit about having systems. She came to me and said, "I really want to talk to you about this whole systems thing. I don't know how to do it."

So we started a relationship and began looking at every aspect of her business. What systems did we need to put in place and what did she already have? We looked at her marketing system, her sales system, and more. Taking the time to document everything in the beginning is where most entrepreneurs get lazy. They don't want to do it. It's not fun. Documenting your systems only becomes fun when you put them in place because then it gives you a little more freedom. And as you grow your team, it gives you a lot more freedom. But I helped Nora most by building her systems.

The following year, Nora came down with an illness and the doctor said she had to be off for sixteen weeks. That's a long time for a small business owner to be off and not generating any revenue!

When I checked in on her and asked how she was doing, she said, "I'm doing amazing, but more important, my business is doing amazing." She was so grateful. "Since we put systems in place, I now see the value of all that work we did, because I'm in the hospital and my business is still making money. My assistant is handling my clients. I don't know if I will ever appreciate the work we did as much as I do now because I see the tremendous value of taking the time to build it right."

Building the systems will allow you to go on vacation—or in her instance, to be sick—and still be able to bring in income. So the foundation of your business lives in creating the systems so that your business can enjoy a life of its own. With Nora, systems gave her freedom, security, etc. In sixteen weeks, her business could be gone without systems. But she won't have to face that now or lose her business momentum.

REDUCING RELIANCE ON OTHERS

Sometimes it's not just the business owner who knows everything that needs to be done. A key employee may have created a successful approach to providing a service or winning customers with your business and you need to document that for future employees. Having systems can help us to reduce the reliance on key employees. For example, one of my clients, Leslie, had a business that did well from the jump, earning her first million without a hitch. But then her revenue started slipping; she went from one million in revenue to $800,000 to $700,000. Her business was falling like a lead balloon. After working with her a while, I learned that her key salesperson was holding her hostage because no one could do what he could do. He was the only one who was good at delivering her programs, and every year he demanded more money or he would threaten to leave. She felt she needed the programs so she kept sinking more and more into it.

I said, "Well, we just need to train other people."

She said, "I've tried. I hire really great people who have expertise in business management, but they're just not relating to our customers."

I asked, "What's your training program like?"

"Well, we train them on our product, but I don't really know how to train them to be like this star employee."

"Well, you trained him," I reminded her. "So let's put together a training that relays your ideal customer experience."

Once she got her feet under her, she realized the ideal training regimen just takes time. . . . She was so busy being busy that she became this employee's hostage because she didn't take the time to create her own training manual. What I love about systems is that you can produce extraordinary results from talented, ordinary people. I made her stop and ask, are you willing to do the work? Are you willing to stop a minute and breathe and ask, "What am I willing to put in place so this business can thrive?"

So we ended up releasing the superstar person because his compensation was so out of whack. When I looked at the numbers, she was actually losing about $30,000 annually—between the compensation, the expenses, and the overhead—on that one program she thought she couldn't live without. We later realized it didn't make sense to even be doing that program because we were losing money every time we did it.

I believe that when we are good technicians in the business, we don't stop and reassess and look at the numbers and what the business is doing financially. When we're a smaller business, we could be losing hundreds of thousands of dollars and not know it.

So, in Leslie's case, we raised the price on the program because it wasn't profitable. We put together a training outline that had a script of what to say, so anyone who delivered the content could be successful.

If you really look at it, nearly every great salesperson started with scripts and learned their business on a script. Look at the big training and development companies like Dale Carnegie or Ken Blanchard. They all train off of scripts so they don't have to have presentation slides and just wing it. I still use a script in my sales conversations. Even though I've been doing it for twenty years, I just pull up the script to stay focused on not getting distracted. I script it so other people will know what I say to get a 50 percent closing ratio.

It's imperative to grow your business and to keep your fingerprint on it—your voice, your sound, your culture—otherwise every time somebody comes in, your business model will change. That happens a lot in small businesses. Part of having someone else come in is freeing for the owner because you're like, "Whew, somebody else is helping me." But then all of a sudden it's not your business anymore. You might be paying the bills, but you're not running the business. Having systems, like a script for what your team should say, helps to keep your fingerprint on the business while creating systematic results.

BUILDING THE FUNCTIONAL ORGANIZATIONAL PLAN

If you were to think of your business with the ultimate goal in mind, what roles, functions, departments, processes, etc., would need to be in place? This doesn't have to be complicated. If you don't know how to write training or procedures manual, or you feel you don't know how to systematize things, just start with lists. That's what I did. I would ask, what are the things others would need to know to do this? I would write this down and create it as a checklist. Eventually, over time, I became more sophisticated with it.

For example, when I owned a salon and spa, I had a system for folding the towels. (Yes, even that!) I discovered that if I didn't create a system,

Your CRM might be as simple as using a software program to document each of your prospects and customers and their interactions with you. Or it could be a combination of your sales funnel and auto-responder software. Or it could be using cloud-based note software like Evernote or OneNote. Whatever you use must be simple enough to incorporate into your regular routine so that it stays up to date.

Your start-up sales system may be the flowchart of questions that you lead your prospects through to help them decide to use your solutions. Your binder will hold your sales goals per quarter so you can track your performance. It may be an online option form on your website that connects prospects to your auto-responder that provides valuable content on a regular basis. It may include the Sales Member Analysis Worksheet (see Chapter 6) to provide clarity, accountability, and training for your sales representatives. If you have physical products, you might also use the inventory management section of your accounting software to track inventory. Your sales system need only include what you need to sell successfully in your business at this time because it can grow as your business grows.

Your initial social media system may include having a Hootsuite account through which you post three tweets per day on Twitter, two posts per day on Facebook, and three pictures per day on Instagram. Your binder might include a monthly schedule of themes and posts to use for this purpose. Your system will also have social media engagement goals that you can refer to at any moment. Of course, your binder can also include all the account access information as well.

BUILDING SCALABLE SYSTEMS

The reason I started putting systems in place is that I'm a butterfly. I'm naturally disorganized. I used to follow the sparkle and take on too many projects. I couldn't keep things on track, I had inconsistent income, and clients would just come and go. I didn't want my schedule to control me. As a single mom raising two kids, I had to figure out how to work and provide for them and be a good mom at the same time. Back then, I was at a loss, so I had to look at how I could create predictable results in everything.

In my consultations, some days would be mystery days, and others would be amazing where everyone said yes, and I needed to figure out what I did to make that happen. What did I say? Homing in on systems allowed me more freedom. Following structure allowed me to be more creative (not less) and actually gave me more time with my family because I was no longer trying to do all the last-minute stuff that comes with following the sparkle.

As your business grows, all of the tracking systems you have in place for each functional area of your business may grow to include tabs for each department of your growing business. You may also have systems by program or by service area—be flexible in creating and modifying systems as time passes. Talent management and personnel systems will need to be added as you expand. These will include job or project descriptions so that new team members can be on the same page and so you can manage expectations.

At the beginning, you do not have to create every system for a long-term end result. You can have a plan that includes and leads to that end result, but you don't have to have everything in place all at once. Allow yourself and your business to grow organically yet strategically. Start slowly and build bread crumbs into your operation. Work from the philosophy that this is something that somebody else can or will do, so document all your processes for future growth. (Remember, you are going to ask yourself, "What is the highest income-producing thing only I can do?" and then delegate the remaining tasks to others. You will need to document those tasks.) When you know your business goals, you can ask yourself what you need to have in place or at the ready to achieve them. In your documentation, you can also include the scope of your projects, your strategies, and who will do what by when. Additionally, identify the potential obstacles. What could get in the way of your success? Write out the obstacles and their workarounds so they will be accessible when needed.

BUSINESS SPOTLIGHT:
BENEFITS OF CONSISTENT OPERATIONAL SYSTEMS

Operations are the foundation and the heart and soul of any business. When set up correctly, operations keep the business running smoothly and allow the owner to focus on strategies and finances, instead of the day-to-day. A solid operational plan creates consistency in the business, and this allows ordinary people to create extraordinary results.

Think about any successful company that has multiple locations, like Starbucks. Walk into any Starbucks across the country or around the world, and you will have the same experience from store to store. Your coffee is the same, the names of products are the same, the furniture is the same, the retail items are the same, and the motif is the same. The only thing that may be different is pricing and the employees' faces. I travel a lot for business and often travel alone. The first thing I do when I get to a new town or country is find the local Starbucks. Why? First, I like the coffee, and second, it feels familiar—like home.

Though you may not open several businesses, you need to set your business up as if you were planning to franchise it. The more systematic you are in your approach to operations, the easier it is to train your employees and replicate the experience. Like Starbucks, you want to provide the familiar experience that keeps customers or clients coming back for more.

DOCUMENTING THE STRUCTURE: SOPs AND MORE

To grow your business and maintain consistency in providing a quality service to your clients and customers, create a process for each activity in your business. What is the workflow? Whose hands need to touch the project as it moves through? Chart that path and document it in a standard operating procedures (SOP) manual. Even if you are the only one working in your company right now, having this documentation will be advantageous when you start to grow. When you are ready to hire or outsource, you will have this documentation ready. It is also beneficial if you have an unexpected absence and someone has to step in for you (like my client Nora, whom I mentioned earlier in this chapter).

In addition to having operating procedures, make sure that you create and have an up-to-date organizational chart at all times. It is necessary for the team to understand to whom they report and to whom they are accountable. In many organizations, the owner puts managers in place, but the owner ends up doing what we call skip management, which means they end up getting involved in projects with a team member, skipping over the manager, and confusing the team member on who is really the boss. Keep the lines clear with an organizational chart.

CREATING STANDARD OPERATING PROCEDURES (SOPs)

When creating SOPs, I use a project management sheet. This is a form that includes an action item, who is responsible for it, and by when. It shows everything that needs to occur in the project management process to be successful in that area. See the snippet of the form in the image below.

SAMPLE STANDARD OPERATION
PROCEDURES ACTION PLAN

Team: Sierra and Phillip

Objective: To maximize the efficiency and effectiveness of the internal processes/operations of XYZ Inc.

Action Items	Project Leader(s)	By When?
SOP for biweekly blog posting	Sierra	04/30
• Create editorial calendar for blogs	Sierra	04/15
• Develop image folder	Phillip	04/17
• Manage content creation	Sierra	04/19
• Identify keywords, tags, and categories	Phillip	04/25

The first column shows the actual *Action Item*. The next column shows the *Project Leader(s)* or who is responsible or accountable. The final column is the *By-When* date. These words become magic; you will double the efficiency of your organization just by adding these words to any task you delegate.

When managing this process, it is important to be mindful of the *By-When* dates. Since many projects are over and above regular job duties, it may not be possible to complete them all within the same week. You may have to stretch out the timelines among the everyday workflow, so that special projects can be successful. It is better to underpromise and overdeliver than the other way around.

The key to success in this model is to make sure the dates are set in stone, meaning you can't keep moving and changing them. If you allow people to constantly change their commitments, the commitments stop meaning anything. There are exceptions to the rule, but be wary of changing deliverable dates. An exception to changing dates is to help the team member discern whether or not he or she overcommitted and to help the project manager plan more thoroughly.

I recommend that you frequently check the accuracy of the project flow. When learning how to be an effective project manager, it can be easy to leave out important steps. Make sure every step that needs to occur in a project is written, and have the project manager review the action plan with several key team members to check for accuracy. It can be easy to lump projects under one heading, so be mindful.

In elementary school, my daughters were asked to write out each step that it would take to make cookies. Another student would then have to follow the directions step-by-step without filling in any blanks. It had to be explained as if you were telling an alien from another planet how to make the cookies. So you couldn't just say "Take the flour and mix it with the sugar"; you had to be explicit with every step. What would you put the flour in? How much do you mix? With what utensil? It is easy to assume that something is obvious, but when someone has to follow the steps verbatim, it matters when something is missing. The same will be true for your SOPs.

THE SECRET BENEFIT OF SOPs

Clients often ask me how much they need to include in their SOPs and why they are necessary for an existing team. They already know how to do their jobs.

One reason you should have SOPs is that you don't want every person under you running to you for the answers to all the questions. You don't need constant interruptions or delays because they need to know next steps. An SOP gives you freedom in knowing that your people can do what their job requires without your direct oversight. Most important, however, is that the SOP gives you a business to sell! It is a system that becomes part of your exit strategy.

If you have to be in your business every day for the business to prosper, you don't own a business—you own a job! If you have to worry whether all the questions will be answered or if there will be a business when you return, you have trouble brewing. If your team can't handle business effortlessly without your being there every day, you have a lot of work in front of you to create your business. By using SOPs and having your team follow them, you can trust that business is being handled correctly, whether you are at the helm in person or not.

This is another reason that choosing your team wisely, treating them as you would your best client, and understanding the dynamics in their development are so important. They may be representing you when you are away from the business, and you want them to have all the tools they need to do that successfully.

One of my clients had taken her business as far as she could go on her own. She had to grow in size in order to reach the next level of sales/revenue. She decided to hire consultants who could serve her clients, but she didn't have systems in place to allow them to do their best work. She had to learn not to fear the system so she could grow. With my guidance, she decided to set her business up as if she wanted to franchise it. She created systems so each consultant could step in and produce positive results because they understood, "This is how we do it." The result of creating sales systems for her new consultants added $250,000 to her bottom line. That is nothing to be afraid of!

"I feel sorry for the person who can't get genuinely excited about his work because he doesn't understand his role. Not only will he never be satisfied, but he will never achieve anything worthwhile."
—WALTER CHRYSLER

ACCOUNTABILITY AND SOPs

The business system is only as good as the team that incorporates it or the leader who holds them accountable to it. I have a client who is very successful, but there's so much chaos around the business because she won't hold people accountable to following the system. They're always reinventing how to do something that is predictable—it's basically doing the same thing over and over, but she lets them do it in whatever way they want each time. Then she won't train people and they don't want to take the time to find someone to show them how to do it when she's busy going to the next thing. So what happens is they waste a ton of time and a ton of money reinventing things.

Some team members are saying, "We've already created this, why are we doing this again?" So instead of tweaking things, they're re-creating things. But if you have systems in place and people are following them, you'll naturally update those processes as your business grows instead of starting from scratch all the time. This could save you thousands of dollars.

A start-up business is different from a $250,000 business. As you grow, your systems will change a bit. Your hiring procedure, your interview process, your vetting process as you bring on additional people, how you interview people for the team, how you deliver your product or service—all of these can change over time.

Take putting a marketing plan or campaign in place. If that campaign works well, keep refining it and keep making it better. Don't just say, "Oh, now let's try this instead, and next let's try that." You may do a little of that in the beginning, but after a while you'll see something work and then stick with what works. Now, that may not be as fun—repeating the same thing can be boring for some entrepreneurs. But for me, the growth and scalability is the fun and exciting part. I like finding out how to grow with the least amount of chaos.

Bear in mind that business is designed to have conflict and chaos. The finance department is always saying, "No, you can't spend money." The marketing department always wants you to spend money. Salespeople always want to make more money. So there is this constant conflict either with yourself or with your team. If you're just starting out, you're in the conflict with yourself, saying, "I need to spend money; I have no money. I need to spend money; I have no money." Calm your chaos with systems.

CLIENT MANAGEMENT SYSTEM

One system that is important for every business, regardless of size, is how you manage your client relationships. In the early days with my salon and spa, I just had a phone and appointment book. By the time I sold the salon, I had a software system in place. In my training company, I used software called ACT, which allowed me to keep track of contacts, correspondence, and next steps. Now my current company uses Keap (formerly Infusionsoft). You have to decide what is best for you given the client relationships you want to have and information you need to manage. How will you communicate with your clients? What do you need to track? I have had clients keep their client data in an Excel spreadsheet. We later uploaded them into a client relationship management (CRM) program, but as long as the system isn't sticking business cards in a drawer, most anything will work if you use it.

MANAGING THE JOURNEY

My chaos client from above not only failed to hold people accountable, but she also didn't have a client journey. The journey means when the client comes into your organization, it defines how you take care of them, what conversations you want to have with them, and what is the first contact, second contact, third contact, or fourth contact. It is what you want people to experience. It might be the communication that says, "It was great meeting you, here is who we are and what we do, and if I can be of service to you and your community, let me know."

You want to sit down and think about "How are we going to have a conversation with this client throughout the journey of our relationship? How am I going to check in with a client and build trust?" Putting together a client's journey allows the customer to feel touched even though the communication was automated (like an email). I have clients who respond to my automated emails just thanking me for touching base. I love that! It just always tickles me when they respond back to me and say, "Thank you so much. I appreciate you keeping me in the loop."

In addition to planning and knowing when a client has been touched by a newsletter or a video or a blog post that you send out, you should really be taking and keeping notes in your database about each client. Notes are so important, especially as you get more removed from your customer experience (where your team has most of the direct contact). If your notes aren't in your database, for example, what you said to the customer or the emails that you've sent to them, if there's a complaint, or if there's a challenge, you have no data to fall back on. You want to be able to say, "Oh, well we sent you an email on this day and we communicated on that day and my finance department talked to you on this day." And you could be all those people, right, but you've had and documented all of those conversations. It protects your business by keeping that data. Especially when you get bigger and have more people on your team, it is hard to manage all of those interactions. But now software is so sophisticated that you can email from that database and it automatically logs that and tracks those conversations and tasks so everyone on your team can see them.

I learned the hard way because I've had clients who would complain about my service or complain about the way a staff member treated them, and I didn't know what to say because there was no evidence. I would have to go and search for the evidence and waste time going to check people's emails when a client said that she didn't hear from my team, and then they would have to search their emails to try to find that email because they know that they communicated with the client. How much time and money did we waste because we just didn't take the time—in the moment—to update the notes? I think we've all had that experience or one of having to search emails to find something that we know we sent or did. It's just a waste of time and money and it's frustrating. Having consistently used systems in place will help eliminate or diminish that.

It may seem like a lot. It takes ten units of energy to get it going, but once you get everything in place, it will only take one unit of energy to keep the flow. The business/systems building process can take one to three years, one to five years for some people, depending on how you're building and depending on what you're doing. You have to have patience and grace with yourself and know this will pay off in the end. This will make a big difference.

JOB DESCRIPTIONS

In my more than twenty years consulting with businesses, I am amazed by how many businesses do not have clear job descriptions with specific measurable goals and responsibilities. The success of your business depends on your frontline employees who interact directly with your customers, suppliers, and others. If they don't get things right, your business suffers. It is in your best interest to make their jobs as easy for them as possible. Start with a clear job description.

One model of a job description could include a list of the skills a person absolutely must have to perform at an optimal level. For example, leadership skills, time management skills, project management skills, and comprehensive spreadsheet skills may be necessary. If the person you are hiring doesn't possess these skills, you have a choice: hire and train them or hire someone else.

The job description can also include the percentage of time that will be devoted to each area of responsibility (for example, 20 percent of time in coaching team members, 30 percent of the time in strategy, and 50 percent of time is spent producing). Lastly, what is the work value that needs to be in place to succeed? Where do you focus your efforts? If you are a new manager, you have to weigh spending time on coaching against developing others. It's hard to train a new manager about the fact that production isn't the number-one priority. But in today's world, it's not.

Here is a sample job description for a marketing manager, to give you an idea of what could be included.

JOB DESCRIPTION

Position:	Director of Marketing
Reports to:	Executive Director; consultation from Marketing Partner(s)
Status:	Exempt

Position Responsibilities:

Direct firm's overall marketing and strategic planning programs, and corporate communications. Facilitate client development through marketing and client services programs.

Duties and responsibilities include but are not limited to:

1. Design, implement, and facilitate annual marketing plan for the firm to ensure we hit the financial goals. Support and facilitate development and implementation of section business/marketing plans.
2. Plan and administer the firm's Marketing Operations budget; support development of regional marketing budgets.

3. Oversee the Charitable Contributions Foundation.

4. Organize and implement client relations including:
   * Client satisfaction surveys
   * Client development activities
   * Client skills training
   * Special events

5. Supervise the firm's RFP protocol process, including soliciting RFPs from desirable prospective clients and writing proposals for new business; participate in planning and presentation sessions, when assigned.

6. Oversee business development activities, including:
   * Efforts through Business Development Coordinator
   * Assisting attorneys in strategic planning for client presentations
   * Offer coaching for prospective client meetings, presentations, etc.
   * Work with regional offices on designing and implementing prospecting and client contact systems.

7. Oversee corporate communications activities through Communications Coordinator, including:
   * External communications and systems
   * Internal communications and systems
   * Public relations efforts
   * External vendors and consultants

8. Develop and administer marketing database that includes client and prospect information, mailing list applications, access to financial reports, etc.

9. Assist with and support firm's involvement in various networks, including coordinating business development and marketing activities via these relationships.

10. Design and plan quarterly marketing training seminars for staff.

11. Oversee firm's electronic marketing efforts, including supervision of website design and maintenance.

12. Supervise Marketing Assistant, Client Services Administrator, Communications Manager, Practice Development Manager, and Regional Marketing Manager(s). Make staffing and hiring decisions within marketing department.

Employment Standards

Education:	College degree required. Concentration in Marketing, Business, or Communications preferred.
Experience:	At least five years in marketing director role within professional development environment. Strong leadership and consensus building skills; marketing management and strategic planning experience; a proven track record in developing and administering a marketing program.
Required Skills:	Must be a self-starter, highly organized, and able to work well with team members at all levels in the organization. Polished presentation and interpersonal skills. Must possess top-level business management, interpersonal, and facilitation skills. Needs good knowledge of Microsoft Office and Windows-based computer applications.
Special Skills:	Background in business marketing and knowledge of Business Practice Development System a plus.
Time allocated:	50% Marketing Tasks 20% Strategic Goals, objectives, and partnerships 20% Managing others 10% Admin tasks

Most individuals fail at their jobs because they are not clear on what they were hired to do. Job descriptions become so general that they are useless or the job morphs into something completely different. It is critical for everyone on your team, even for you, to have clear responsibilities. Do you have job descriptions in place for all of the positions in your organization chart? Do they include not only what the overall objective of the position is, but the skills required and time applications? Be sure to write the job description for the position and not for a particular person you have or want to have in the position.

If you are at an early stage with your business, the percentages of time allocated are more like 50 percent if you're a business owner/technical work, then you have 30 percent as CEO, and then 20 percent admin. Right? So I'll find that people say, "Oh, I'm the CEO." Well, you're not always the CEO. There is a percentage of time when you are acting in that role. Even in my business right now, 70 percent of my time is spent as a technician and then 30 percent is working on the business (I want to balance that more at 50/50). As I bring people on, the technician percentage will be less, and the CEO will be more.

You have to realize that 100 percent of your time cannot just be as technician. You've got to spend time managing yourself, managing the business, and managing processes. That's why people feel like they're working sixteen hours a day or longer, because they are . . . all day they're the technician, and all night they're trying to figure out, what systems do I need to put in place? Well, if you know that from the beginning, let's outline your day that way and say, "Oh, I've got to put in fifty percent as the technician and then fifty percent running my business. How am I doing that? How does that other fifty percent of the time measure up?"

Perhaps creating job descriptions that are results oriented versus task oriented could help. "Make sales calls" is a task, "Make thirty sales calls a day" is a result. You can say, "I made sales calls this week," and that could be two sales calls. But if I know you need to make thirty calls a day, that's a result that I can manage.

EVALUATING YOUR BUSINESS SYSTEMS

This systems checklist is probably one of the best tools that I give my clients. When I started my training company in 1995, I started accumulating the systems I was using to build a multimillion-dollar business. As I shared earlier, I created something called the Management Tools Binder, and in that binder was every system I needed to run my business, from sales, to marketing, to operations, to finance, etc. I put it all in this binder. My clients at the time were visual, creative entrepreneurs, so I brought this management tool in to show my clients what they needed to put together. In the training session, I referred to this binder. And several people raised their hands. I called on them and said, "Yes?"

"Can we buy that?"

I looked at my binder and asked, "You want to buy this?"

They replied, "Yeah, could we buy that?"

I told them, "Well, no, it's mine for my business, and it has all my systems."

"Yeah, we don't care. We want to buy that one."

I was caught off guard. So I asked, "Well, how much will you pay for that?" I had no idea what to charge. I wasn't planning on selling it.

They said, "We'll pay $900."

Surprised (yet delighted), I asked, "How many of you would pay $900?" And a big group raised their hands. So I said, "Okay, sold, $900. I will make you a copy, but I'm not changing anything. It's going to have all my information in it, so you'll get all the papers exactly as I have here."

They said in unison, "We don't care. We want it."

I was amazed. That's when I saw the value of just giving people the "it," the tool. Not the concept but the "it," the systems. What's the "it" you need to have in place to grow a multimillion-dollar business? Whether it's a six-figure business or a seven-figure business or an eight-figure business, what do you need to put together? Those are the business systems you want to have in your Management Tools Binder.

To understand where my clients are in the development and use of their organizational structures, I have them review a list of processes or systems and identify what they have and what they need. Take a look at the list below and put a check mark by those you have in place and those you know you will need later; write "N/A" on those that do not apply to your business. Note that already having a checklist or step-by-step process documented is worthy of a check mark.

- ☐ Administration—Entity creation, licensing, and regulations
- ☐ Agreements—With clients, contractors, landlords, event planners, affiliates, etc.
- ☐ Business plan—The plan for your business that you created or tweaked in Chapter 3
- ☐ Customer service—The experience you want customers to have and delivery system
- ☐ Database management (+ CRM)—Process for acquiring, storing, and reviewing data, especially for client management
- ☐ Employee and team handbooks—Regulations for employees to abide by and be held accountable for. May also include hiring, vetting, and onboarding processes
- ☐ Financial management—A system and schedule for producing and reviewing profit and loss reports, operating budgets, cash flow projections/calculators, taxes, and payroll
- ☐ Inventory control—If you sell products, plan to have enough on hand to meet sales projections and address seasonality
- ☐ Job descriptions—Roles and responsibilities for each position in the company (vacant or filled)

- ❏ Lease negotiations—Rental agreements for equipment and real property
- ❏ Marketing and promotion—Budgets, campaigns, branding, collateral, and strategies
- ❏ Meeting minutes and notes—Documentation from staff and board meetings
- ❏ Pricing—Base price calculations to ensure profitability; setting prices for growth
- ❏ Professional development—Training for you and your team to grow and improve
- ❏ Programs/Products/Services—Sales process, product knowledge, sales tools
- ❏ Sales systems—A systematic process to sales that removes the pain and makes it fun to convert prospects to sales (including sales funnels)
- ❏ Travel—Process for petty cash, per diems, reservations, travel plans/accounts, packing lists
- ❏ Weekly reporting/accountability—Tracking key success indicators (average ticket, lead generation, lead conversion, social media growth, sales member analysis)

Visualize your business a few years from now; what systems will it need to have in place to be successful then? Plan for them now.

Step into the Big Time: How Strong are Your Systems? An Assessment

Now it is time to take a look at where you are and where you want to go. I don't know about you, but I have terrible test anxiety. I hated tests in school. I would freak out and sweat. Even if I knew the information, I wouldn't pass the test because of the test anxiety.

I remember when I had to renew my driver's license. I went to the DMV and had to take a test. The first time I took the test, I missed six questions. The lady said to me, "You can take it again."

So I said, "I'm taking it again."

I took the test again and had six wrong again. But this time they were completely different wrong answers than the time before!

The lady said, "Ma'am, you had these answers right before."

I asked, "Well, can I just use that? Can we just combine them?"

"No."

"Well, can I take it again?"

She says, "You can take it again."

So I went back, and I took it again. I came back, and again I had six wrong. And again, you can only have five wrong. This time, some of them were the same and some of them were different.

She said, "Ma'am, you know this information."

"I know that I know, and you know that I know. Can we just say that I know?"

She said with a heavy sigh, "My God, yes, you can."

Luckily, by the grace of God, she let me through because I wasn't allowed to take it a fourth time. I would have had to come back. I just have such test anxiety and it keeps building.

Note that I am giving you assessments inside this book, but I want to make sure that you are aware that they're not meant to be judgments or measurements of your worth as a businessperson. I'm not looking at whether you're "good enough." For me, assessments allow us to see we are here (at this particular point) and that's a fine place to start. You can then know this area is what you need to work on and this area is what you're really good at.

I want to free you up to not measure yourself, and allow yourself to let go of the emotional baggage you have around doing tests. Breathe and give yourself grace. If you get zeros, you get zeros, whatever. Let's just work on increasing those numbers and increasing those scores versus beating ourselves up. There are too many times in life where we focus on what we didn't do instead of celebrating what we did accomplish. What I want to celebrate in all the assessments is that we're taking action. And as Joan Baez says, "Action is the antidote for despair." Make sure that you are celebrating this process versus resisting this process. So, remember, if you ever get tense and contract while doing an assessment, celebrate, don't resist.

Now, this assessment will help you to determine the broad areas where you might need systems in place for your business. Again, be honest with yourself in your responses. This is all about and for you. You can strengthen your systems once you are clear on what is needed.

As you look through each of the ten items below, rate yourself on a scale of 1 to 10, with 1 being the furthest from the truth, and 10 being "It's in there!" After you finish rating yourself in each area, add all of your points (there can be no more than 100 points).

Systems Self-Assessment

Rate the strength of your systems from 1 to 10, with 10 meaning that you have everything you need to be successful in this area.

I have . . .
1. Effective Monthly Promotions (e.g., marketing calendar) _____
2. Policy and Procedures Manual _____
3. Agreements _____
4. Team Coaching Systems (monthly/weekly accountability) _____
5. Advertising Campaign Strategy _____
6. Ongoing Recruitment Strategy (website, ads, etc.) _____
7. Retailing and Service System _____
8. Customer Service Scripts (for all departments) _____

   9. Pricing Structure/Menu Development   _____

10. Owner Support System (P&L review, coaching,

     budgets, etc.)   _____

                                Grand total = _____

Did you find that you had several low numbers? If you did, you already know you are in good company. If you came in around the 10–25 point range, let's look at the most important system you can put into place. For me, item #10, the owner support system, which is my profit and loss review, my budget, would be one of the first things that I want to work on. If I look at the second thing, it would be item #2, policy and procedures. How do we do it here? Right? The third thing would be item #9, pricing and menu development, or product suite. What are we offering and at what price?

Take baby steps. Don't think you have to do this all at one time. I didn't do this all at one time. This is years and years of processing and failing and getting sued and not having information or wanting to train somebody. How do I train someone in a predictable manner? So be gentle on yourself. The important thing is to know that you need to know it. That's the beauty of this for me. The self-assessment is "now I know what I need to do, where before I didn't even know that. I didn't even know that I needed to do it." For me, these are just the most important ones to start building an efficient organization.

So breathe; it's not going to be built in a day. It's a process. The first person I always hire in a company is the operations person. I know I can sell, I know I can deliver the service, and the highest income-producing activity for me is that. So let me make more money to hire someone to do this stuff. If you don't like doing it, don't suffer through it. Go sell more so you can hire someone to do the things you don't like to do. Remember, knowing you have a gap is great information to have so you can address missing areas before you need them.

If you are in the 26–40 point range, it may be time to invest in yourself so you can take things to the next level. What areas can you improve in? Take your two lowest scores and take a closer look. Where could you tighten up your information, forms, or processes? The next time you work through a regular system for serving clients or completing a business transaction, document it and add it to your Management Tools Binder.

If you are in the top 5 percent, you are clearly ready to move ahead with your solid business systems. Use those systems to train your team so they can make every business experience a familiar one for your clients.

Chapter Six

SELLING YOUR PRODUCTS AND SERVICES

DOES LOVE EQUAL MONEY?

What good is it to have your community fall in love with you when they never buy? I work with a lot of clients who love what they do. They are passionate about the product or service they provide, but they are afraid to ask for the sale, so they can't get a yes. If you provide a great product or service, but you don't ask your client for the sale, who wins? No one! You have to ask for the sale or be proactive in selling to get to that powerful yes or that powerful no. You want them in or out and you have to be okay with whichever one it is.

Let's talk about that for a moment: being okay with the powerful yes or the powerful no. I remember being enrolled in a leadership class, and they were big on being on time. I am a time stickler, but they were *really* time sticklers. One time I was going to be late. Driving in, I panicked about being late. I remember thinking, *I'm going to get in trouble, because I'm late. I'm going to get in trouble because I haven't communicated that I can't be there on time. They're going to yell at me or lecture me.*

And I had to take a minute, breathe, and say, "Wait a minute. I'm an adult. I could just communicate. I could communicate that I am going to be late and give them my arrival time." And I had to be really clear what the arrival time was, so I padded it by an extra ten minutes.

And then I listened to what they had to say. Their job was to hold me accountable to a higher standard because they were training me to be an extraordinary leader.

I thought, *Okay, whatever they say, I can't make that mean something more than it is. I can't make it mean I'm not good enough. I can't make it mean I suck. I can't make it mean I'm a loser.* I had all that mind chatter that we run through when we have to have hard conversations and we're afraid to have them.

So inside of looking at your money and your sales, I want us to start developing our truth—our truth for us. People may not agree with you as a leader. They might not like you as a leader, but at the end of the day, they will respect you as a leader.

Here we have to get our ego out of the way so we can focus on the business and serving our client. The yes or no is not about you. It is about whether you have expressed enough value to your client (marketing) to compel them to a decision to work with you (sales). But if you never ask them to work with you, you don't make the sale and they don't get the solution.

So what keeps you from asking them to work with you? Yes, it is often fear. It is often the fear of being rejected, fear of sounding salesy, fear of success, and the like. That fear is grounded in the ego that you need to step out of. Let that go. Release on that fear so you can confidently invite your clients to accept the solution that your business provides. Think of your client here. You have identified that they have a problem. You have identified that you have a solution, and you are not inviting them to use it! This is one area where I add a lot of value to my clients. I help them to uncover areas where they are not asking for the sale, I show them the economic impact of not asking, I help them to establish their sales process, including the ask, and I hold them accountable for doing so.

I'm not going to lie to you. I also have an accountability coach. My excuses can be sexy; I can hide and manipulate with the best of them. I need someone helping me to stay in my greatness and to stay in my lane of action, but I don't have to do it alone. I suggest you not try to do this alone. Personally, I am a recovering supermom, superworker, superwoman trying to do it all, be it all. So it's important that you find a coach—whether it's a business coach, an accountability coach, or whatever is the best fit for you—who is willing to hold you accountable and hold you to your greatness. You want coaches who are willing to tell you the truth. I find too many times that coaches are just "yes" people who agree with you about everything. My job as a coach is to make you uncomfortable. My job is to hold you to your greatness. My job is to be a stand for you when you can't be a stand for yourself.

You want to find a coach with synergy who can match you power to power. Don't find someone you can manipulate. Don't find someone who isn't willing to call you on your stuff because they're afraid to lose the account or lose the money. When you get in a coaching relationship like that, it's incredibly dysfunctional. As much as I hate when my coach holds me accountable, I love it. I don't love it in the moment, but I love it on the other side.

TAKING A STAND FOR YOUR MONEY

Being a stand for my clients reminds me of Melanie. When I first started working with Melanie, her training and development company had a love for what they did and they were really good at it, but they were really uncomfortable talking about the investment that needed to be made to pay for themselves. I remember when I started coaching her;

she would get so mad at me when I would have her set her financial goals. These were the sales goals she was going to sell from this month to next month. She was really picky with me and would say, "You're so mean to me. You always make me sell."

I would remind her, "If we don't sell, then we make no money. If we make no money, you can't pay your overhead and you can't pay me. We have to have a breakthrough in this." So we started looking at what was really there for her and started to uncover that she didn't feel worthy of the price that she needed to charge. And she didn't know what that price was. She hadn't looked into that.

So we looked at how much we had to charge in order to pay all her overhead and expenses and herself. She could now see that if she didn't charge this, it was basically equivalent to giving the customer money! It probably took us six months of her fighting me, me holding her accountable, and her getting mad at me, but every week we'd have a conversation. Each week she would hit or exceed her sales goal, so we would raise the goal for the next time.

Again she would say, "You're so mean to me. You keep raising the goal."

"I know," I would reply, "because you keep achieving the goal."

"If you keep raising it, it's just going to make me not want to achieve it."

I said, "How silly. You are willing *not* to achieve your goal so that you do not have to do your homework."

When we looked at the financial impact of her hitting her goals, she had grown from $50,000 a year to more than $300,000 by doing what she was doing. Sometimes I just have to take a stand for my clients, even when they are tempted not to take a stand for themselves.

BUSINESS SPOTLIGHT: LINDA WEARS MASKS FOR MONEY

It's funny how our limitations and our self-esteem and self-worth are tied to the ability to talk about pricing.

My client Linda had such a strong issue with having a money conversation with her clients that she created an alter ego, Laverne. Laverne would call prospects on behalf of Linda to talk about sales. She could do that better than calling for herself. It sounds silly, but she had to figure out how to have the sales conversation. If selling is hard, perhaps you are able to talk from the third person. To the prospect, she is Laverne who is calling on behalf of Linda. The prospect didn't know the difference. (If she conducted her sales calls via Zoom with video, she wouldn't be able to do it this way.)

How do you have the sales conversation and what's going to empower you most to have it? I find when you're first building sales, you have to be your own best salesperson. You may find yourself wanting to delegate that to somebody else, but the reality is you have to do it first and then you can train someone else to do it. It may take a little time to get comfortable with, but be patient with yourself. Be gracious with yourself. Sometimes, following up as yourself is hard to do. Okay, so then let's create an alter ego so you can talk about yourself in the third person. But if you can remember that you are really selling the results to your clients, not yourself, it is like having your own Laverne.

How can you discover the weakness in your sales process? We are going to talk about several key issues that will help you find pockets of money that you are either losing or not using. Looking at your current sales can help you to make more money without even winning new clients.

FOLLOWING YOUR MONEY

Take a look at your profit and loss statement (P&L, aka your income statement). If you don't know what this is, or you've never spent time putting it together, make a commitment to yourself that you will make this a priority. You can't run your business without a P&L. It's an entrepreneur's road map. It's equivalent to getting the car and driving to my house when you don't know where I live. You don't know what city. You don't know if I'll be home. You need to know that I'll be home. That's your P&L. Your P&L is the foundation of everything else in your business, so make it a priority. Find an accountant or bookkeeper who can help you organize that. A simple example of a P&L follows so you can hold a mental picture of it as we talk about it.

SAMPLE INCOME STATEMENT (P&L)

Revenue (Income)

Coaching	$75,000
In-house Training	55,000
Speaking Engagements	25,000
Publishing	15,000
Total Revenue	**$170,000**
Direct Costs (Cost of Sales)	−25,000
Gross Profit	**$145,000**

Operating Expenses

Salary and wages	75,000
Employee-related expenses	10,000
Internet	2,500
Dues and Subscriptions	300
Office supplies	500
Phone and utilities	4,200
Marketing	7,500
Meals and entertainment	500
Transportation and tolls	200
Postage	50
Contribution	7,500
Printing and production	400
Bank fees	3,650
Professional services	1,000
Rent	6,000
Total Operating Expenses	**$113,300**
Operating Income	**31,700**
Interest & Taxes	6,000
Net Profit	**$25,700**

On your P&L, you will see the revenue numbers and the expenses it took to generate that revenue. Now I want you to look deeper into the revenue line items. What specific streams of income do you have? Where are all the sales coming from? Can you break those sales down by category and by salespeople? What is their average ticket? How many clients or customers do those sales figures represent?

Taking a deep dive into your sales figures will help you to discover a lot about your business. Unfortunately, many business owners don't feel they have the time to look deeply into their dollars. They might say "Well, money is coming in, and money is going out, and there is still money in the account, so I guess we are doing all right." No, that's not okay! Multimillion-dollar businesses lose millions each year by not looking deeply into their sales numbers, processes, and strategy. And they wonder why they keep bleeding money. I don't want that to be you.

You can be losing money and not realize how much it is costing you. In business, it's what we call a slow bleeder. You haven't lost a limb all at once, but at the end of the year, you essentially have. When you bleed money throughout the year, and you don't know where the bleeding is coming from, you get to the end of the year and you're like "Whoa, what happened? Where are all my profits?"

Chances are, that leak is either in the productivity of your technicians (team members who are providing your product or service), your pricing structure, or your capacity versus demand. Let me give you an example.

CLIENT SPOTLIGHT: FINDING THE MONEY

Recently I was talking with a client about his salon business. It is a fabulous salon earning $1.5 million in sales each year (which translates to $125,000 per month), but it couldn't even keep up with the monthly rent on the building. When I asked the client what was going on, he said, "I just can't figure it out." So he asked me to take a look.

I looked at his sales numbers, looked at his productivity, and examined his costs per hairstylist. Each stylist was expected to book $3,100 of business per week, but, on average, they were only selling $2,500 per week. That's a big deficit. That's a loss of $600 per week per person (he had thirty) for a total loss of $18,000 per week. You multiply that out and it equates to $72,000 per month and $864,000 per year. That is a huge limb to lose. It started with a small bleed of $600, and ballooned to a whopping $864,000 by year-end!

So, I told him there were a couple of things he could do. One was to sit down with every single stylist and demand that they meet the $3,100 figure or they couldn't work for him. The other option was to share the reality that we can't keep losing $864,000 a year. It makes no business sense. Having those conversations can be tough, but do you want to keep losing money, or do you want to sit your team down for a serious talk? For him, it was like parting the Red Sea. He said, "Oh, I see now."

Isn't that delicious? Just by looking at one key indicator, I was able to help him find $864,000 in lost sales.

Let me give you a tool you can use to follow your money. I created this tool because my coach kept telling me, "Susie, quit managing your team members' feelings. You have to manage the results. Look at the numbers of what your team member is doing or what they're not doing, and quit being lazy."

If you want to own a business, your work now is to ask, "How do I get my team to the highest level of production?" The only way you're going to do that is by measuring. The tool I describe below allows us to see where we are and where we need to go. I use this Sales Member Analysis tool/form with my clients to help them determine what each of their team members should be generating in revenue to support their position. I will include a full, blank version of the form for your use and review, and then I will break down each section with an example so you can learn how to use it.

SALES MEMBER ANALYSIS WORKSHEET

This worksheet is designed to help you calculate your "Sales Member Analysis." This is the dollar amount each *person* needs to meet to break even in your business.

Calculating Sales Member Analysis

STEP 1: ENTER THE INFORMATION		
Line 1:	**TOTAL MONTHLY EXPENSES** *(Enter ALL monthly expenses together.)*	$_____
Line 2:	**PROJECTED MONTHLY PROFIT** *(Actual or 10% of gross sales)*	$_____
Line 3:	**TOTAL # of SALES MEMBERS**	_____
STEP 2: CALCULATE THE INFORMATION		
Line 4:	**TOTAL PROJECTED EXPENSES** *(Line 1, Total Monthly Expenses added to Line 2, Projected Monthly Profit)*	$_____
Line 5:	**SALES MEMBER PROJECTED SALES** *(Line 4, Total Projected Expenses divided by Line 3, Total # of Sales Members)*	$_____

Line 6:	**WEEKLY PROJECTED SALES** *(Line 5, Sales Member Projected Sales divided by 4 weeks)*	$_____

STEP 3: UNDERSTAND THE INFORMATION

This formula allows your business to determine what each salesperson needs to produce for *your* business. If your sales are below the "Recommended Sales Member Analysis," you need to share this with your team. People will support what they help create.

If numbers are low, you have two options. Have each salesperson sell more customers or work smarter with each customer. It is recommended that you do an average ticket worksheet on each sales member to support him or her in achieving this goal.

It is easier to manage results than people's behavior.

CALCULATING SALES MEMBER ANALYSIS

In the example table below, which is Step 1 in the Sales Member Analysis Worksheet, enter your total monthly expenses on line 1. This dollar figure will represent all of the costs you have in your business, on average, in a given month. It will include rent, utilities, office supplies, internet, maintenance, etc. You should be, or become, very comfortable knowing this number for your business. For our example, we will enter small round numbers to keep it simple.

On line 2, enter your projected monthly profit. Here, if you know the percentage of sales that your business usually has left to invest, put it in dollars. If you do not know, and do not have an industry average you can use, just enter 10% of your gross sales figure here (gross sales dollars × .10 = projected monthly profit in dollars).

On line 3, enter how many sales members you have working in your business. These are only those out generating sales revenue for you by selling a product or service for the business. If you are the only one, put a 1 here. If you only have an administrative assistant who does not generate sales leads and dollars, still enter 1 here (you).

STEP 1: ENTER THE INFORMATION		
Line 1:	**TOTAL MONTHLY EXPENSES** *(Enter ALL monthly expenses together.)*	$8,000
Line 2:	**PROJECTED MONTHLY PROFIT** *(Actual or 10% of gross sales)*	$4,000
Line 3:	**TOTAL # of SALES MEMBERS**	5

Now, using the numbers from lines 1–3 above, we can calculate your total projected expenses for the business on line 4. If we need to cover $8,000 in expenses and still generate $4,000 in monthly profit, then our total project expenses combines the two ($12,000).

On line 5, we calculate what that means: each of our sales members needs to generate in order to meet our profit goal each month. The total projected expenses are divided by the number of salespeople we have.

To bring this down to a manageable level, you can divide line 5 by four weeks to find the weekly sales that need to be generated by each sales member on our team. Now we can talk!

STEP 2: CALCULATE THE INFORMATION		
Line 4:	**TOTAL PROJECTED EXPENSES** *(Line 1, Total Monthly Expenses added to Line 2, Projected Monthly Profit)*	$12,000
Line 5:	**PROJECTED SALES BY SALES MEMBER** *(Line 4, Total Projected Expenses divided by Line 3, Total # of Sales Members)*	$2,400

Line 6:	**WEEKLY PROJECTED SALES** *(Line 5, Projected Sales by Sales Member divided by 4 weeks)*	$600
STEP 3: UNDERSTAND THE INFORMATION		

This formula allows you to determine what each salesperson needs to produce for *your* business, not the business down the street. In the example above, your team members need to generate $2,400 in sales per month or $600 per week. If your sales or those of your team fall below this "Recommended Sales Member Analysis," you need to share this with your team. People will support what they help create. Work through the numbers with them so they can see how they are generated and how important meeting those numbers is to the company's overall financial health.

Let's say you are the only salesperson right now, but you want to hire someone on commission. This worksheet shows how much that commissioned salesperson needs to generate from the start to meet your business's goals. By breaking it down by the team member and by the week, it makes it easy to see what is expected.

If they are underperforming, you have two options. Have each salesperson sell more customers or work smarter with each customer. They may need to make more sales calls, increase their closing rate, or improve the qualified leads that are ready and able to buy your products or services. To support each sales team member in achieving the projected sales goal, I recommend that you do an average ticket worksheet (we will review this later). Remember our salon owner example from earlier: one simple leak of $600 per week turned into an annual hemorrhage of $864,000.

Before you point any fingers, be sure to check yourself. As the owner of the business, you might think you can quit selling when you have a sales team in place. You have to remember that you are essential to the growth and sustainability of your business. You must always "be selling." I am always selling. In every conversation I am having at every event that I am doing, I am selling. Now it is second nature for me. I expect that of myself.

I am also holding other people accountable for meeting the minimum acceptable level of sales. Using the Sales Member Analysis Worksheet, I can measure people by that number. Did you hit it? Did you not? Why not? If they didn't hit it, their results are going to show us what they are not doing. It could be they are not doing enough sales calls. If it takes you six clients to reach the $600 per week in sales (from the example above), are you making sixty calls per week to reach that number? Note here, if your closing rate is higher than 10 percent, you can get away with making fewer than sixty calls. I am just using an average return of 10 percent on energy expended.

If they are cranking on the sales calls, but their results are still not up to par, are they getting ahold of people and following up? If they are getting ahold of people, but they're not closing anything, then I'm going to say they don't know how to close people. They don't know how to have a closing conversation and we need to work on that.

It could be a qualified lead challenge. You could be talking to a lot of people, but nobody has the money. So the salesperson has to really take notes and put that in a data management system. (You can use a system like Salesforce or Agile CRM to keep those notes.) If we've had sixty calls, and out of those sixty calls we got ahold of ten people, and ten people had no money, what can that tell us? Did they really not have money? "We have no money." That's what we all say, unless we really want it, and then we find the money. We have to show our prospects the value of our products and services so they will seize the investment opportunity. If we are talking to the wrong people, all the calls in the world won't help us to meet our sales targets.

When we bring on new salespeople, we know we are going to have to put a lot of energy into them without a lot of results at first. But using tools like the Sales Member Analysis Worksheet, we can help them to be successful by working the CAT system: providing *clarity* and *accountability*, and then the *training* they need to meet the company's goals. This allows salespeople to take responsibility for their own success. They are clear on what goals they are here to hit, their accountability shows in their results, and when they miss the mark, we evaluate what is missing and train them so they can hit the target going forward.

I give my sales team three months to get up to speed in training. I have found that it takes about three months to really understand the business culture. As a leader, I have to have grace during that time period, but I have to make it clear what I want them to produce, and I hold them accountable for it. I give them training before I start evaluating. If I am not clear, and I don't hold people accountable, and I don't train them, I cannot be upset when they don't produce the results I was hoping to see. But if I have put in the C, A, and T and they are still not achieving the desired results, I must decide if they are a good fit for the company.

This whole conversation and training can come out of using this worksheet tool and working through to see where the results falter. It is easier to manage results than people's behavior. Follow the money (and the numbers) so they can see where it leads.

EXERCISE: YOUR SALES MEMBER ANALYSIS

Now it is your turn to calculate your Sales Member Analysis. It will be a great tool for helping you to get or stay on track with your sales needs, and it will provide a way to hold your sales team accountable. (Remember the CAT: Clarity, Accountability, and Training.) Gather the information you will need to complete this exercise:

* Monthly income statement with line item detail for sales
* Monthly income statement/cash budget showing all monthly business expenses
* Monthly income statement showing profit as a percent of sales (or industry standard profit percentage if new business; otherwise use 10 percent)
* Staff data: number of sales members on your team (include yourself)
* Client data: number of unique clients per product line: retail and service

Now use the Sales Member Analysis Form to find your weekly projected sales numbers that each sales team member must meet to justify their position and keep the business generating the income it needs to grow. Note that you can use the printed form in this book or contact me for a spreadsheet version that will do the calculations for you when you enter your data. If your sales numbers are below the final number on line 6 of the form, you need to share this with your sales team and work together to sell more customers or work smarter with each customer. You cannot afford to allow sales members to keep producing less than your minimum. Remember, you don't want to bleed out. A small leak now can lead to a hemorrhage later. And if you are going to take your business to powerful profits, you cannot afford that. Your team must perform or transition out.

STEP 1: ENTER THE INFORMATION		
Line 1:	**TOTAL MONTHLY EXPENSES** *(Enter ALL monthly expenses together.)*	$_____

Line 2:	**PROJECTED MONTHLY PROFIT** *(Actual or 10% of gross sales)*	$_____
Line 3:	**TOTAL # of SALES MEMBERS**	_____
STEP 2: CALCULATE THE INFORMATION		
Line 4:	**TOTAL PROJECTED EXPENSES** *(Line 1, Total Monthly Expenses added to Line 2, Projected Monthly Profit)*	$_____
Line 5:	**SALES MEMBER PROJECTED SALES** *(Line 4, Total Projected Expenses divided by Line 3, Total # of Sales Members)*	$_____
Line 6:	**WEEKLY PROJECTED SALES** *(Line 5, Sales Member Projected Sales divided by 4 weeks)*	$_____
STEP 3: UNDERSTAND THE INFORMATION		

This formula allows your business to determine what each salesperson needs to produce for *your* business. If your sales are below the projected sales, you need to share this with your team. People will support what they help create.

If numbers are low, you have two options. Have each salesperson sell more customers or work smarter with each customer. It is recommended that you do an average ticket worksheet on each sales member to support him or her in achieving this goal.

It is easier to manage results than people's behavior.

BUILDING IN MULTIPLE STREAMS OF INCOME ("BACK OF THE HEAD" MONEY)

Another thing you can find when looking at your revenue streams is where your sales are coming from. This next tool is a game changer. This tool allows me to find the money in my clients' businesses and my own. This tool is the truth teller. What I have learned to love about math is that numbers don't lie. We all want to think we're doing more than we're doing, so be ready to have some eye-opening experiences with this one. This tool will enable you to get real with your numbers and with what's occurring and not occurring.

Ask yourself how many products and service lines are active in your business, how much do they generate in income, and how much does it cost to generate that income per line item?

Many clients I meet know their products or services, but they don't know how each of them contributes to the business as a whole. As such, they spend ad dollars, human resources, and other energy selling each of those products or services, when all of those products or services aren't even making a return on that investment.

Yes, you probably understand the concept of a loss leader (selling merchandise at a discount to draw in customers), but when you are not doing that strategically, you are just selling something because you have always sold something, not because it adds profit to your bottom line. You have to look at each line item and make a go/no-go decision on whether it is earning significant enough revenue to keep promoting and selling that product. Just because you like that training course doesn't mean that it makes sense for your company to sell that training course.

If you find products that are not holding their own, it is an opportunity to release them from your sales inventory and reinvest that energy and those resources into your more profitable products and services. This one move can help boost your sales significantly. Energy flows where attention goes. Focus your energy where your profitability lies and you will make more money.

For example, my client Nicole is an interior decorator. When she came to us early in her business, she was her own best client because she was spending more money on her own interiors than anyone else. When she did have a client, she was actually investing some of her money because she didn't know how to charge. She didn't know how to leverage referrals. One of the things that we shifted was that on everything that she was referring to the clients, she should get a percentage. So if she were hiring someone to come in and do blinds, she would get a percentage of that. If she bought a couch, she would get a percentage of that. If she bought a chair, or a lamp, or a desk—anything that she recommended to the client, she would do revenue share on that.

So now fast-forward seven years. Thirty percent of her income comes from a revenue share on those other items, where before it was just a complete pass-through. Now she negotiates better on behalf of herself and her clients, and she gets a percentage of everything that she sells.

When does it make sense to have multiple items to sell, even when they are not huge winners? When they build your community by creating a sales funnel. If you can drive new clients into your fold, and have those clients move swiftly into higher-priced programs or service plans, it may make sense to offer products with a lower return. We will talk more about that when we discuss the Momentum Map later in this chapter, but for now, let's look at how existing income streams are performing.

THE STREAM WITHIN THE WATER

Evaluating your sales numbers can also lead you to find money where money already exists. It is the stream within the water that is already flowing. This is where understanding your average ticket can come in handy. By that I mean, for each customer you have, take a look at what the average sales ticket is for each of them. You may sell a $50,000 annual program on the high end, and a $997 product on the low end, but your average ticket may be something like $1,500.

What if you could double that average? How would that impact your business?

How could you double your sales without selling even one more customer and without increasing your sales staff? By being more effective with every single customer.

Before we can do this, we have to know what our average ticket is. When working with my private clients, I provide an Average Ticket Worksheet that helps them to calculate their average ticket per week, and to evaluate the impact that small improvements can make on their weekly and annual income stream. As you can see in the example below, you find out how much income you make in a week in your service lines and retail lines, separately. Then you total the number of clients it took to generate those weekly sales. This gives you your average weekly ticket in both categories. Additionally, you can then project your annual sales based on this information.

Sample Business

Follow the steps below to find out your average ticket:

Step 1) ENTERING THE INFORMATION: _____

TOTAL SERVICE DOLLARS
(enter the TOTAL amount spent in the business on SERVICES for the week in this box) | $5,000.00 |

TOTAL RETAIL DOLLARS
(enter the TOTAL amount spent in the business on RETAIL for the week in this box) | $200.00 |

TOTAL # OF CLIENTS
(enter the TOTAL # of clients who visited the business for the week in this box) | 5 |

Step 2) CALCULATIONS BELOW: _____

AVERAGE SERVICE TICKET:	$1,000.00
AVERAGE RETAIL TICKET:	$40.00

CURRENT PROJECTIONS

TOTAL AVERAGE TICKET	# OF CLIENTS PER WEEK	TOTAL SERVICE SALES PER WEEK	TOTAL RETAIL SALES PER WEEK	TOTAL SALES PER YEAR
$1,040.00	5	$5,000.00	$200.00	$270,400.00

As you can see in the example above, the average total ticket for both service and retail is $1,040 per week. This equates to $270,400 in annual sales per year. If you keep doing what you are doing, you will make $270,400 by the end of the year. Depending on where you are in your business, that could be great. But what if you want to step it up a notch? Using the information above, we can now do sensitivity analysis to project how our sales revenue can change with incremental changes in the average spend each of our customers makes. Let's put it into the form so we can calculate it.

As an example, if we just increase our average service ticket by $30 per week, we could add $7,800 to our annual revenue. That extra $30 in service raises our total average ticket to $1,070. Multiply that by our same five clients per week and we now make $5,350 ($5,150 in service and $200 in retail) per week instead of just $5,200 ($5,000 in service and $200 in retail). Now multiply that weekly income over the year (52 weeks) and you have made $278,200 (which is $7,800 more than our original $270,400). What starts as just a small increase in sales per client ($30) turns into much bigger revenue over the course of the year!

AVERAGE SERVICE TICKET:	$1,030.00
AVERAGE RETAIL TICKET:	$40.00

CURRENT PROJECTIONS

TOTAL AVERAGE TICKET	# OF CLIENTS PER WEEK	TOTAL SERVICE SALES PER WEEK	TOTAL RETAIL SALES PER WEEK	TOTAL SALES PER YEAR
$1,070.00	5	$5,150.00	$200.00	$278,200.00

Let's have some more fun! Increase that same ticket by $50, and your increase in sales jumps to $5,600 total per week ($5,400 in service and the same $200 in retail) or $291,200 per year, an increase of $13,000. That's a small lever that produces a big result! And we didn't need any additional sales staff or clients to grow that money. Isn't that beautiful?

AVERAGE SERVICE TICKET:	$1,080.00
AVERAGE RETAIL TICKET:	$40.00

CURRENT PROJECTIONS

TOTAL AVERAGE TICKET	# OF CLIENTS PER WEEK	TOTAL SERVICE SALES PER WEEK	TOTAL RETAIL SALES PER WEEK	TOTAL SALES PER YEAR
$1,120.00	5	$5,400.00	$200.00	$291,200.00

CLIENT SPOTLIGHT: FILLING THE STREAM

I tasked a client of mine with doubling her average ticket. We'll call her Jane. To do this, Jane had to get her sales numbers together and divide that number by the number of clients served to generate those sales, just like we did in our Average Ticket Worksheet example. This gave her the average ticket. Now she had to double it.

Jane had no capacity to expand. She could not take on any more clients to raise her revenue, so she was going to have to serve each client she already had more efficiently to maximize their spend with the company.

After going through this exercise, Jane determined how much more per ticket she would need to reach her new sales goals. (Half the battle is in just knowing where you want to go.) What she found was that with a clear target in mind, and a renewed sense of purpose (to allow each client to buy more services), she could achieve her objective.

Jane is a homeopathic MD. So we looked at a couple of things. One, what other services does each customer need? And two, what products would we recommend based on their needs? So just by looking at her customers, could they benefit from getting IV therapy, or getting booster shots like vitamin B_{12}, or could they come in one more time per year? We strategically looked at offering retail items to the customer and offering additional services, whether that was vitamin B_{12} shots or energy shots or liver shots or coming in to address their concerns one more time per year. All those actions raised the average ticket.

In three months' time, Jane tripled her average ticket, and then doubled her overall sales without any more clients and with no more staff. Her business grew from $1.2 million to $2.4 million in revenue just by doing this exercise.

Having my clients produce results like this is why I always say that there is money everywhere. You just need to learn how to find it. We all get stuck in our boxes? We get stuck in our own limitations. So what I do is help you to open that box.

I may ask, "Well, okay, where are the strategic partners? What is the next logical service? What else is your customer asking for?" A customer has asked for every product I have ever created. My next client question after that is usually "Well, how much would they pay for that?" And we may create a new slice of the revenue pie to address that client need or add on to an existing program or provide additional training that was previously in another form (turning a book into a course, for example).

In Jane's case, however, we only needed to serve the client more effectively to increase the dollar spent per client. When you allow yourself to get creative and think out of the box, you can make great things happen. We also taught Jane and her staff about needs analysis, so not only was Jane making recommendations to her clients, but her staff was making recommendations as well. But again, they were selling from the need; they were not just selling stuff.

For example, if before I'm ready to get on a call with a client, I ask myself, *What are their biggest challenges and how can I be the solution?* the solution is my products and services. So for Jane, because she was in health care, what were the solutions every client was looking for? They wanted to feel better and be healthier and have more energy and vitality. So what products and services does Jane offer that can be that solution?

So now if you take fifteen minutes before you start your day and think about what your clients need, and then make those recommendations, your sales will go up.

No matter what industry you are in, there are examples. If you were a hairdresser, you would have the haircut, the color, and the conditioner. If you were a graphic designer, you would have the website, your brand identity, business cards, and program flyers. Find out what else the customer needs that maybe they're not aware of and really comes from a place of total service. A mechanic may recommend rotating your tires, and do an oil change, and do a thirty-point maintenance check to make sure your systems are working. A landscaper may not only trim your trees but also look at your watering system. Every technician sees something a customer needs, but they're shy to make that recommendation. Our job is to recommend, and the client's job is to say yes or no. You'll get a no, but you'll get yesses as well. Your job is making the recommendation and being consistent in your recommendation because every client isn't going to say no every time. If you're consistent, and you believe that's what they need, eventually they'll come around. But come from a place of service and help them to get what they need.

If, when thinking about your clients and their needs, you discover you need to create new products to be that solution, look at the revenue wheel in Chapter 8 and see what the next product is that makes the most financial sense to launch.

DEVELOPING YOUR SALES STRATEGY: HOW TO GET WHAT YOU WANT

Before delving too deep into your sales strategy, it is a good idea to evaluate where you, as the business owner, stand in your effectiveness as a sales consultant. Regardless of what you do as a business, you have to sell your products or services or you don't have a business. But it is important to note that a sales consultant is different from a salesperson. A consultant is finding a need and filling a need. When you stand in service, your clients will look at you differently versus just a salesperson. The goal is that clients rely on you to help them in their business or their personal life or their service needs. That's why I am a sales consultant and not a salesperson. The salesperson is selling to get the sale and to get the most money they can from each customer. I am coming from a place of "Which products and services will help this customer and serve this customer?"

Remember, no matter how much your business grows, you should always be selling. How effectively do you do that? And are you coming from a place of service?

STAIR-STEP PROCESS FOR SYSTEMATIC SALES

In 1995, one of my first business coaches and mentors was a man named Doug Carter. Doug was one of Dale Carnegie's top trainers, and he was one of the top sales trainers in the world (the results he produced were higher than anyone else's results inside that organization). We would meet every Thursday at my house, and he would teach me modules on selling, presenting, and the whole behind-the-scenes of what it takes to be a powerful presenter, speaker, trainer, and salesperson.

One of the tools Doug gave me was the stair-step question process and it forever changed my life. (Another name I hear for this tool is Spin Selling Questions. You may be familiar with that.) I never get on a sales call without using this process. This process is diamond. You have to make sure you don't change it. You don't add your own words. You don't change the flow of the process. The process is designed in a systematic way to allow you to get the customer to a powerful yes or a powerful no. Inside the stair-step questions, you want to go deep with your clients. You want them to really dig in in each section.

"Stair-Step Questions"
A system for tapping into people's emotions!

Situation:
1. What is your position in the business?
2. How did you get started? (This is when you want to hear their "story." What was your original plan and thinking when you opened?) (Repeat what you heard them say; they need to know you get their story.)

Need:

3. What is your greatest frustration with your business at this point?

4. What do you *know* the business needs right now?

5. How do you know this is something you need? (What is your evidence?)

6. When was the last time something like this happened? (Tell me about a situation so I can relate to what you are saying.)

Implication:

7. What do you know will happen if you don't improve on these or this?

8. Ultimately, what's the long-range impact on you, the business, the staff?

Payoff:

9. Let's say we can improve on this situation; how would this help you?

10. What would that mean?

11. Ultimately, what would this mean to you?

12. The ultimate question is: Are you willing to do the work to have what you want?

Recommendation:

May I make a recommendation?

What I recommend is . . .

Why I recommend it is . . .

How you will implement or use this service is . . .

Your investment for this is . . .

Source: *Bootstrap to Big Time,* by Susie Carder

Copyright of R. Douglas Carter, 1993

The first part of the questions is called the Situation. The situation allows us to look at where the client is right now, and it allows you to build rapport. We build rapport by relating to someone's history, emotionally, by pacing his or her tone, tempo, and word speed (mirroring). The more we have in common with that client, the more related they feel to us. This first part of the questions is all about getting related.

The second part of the questions is eliciting the problem or the Need. What are their pain points? What's their single greatest challenge?

It is important that throughout this process you let the client speak. Hold back on coaching. One of the hardest things for me to do is keep my mouth shut and not respond, or try to fix things, or coach. So keep asking the questions and take copious notes. This helps you to remember and really pay attention.

After we identify the problem or need, we look at the Implications of the issue. These questions assess the relative impact of the problem area. What would be the impact if this didn't get fixed (on the business and them personally)? What would the cost be? What would it cost you? Allow them to go deep in the valley of seeing that if they maintain the status quo it will have a negative outcome. They're going to be unhappy or they're not going to have their relationships. You help them to see the outcome if they keep traveling on the same path.

The last phase is the Payoff. These questions get the customer to explain the benefits of improving the issue. Why would it be important for you to fix whatever the problem is? How would you see yourself if we solve this problem? What would you do if we could turn it around?

Many people glide through to this part really well, and then they leave you hanging out there like a big meatball. The final part is key—it is your Recommendation. Here is the power inside of a needs assessment.

There is something called agreement pacing: when you tell a person three relevant things they know or believe to be true, the fourth thing you say will be accepted without question. So it's imperative that you repeat back everything that you heard them say throughout the first part of the stair-step questions, the Situation, the Needs, the Implication, and the Payoff. After you get confirmation that yes, that's everything that they said, your next statement is "May I make a recommendation?" And then your recommendation is what programs you want to service them with.

It is important for you to know that you can use these powers for good or evil. I recommend you use them for good. Don't get money hungry and just sell someone your highest-level program because you need money. Really find the need and fill it. What do they need? And then make that recommendation.

Inside of the recommendation, there is also a three-step process. You share what you recommend, why you recommend it, and how they will implement or use that service. You then share what the investment is (how much it costs). Don't be afraid of your pricing. What you charge is not the value of you personally; it is just what you charge. And too many times we as business owners mistakenly believe our pricing determines our value. Our pricing doesn't determine our value. Our results determine our value. What results do I help my clients produce? Approached this way, you can stay in your authority around your pricing. (If you start to doubt yourself, go back to the chapter on mindset.)

I want you to make a goal of practicing the stair-step questions with three people. Don't do your mom or your dad. I want you to practice on someone who would really be interested in your service, and let him or her know you're just practicing. And I guarantee you: one of the three might possibly jump in and enroll in your program.

I have had several clients say, "Well, it works for you, Susie. But it won't work for me." I promise you, it will work for you. It works in any industry. I've used this closing with someone who owned a machine shop, a graphic designer, a car dealership, a doctor's office, a photographer's workshop, and more. I have used it in every industry. It's about getting that human connection, having somebody see the biggest pain point in their business, and creating a plan of action that you are the solution for. The only reason it would not work is if you don't follow the script, and you don't make a recommendation.

CLIENT SPOTLIGHT:
FEEL THE FEAR AND TAKE THE STAIRS ANYWAY

I have a client, Katy, who was so afraid to do the stair-step questions that I gave her homework to call ten clients and do the questions. She needed to close sales, but she was so afraid.

On a coaching call, I said, "Okay. Great, I want you to make a call right now."

"What?"

"I want you to call right now."

"While you're on the phone?" she asked.

"Absolutely, call right now." So I stayed on the phone while she called her client. It was an amazing call. She followed the process. He didn't have business for her, but he ended up giving her five hot referrals of people who needed her service. (She does diversity training in the film and television industry.) When they hung up the phone, I asked, "How did that feel?"

She said, "It was scary, but it felt so natural and so easy and I can't believe he gave me referrals."

"Okay, great, now let's pick up the next phone call."

"Again?"

I said, "Again, you do it while it's exciting; do it while you're in the high. Don't just sit back now and go, 'Okay, I'm done.' We're not done. We're not done until we make a sale." Sometimes you need a little hand-holding. At the end of the coaching call, I said, "Katy, what was the value?"

She said, "Well, the value was that was amazing, but this was an expensive phone call. I need to get over my fear."

We all need help. We just have to jump in, and practice, and just do it. It's not magically going to happen by itself. But when you take the initiative and do it, it will work like magic.

MOMENTUM MAP

I am not a marketer. I'm a small business owner, and I'm a small business owner who is managing details. Part of your success in moving away from selling your time is creating a powerful online platform. This was probably one of the hardest things I had to dissect and understand in launching my own businesses and my clients' businesses. This is a framework of what needs to be put in place.

You may want to hire a marketing expert. I have a marketing manager who works with me to put my funnels and campaigns together, and then I have the team that does the back-end support. Again, I'm not trying to be the end-all and do-it-all, but I still need to know it all and understand it. I have to be responsible for each piece of my business and know enough that if something is broken, I can bring it to my team.

My team is virtual. You might have team members on-site with you. The companies I support are both virtual and employee teams, so whatever level you are on or wherever you want to be, this section becomes imperative in building your wealth strategy and your business strategy. Please note, however, I don't want people calling me and asking, "Will you build me a funnel?" No, I don't do that.

Now, when your sales members go out there generating business, you don't want them to try to sell everything to everybody. Not all of your products are appropriate for everyone, and certain products or services have specific target markets. One way to segment your product flow is to mix and distribute them to the appropriate target market is to use a Momentum Map.

Here the concept is to get really deep and wide, providing your core product or service so your prospects can grow with you from initial interest through paying customer to raving fan. You build momentum through this process by creating funnels through which your community will travel. Your community consists of people in your prospect and client databases who ask to receive your information, buy your products, attend your events, and subscribe to your fan pages. These are those you will serve with your products and services. They are the reason you are so successful.

One of the best uses for the Momentum Map is to reduce client attrition. We lose 30 percent of our customers every year. Thirty percent! Yet we spend tons of money trying to win new clients each year. If we just invested our money and energy into our previous clients, we would not need to dump so much into gaining new leads. So our question becomes, "How else can I serve that client?" instead of "Where do I get a new client?" This is exactly what my client "Jane" did when she wanted to increase her average ticket per client: she asked, "What else can I do to serve my existing clients?" And remember, she doubled her $1.2 million in sales!

Money loves momentum. So our goal with the Momentum Map is to nurture your clients, your community, so that they eventually come back to your business and spend more money with you. What will make your customer come back to you the next time they need your solution? Keeping in front of them and talking about other successes that you are having will help you to be front of mind when they need you.

LAUNCH ONE—THE LEADS FUNNEL

If you have been exposed to the concept of marketing funnels, this Momentum Map process will look familiar to you. This Momentum Map clearly outlines the execution steps for three major types of launches that will allow you to market like a boss. Let's look at the first launch phase of our Momentum Map—the leads funnel.

Even if you are not an online business, you can use this approach to generate leads, attract prospects to your community or list, and nurture them. This leads funnel helps you to become seen and heard in your market and to start building your database of clients and prospects. It will help you to build credibility and be seen as an expert in your niche.

Let's use my website, for example (www.SusieCarder.com). When I started my own coaching company, I essentially became a start-up again. So I created a leads funnel through my website.

There's a tagline to draw attention, "Wealth is your birthright." Then it provides an invitation to sample something juicy—a free ten-point business planning assessment and companion video training that will help you to assess your company's health in ten mission-critical areas to spot breakdowns before they happen. That's right on the home page. This is the opening of the funnel. It is an invitation to gain something of value for free so we can start a relationship.

Your invitation may be in the form of videos, a free lead magnet report or e-book, a checklist, or a specific tool for your industry (a quiz or spreadsheet tool, for example). It should be something of value for which your prospects would be willing to give their name and email address. It says, "Join me."

Whatever you want to offer to your prospect should be related to the value you can add to them once they start working with you. You want your giveaway to be something the client needs and wants. You don't want this freebie to be low-quality or "taste" like it is free—you want it to be juicy and have people saying, "Wow, she gave me so much value in this one thing. I wonder what else she has to offer."

Once the lead accepts your invitation, they will be taken to a squeeze page, where they will learn more about you and gain access to your lead magnet. As you can see in my funnel, they "click here to get access." When they click, they provide their name and email address so I can send them their free giveaway. I give out a podcast and training video that encourages people to watch and start building a relationship. There's an assessment (I told you I like assessments!) and a video for the free giveaway. This step also gives them access to my "Playbook," which they can purchase for $97, if they choose.

You want your call to action to inspire your lead to do something—to click for your free giveaway. You have probably seen many of these call-to-action buttons on websites. They say, "click here," or "grab your seat," or "send my book now," or some active phrase that makes you want to take action.

After they take advantage of what you are offering, they will be taken to a thank-you page, where you will continue to make them feel valued while sharing your value. It might take them to other pages that have offers they can choose to be fed or not. You thank them for taking action, and then they go into the fulfillment sequence.

If it makes sense for your business, you might include a low-cost product in your fulfillment sequence for your community to test the waters. They have already received a valuable free item from which they have gained a benefit. Now they can make a small investment in another offer. Whether they do or not, you will continue to nurture them and provide valuable content that keeps them engaged and you in front of them. How you nurture them will depend on whether they have said yes or no to your business opportunities.

In my case, fulfillment includes sending my newsletter—*Susie Snacks*—which contains announcements of any online summits, emails with juicy content, or information I want them to know about, which will benefit them. That's the fulfillment sequence. It nurtures and builds the relationship.

This leads funnel replaces and automates the old process of when a client walks into your business and is scouting prices. In the old days, the client would physically have to go into somebody's business, find out what the offers were, and then decide. Now we can do some form of that online to qualify the lead and communicate automatically. So our goal is to answer the questions "What can you automate in your business? What questions can you answer, what processes can you provide, and how can you give people a sample of you and your service?" That's what a good lead generator will do. That's why you want your lead generator to have value.

LAUNCH TWO AND THREE—THE SALES FUNNEL

In these phases of the Momentum Map you will provide an opportunity for your community to take a bigger dip with you in the pool of beneficial products and services. This is just the next level of service that answers the question "What else can I provide to my client?" or "How else may I serve them?" It is a systematic way of sharing with each of your clients how else you can serve them when you wouldn't have time to tell them each individually otherwise. This can continue to expand as your business grows.

For example, if you are a coach or a consultant, the launch two funnel might include a group-coaching course. This is a program that can really add value to your community. This product will have a higher price tag than that in the leads funnel, but by now you have provided free content of value and have nurtured them through to this stage. They have taken a liking to you and what you have to offer, and they are willing to have you help them to create solutions to their most pressing needs. Your launch three funnel might be a higher-level program that takes your clients to a new level of sales or new state in business. It might have more hands-on work or include intensive sessions that delve deeper than the launch two program. These funnel sequences will look something like this:

As before, the invitation would lead to a squeeze page that might offer a podcast, a training event, a webinar, or a live event. At the squeeze page, people will either opt in for that or go away. Once they opt in, they become a qualified lead. The difference with this is we're adding something for purchase, either service or in this case an event. Notice that the service/event stands out. That is because it has its own sub-funnel that takes your community through the sales/registration process, as shown in the chart below. The event page has the details and asks them to play.

Let me give you a tip: if you have a video on the service/event page (on each one of these pages, actually), you have a higher conversion rate. Meaning, more people will convert from prospects to paying customers.

The service/event page talks about what the services are, what events are coming up, and then will take them to a buy page, which is a sales page. Then they will continue through the sequence.

Once they buy it, they go through a thank-you for buying. (I have a video on that page as well.) Then after you thank them, it goes into "Now what conversation am I going to have with this person in the future?" (Fulfillment and closure.)

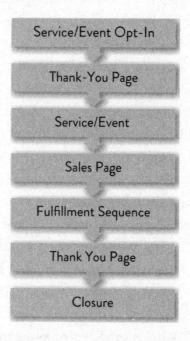

Here is something else that is important for you to know: I have professionals who build these out; I don't do them myself. It's better to hire an expert in this area if you're not an expert at it versus you trying to learn how to do it all. I have a saying, "Don't spend dollar time on penny jobs." You go out there and make the money so you can pay someone to do this job, and then the return on that investment is going to create more clients who are paying more money. Then you can continue to pay for Web/funnel support and services.

Stay in your lane. Find an expert by asking for referrals from those who have had success with it. I've wasted a lot of time hiring the wrong people. Just because they say they can do it doesn't mean they can do it. I was lazy and not doing my due diligence because I got excited that somebody could do it. They couldn't deliver and it cost me twice as much and took twice as long because I was in a hurry and I didn't vet the vendor.

Another important point is it's not the highest priority when you're just starting a business. Your website is a sexy brochure. If you don't know how to get people to come and look at your brochure—look at your business—it's not going to do you any good. It is better for you to go generate some sales, get some money coming in, work on your business, and start delivering your service, and then put this together.

In this Google download world where everybody's online and selling on Facebook, you might ask, "How can I *not* do that if I'm starting a business? I'm gonna look like I'm in the Stone Age."

You'll still have a website, but the sophistication on the website will grow in stages. Your first approach might be a simple website that shows who you are, what you do, your bio, and client testimonials. And then as your revenue grows, as you get more sophisticated, you can put funnels in place.

Step into the Big Time: Selling Success Assessment

Remember when you were little and you were first learning to walk (or have you ever seen a toddler start to walk)? Everybody celebrated you. Even though after the first couple of steps you'd fall down, you'd get back up and everybody would cheer about how great that was. You looked like Frankenstein coming off of the operation table, but everybody celebrated you. If you are a parent, grandparent, aunt, or an uncle, you were part of that cheering squad. What happens as we get older? When we are looking to try new skills or assessing where we are and what we can improve upon, there are no more accolades. There's no more cheering. So when you're looking at our selling assessment, I want you to cheer the things you do well because this tool will allow you to see where you are and where we need to be. And along the way, I want you to hear my voice cheering you on for being honest with yourself, for being honest with your team, and for being honest with the process.

To help you to honestly address potential gaps in your sales strategy, answering the questions on the Selling Success Assessment (SSA) can help. This assessment helps you to identify where to focus your attention right now. It starts to show you the road map for where you need to go in business, but it also highlights the learning, skill sets, and focus needed to help you on that journey.

When you answer these questions, it is best for you to be as brutally honest as possible. That's how it will help you the most.

Selling Success Assessment

Rate your effectiveness as a sales consultant from 1 to 10, with 10 meaning that you rock this.

1. Do you have written sales goals and objectives? _____
2. Do you plan or track your day? _____
3. Do you know your numbers (average ticket per account; per your client roster)? _____
4. Do you have business systems/support skills (business management, job descriptions, recruiting, pricing structures, inventory management, profit analysis)? _____

5. How well do you get the appointment? _____

6. Rate your product knowledge. _____

7. Do you have monthly promotions/incentives for
   retail and service for all accounts? _____

8. Is there a system for prequalifying and cold-calling
   new and current accounts? _____

9. How well do you close the sale? _____

10. How is your follow-up? Is it above and beyond
    (thank-you cards, referral cards, business support
    networks, etc.)? _____

Grand total = _____

Did you find that you have several ones (that would really be zeros, truth be told)? If you did, you are in good company. In my experience, most clients complete this with 20–30 points out of 100 (max is 10 points per question for 10 questions). So if you came in around the 10–25 point range, it might be a good time to plan to take sales classes, attend webinars, or hire a coach to assist you in your area of need and really create a plan. Remember; this is great information to have! We want to close those blind spots. Now you know where gaps are so you can close them.

If you are in the 26–40 point range, think about investing in your business so you can take results to the next level. What areas can you improve in? Where could you take your business with extra support? Reach out to mentors who can help you to grow.

If you are in the top 5 percent, you have mastered this. Kudos! How are you sharing that knowledge and success with others on your team, in your business, or in your industry? Sharing your expertise is a great way to continue to grow. Remember, however, you cannot rest on your laurels. People leave, cultures change, and you add new salespeople; understand that the ecosystem of the business is always changing. As such, your score can change and begin to signal a need for attention. Be open to keeping your pulse on the results of this assessment.

It's like a fish tank. If we don't clean out the fish tank, clean the rocks, and freshen the water, it will just get green and moldy. You'll need to do these assessments in your business continually, not one time. Allow the ecosystem of your business to stay clean and healthy. Where are my integrity leaks? Where is the thing I'm not paying attention to right now? It allows us to be real to assess our business objectively. You should definitely plan to reassess your business when your team changes, but depending on your business, you could plan to revisit it quarterly. A bare minimum would be annually.

So now, how do you use this to *Power Your Profits*? If you scored all sevens and a two, let's focus your attention on the two. This assessment, and others in this book, are designed to light up the road map of where you need to focus your learning, skill set, and attention. Many of the items on the assessment are covered in this book. Review those sections to gain ideas and strategies for addressing issues. Then seek further assistance and resources to help you to master them.

Chapter Seven

MARKETING AND SHARING YOUR MESSAGE

Joe Vitale, a marketing and personal development expert nicknamed "Mr. Fire" for his hypnotic marketing techniques, says that marketing is "sharing your love and passion with the people who want to hear about it." So many business owners confuse marketing and selling and think it is all about getting people to buy your stuff. Not so! If you are like me and love what you do, you can't help but share it with others. This is the easiest way to *be* what people are interested in, as quoted below:

> *"Stop interrupting what people are interested in*
> *and be what people are interested in."*
> —CRAIG DAVIS, FORMER CHIEF CREATIVE OFFICER
> AT J. WALTER THOMPSON

In marketing, you are sharing your solutions to the people who have expressed a problem or need. Looked at this way, it is unfair for you to withhold your products and services from those who need them. Share them with those who are looking for the solution you offer. They cannot tap into it if they don't know about it. Marketing helps your prospects to understand what you have to offer so they can take advantage of it. Selling is closing the deal and doing the transaction. Remember what I said in Chapter 6 about getting that powerful yes or powerful no from your prospects: "It is about whether you have expressed enough value to your client (marketing) to compel them to a decision to work with you (sales)."

YOUR IDEAL CLIENT/AVATAR

You can waste a lot of time and money if you don't know who the clients are that can afford your products and services, and whose likes and preferences are unknown. I have discovered through my many clients that sometimes they don't realize whom they are trying to reach. For example, Motivating the Teen Spirit's market is the teenager, but their ideal client avatar is someone who sponsors teens—those who have the heart and financial well-being to put teens through the program. The teens can't afford the program. They have to go to others who support them.

Another example is my high-end consulting at $10,000 per month with an annual commitment (at the time I write this). I can't pursue people making $50,000 per year because they aren't going to invest more than double their salary to coaching. My avatar is a business owner with a minimum of $750,000 in annual income; leaders; in supportive relationships; want to be held accountable; have kids and have balance; and want to take their business to the next level but they know they are leaving money on the table. They are primarily women, though men are welcome and they do find me. And my clients are generally in the age range of 35–55.

I have a client I'll call Michelle. Her program is law of attraction coaching. My experience with a lot of markets is that personal development training customers don't have the resources to pay for coaching. Personal development is defined by BusinessDictionary.com as:

The process of improving oneself through such activities as enhancing employment skills, increasing consciousness, and building wealth. The growing success of the self-help and personal development movement has assisted many business managers in obtaining more qualified and motivated personnel for their companies, and it has also encouraged more people to go into business for themselves.

The price point tends to be lower for personal development coaching. I find that universally true. However, I did find I have a colleague who offers relationship coaching and charges $250,000 to work with a client for a year. Her outreach goes back to identifying the ideal client. She is charging a quarter of a million dollars a year for relationship coaching, which falls under personal development, but she's really clear on her avatar. Her avatars are entrepreneurs who are high-net-worth individuals who place a high value on relationships. So working on targeting the right avatar when you're putting your packages together makes all the difference in the world. I think when I first started coaching, I didn't know how much to charge, so I just charged $100 an hour, not really understanding pricing because there weren't formulas in place. I slowly raised my prices, but, again, there weren't the tools in place like what you are getting in this book. I had to learn that it goes back to the results that you are creating for your customers.

Okay, back to Michelle and her personal development coaching. We needed to find her market. For her, it would be a professional woman who wants to take her own self-worth to the next level. She has invested in personal development before. It's not a new conversation. She is making $100,000 a year, whether that's personally or in her business. She is a leader, she's open, and she's coachable. Now that Michelle knows who her ideal client is, she can serve her with ease.

Your avatar is the character or ideal client you want to meet. Think of an ideal client you have had or whom you've met, where you thought,

I want more clients like that. I spent years pushing the wrong client uphill trying to help them to get it. Now I just turn them away. All money is not good money. It is too hard to try to convince people or cajole people. I want people who love and adore me and are excited for our calls, not avoiding them.

THE TWO ESSENTIAL TYPES OF MARKETING

When you distill it to its essence, there are two kinds of marketing: results-based marketing and image or branded marketing. A lot of social media is branded marketing. You're giving content, you're giving value, you're building your brand, and you're building your celebrity-hood, if you will. Result-based marketing is when you are asking people to do something, asking for the sale, asking for them to purchase something, or asking them to do something in that domain. What you share in the marketplace is "here's how you do business with us."

> *"Make your marketing so useful, people will pay you for it."*
> —JAY BAER, *NEW YORK TIMES* BESTSELLING AUTHOR

By now you know I am a systems woman; effective marketing requires a systematic approach as well. Sure, you can be creative in your messaging and hire creative copywriters for your marketing campaigns, but there is still a system behind what you do. There is also a brand that can either help or hinder what you are trying to do, whether you realize it or not. Take a look at your current brand—how does it speak to your ideal client? Does it say "Wow" or does it say outdated? I update my brand every couple of years because my business and I have grown, and I want to be in alignment with what I put out in the universe.

Every year, in the month of December, I spend thirty days revising or creating the marketing strategy for my company for the coming year. When you already have a business plan, this process is much easier. You are not starting from scratch here. You are looking at your performance over the past year, identifying areas of opportunity and strength, setting goals for your performance in the coming year, and aligning your marketing strategies to meet those goals.

There are a variety of effective marketing strategies that you can use to meet your business goals. I will cover several of them in this chapter. You may already use some of these strategies. You may have previously disregarded some of them, thinking they don't apply to your type of business. I implore you to reevaluate each of the strategies with a new perspective. I have worked with just about every type of business there is: retail, service, online, offline, large, and small. All of these businesses can benefit from many of these strategies, and some can really stand out from the crowd when they do, because people don't expect to see your type of business using certain strategies.

For example, I have seen HVAC technicians (those who install and repair heating and cooling systems) use video very effectively to empower their market, establish themselves as experts, educate their future clients, and attract new clients. They disrupted the usual "ad on the side of their repair truck" marketing approach with a more tech-savvy and personal approach. They created value first and became the go-to expert later. Do you have a business operating in a market that typically creates awareness in the same way as everyone else? Have you ever thought of rising up out of the crowd but didn't know how? Perhaps this chapter will spark a few ideas for you.

Marketing goals set the agenda for the business and are global in nature. Objectives are more specific and short-term. I suggest you create no more than four to six goals linked to the organization's vision. Make the goals you create count! The reality is that with the day-to-day jobs and responsibilities you already have, adding more to your plate has to be strategic, and they must speak to something that excites you and has you wanting to play bigger.

Use milestones and targets to devise strategies to achieve your goals and objectives. When you break down your goals into bite-sized chunks and assign tasks to different team members, your goals will turn into reality. For each objective, create specific action steps. Factors to consider when creating your goals and objectives are: the company brand, understanding your target audience, lead generation, and your capacity and capabilities. These factors will impact the right strategies and marketing approaches for you. In this chapter, we will break down marketing strategies by category. But first, let's look at your overall brand integrity.

BRAND INTEGRITY GUIDE

When I work with clients, we create something called a Brand Integrity Guide. The Brand Integrity Guide factors in all the ways we are seen in the world, like the colors, the fonts, the color palette of promotional campaigns, and more. Brand integrity looks at these along with alignment in your written marketing language, your website appearance, cohesive-looking flyers, sales collateral, product launches, strategic relationships, and your expression of value. Creating this Brand Integrity Guide will be invaluable when your business grows and you start delegating or outsourcing your marketing strategy implementation to others. Regardless of who is representing your brand, the brand integrity should always stay the same.

When I took over Lisa's company, Motivating the Masses, every flyer was different. All the fonts were different. Nothing was uniform; there was no cohesive look and there was no color pattern. It was a hodgepodge. So we limited the number of fonts and the number of colors so that the brand would look cohesive. This allows you to work smarter with graphic designers. They can use it to create a Brand Integrity Guide. This guide shows you the logos to be used, the fonts and styles, and the colors. I will show a representation of each of mine here, but my designer provided this to me in full color in a three-page document that I will include in the Appendices. The first page had several logo styles in our signature color (sorry, it is black-and-white in this book).

The second page had our font styles for headings and body text. You will see these fonts on our website and in our marketing messages.

HEADING 1

Arcadia

ABCDEFGHIJKLMNOPQRSTUVWXYZ

abcoefghijklmnoporstuvwxyz

HEADING 2

Just lovely

ABCDEFGHIJKLMNOPQRSTUVWXYZ

abcdefghijklmnopqrstuvwxyz

BODY FONT

Greycliff CF Medium

ABCDEFGHIJKLMNOPQRSTUVWXYZ

abcdefghijklmnopqrstuvwxyz

The third page had our color palette. The colors won't appear in this black-and-white print book, but the hexadecimal code for the color and the color name would help designers to use it in our collateral material.

TAN
HEX #c7bdbc

CHARCOAL
HEX #: 3b3b3b

POWER RED
HEX #ae1e29

TEAL
HEX # 5ac4c0

DREAMY BLUE
HEX #cef2ea

Having these three pages together in our Brand Integrity Guide helps us to plan marketing pieces and ensure that we are providing a consistent look in the marketplace.

I really understood the value of a brand guide when I was running a franchise company and we had forty franchisees. Imagine forty small businesses all having an idea of what they want their business to look like. But you have to create consistency. When they would send something over to get approved, we would tell them to go back to the brand guide and follow the guidelines.

Now, you may never want to be a franchise, but you do want to have a big business or a professional persona. When I look back at my early days, whew, no planned guide. I would do the graphics by saying, "Oh, I like that picture. I like this picture," and copy my clip art. It was unprofessional, but I just didn't know. Designers and professionals were not in my budget back then. I had to do it myself. I did the best that I could do. So you can be bootstrapping and you can, you know, stick your neck out and customers will still like you and they'll still pay you. Having a designer and a brand guide is the place to get to; it's not a place you have to start. Be patient with yourself.

When you are ready to build your brand guide, it will come from your graphic designer, the person who's helping you build your website or your branding. There are many different services out there that you can use, but I always ask for referrals. Look for somebody's branding that you like and ask who did it. Where did they have it done? See what you like and inquire.

You need to hire someone specifically to help create your brand. If you have a graphic designer just building a flyer, they won't get you there. This is part of a package. You could go to freelance sites like Fiverr or Upwork. There are many different ones that you can use to find freelancers in many different price ranges. (The one I really like is called 99designs.) Especially when you're first starting out.

Nowadays when I'm building content, I have to ask, "Is this aligned with our brand?" This is an area where stepping out of the box is not advisable. There are certain relationships we don't want to foster if they are out of alignment with our brand. (For example, organizations that support children won't align with a beer company.) There are some things we cannot say if it's not aligned with our brand. You'll learn more about this in the Strategic Partnership and Joint Venture section a little later.

MARKETING STRATEGIES

There are several strategies that can be effective regardless of your industry. Some will obviously be more effective than others. Here I will mention several and share my perspective on how you can make them work for you. There may be many more strategies available to you, but if I don't have anything specific to share about them, I won't take your time to discuss them. You should know that you can use a marketing strategy for blogs, social media, video, print, events, teleseminars, webinars, and more. But remember, you do not have to do everything all at once. Don't overwhelm yourself. Work strategically, find success, then rinse, repeat, and grow.

No matter which strategies you use in your business, it is essential that you understand who your clients are and leverage their demographics (their characteristics like age, gender, education level, etc.). Even more now, I love the psychographics (their psychological characteristics; what makes them tick; values, attitudes, and fears) because I run a global company and demographics and geography are different. In understanding the psychographics of the client, you answer questions like:

* What do they buy?
* How do they buy?
* What are their buying habits?
* How do they want to be spoken to?
* How do they want to be followed up with?

To use a simple example, if you look at how different people respond in a grocery store, they are not all the same. I don't want to wait in line. I'm going to go to self-checkout. But there are people who still want others to wait on them. They don't want to scan their own products. I don't care. I want to get out of there. It's just better and faster for me. So understanding my buying habits is important for the store so they can have those self-checkout counters available for people like me.

If our society has turned into a self-serve society, you have to ask if your business is still full-service based? Have you made the adjustment to give your customers the self-service they want?

Where and how do you find out the psychographics? One way is to use a focus group of your best clients that you've had in the past. Identify a few people who would be your ideal client and ask them to join you in a private Facebook group. Tell them you really just want to find out what their likes are, what their dislikes are, what their buying habits are, how much would they spend (on your product or service), where they hang out, and where they find their resources and information for whatever your service or product is.

I did mine based on my experience with my clients and working with clients over the years. I was able to create an avatar from my favorite clients. I've also had some clients who can afford me, but they were a nightmare. They weren't fun to work with. They were always complaining no matter how hard I tried to please them. I just decided I wasn't going to do business with clients who didn't love and adore me, and whom I didn't love and adore because it was too much work; it was too painful.

In the beginning, I felt I had to take all clients because I needed the money. But as my business got more mature and I could actually decide and choose, it gave me the freedom to tell someone, "You're not my ideal client." And those clients who have quit in the past or have asked for refunds in the past—my gut knew maybe I shouldn't take this, but I thought I needed the money, but it was not worth the hassle.

Okay, assuming you know who your customers are, how they want to buy, where they gain information about your products or services, and how best to reach them, let's look at some of the ways you can tap into them.

THE POWER OF PUBLIC RELATIONS

Public relations (PR) is sometimes called earned media because you garner media attention by providing content of interest to the recipient (newspaper, journal, TV newscast, etc.). You don't pay to be featured in these media outlets, but you have to have something of interest to share with their viewing, listening, or reading audiences. When you don't have a large PR budget (money to pay others to create or manage your PR), start by being consistent in reaching out to editors and publishers of relevant publications. This is something you can delegate to an assistant. My girlfriend Jill Lublin literally wrote the book on *Guerrilla Publicity*[1] and has lots of strategies you can use to get seen, get heard, and get paid. Another way to stay relevant is to sign up with HARO (Help a Reporter Out), which provides daily updates on what reporters are looking to interview for. Responding to their posts can help you to gain exposure.

There are many resources available on publicity and public relations, so I won't rehash what is already available to you. I just want you to be aware that having a public relations strategy can be advantageous to many different businesses. It can be a great way to grow your expert status, stay relevant in the marketplace, launch your book or program, and stay connected to current events. Please bear in mind, however, that presenting your announcements like advertisements is *not* how to endear yourself to a media professional. You have to make your news relevant to their audiences.

Using a press/media release can help you to get your message to the appropriate source in a succinct way. Remember, newspapers, magazines, and other media sources need information and stories on a regular basis to stay relevant themselves. You can help them by providing information in a way that captivates their audiences and makes the reporting even easier to do. Providing images with stories is helpful so their producers don't have to acquire images themselves. Providing quotes, offering clips, and providing access to individuals they can interview for the story are all ways to encourage having your press release picked up. Writing your release starting with the who, what, where, when, and how is a good habit as well. Pack as much punch in the first paragraph in case space limits what can be included in print articles. The longer your release, the less likely the last few paragraphs will be used, so put the meat in early for it to be devoured.

Plan your PR on a monthly calendar. Include the topics for the release and the media source. Tie in to known events in your market as well as current events in the news. For instance, if you are a builder, you could have relevant PR during your regional builders association parade of homes, be featured in the local association of Realtors' paper, and share tips and resources for home buyers in a local news segment. Strive to become the go-to source for news in your area of expertise. One thing that entrepreneurs are afraid to do in their communities is call up an association, tell them their idea, and ask if they can give tips to home buyers. You could find out their media calendar and write something specifically for that and send it over. They may not respond right away, but consistency and persistence are your friends. Keep pitching because they will learn that you have information they need or can use. Then they may call on you whenever they need that type of information. So, post these events on your PR calendar, and write the basics of the release in advance to help you to tap in when it is relevant.

TAKING ON TELESUMMITS

Telesummits are one of my favorite ways to build my list and gain exposure. This is one area that many business marketers may overlook. A telesummit is where a select group of experts come together in an online training event or virtual conference to share their expertise in a particular subject area. Telesummits often last for several days to a week (sometimes longer). Registered participants can listen in to the telesummit at specific times by phone, by computer audio, and sometimes via videoconference. No one has to travel (I can stay in my own bed!), but each of the speakers has the opportunity to share their expertise, raise awareness for their brand, be marketed by the others on the telesummit, and potentially gain new followers and customers.

When I receive invitations to be a guest speaker on a telesummit, I am willing to play full out and say yes because I may find my clients in their audiences. One great resource that I use for inspiring invitations to speak is Speakertunity, founded by Jackie Lapin. They give you a list of upcoming summits that fit your ideal client. It can also be used for radio shows and smaller speaking events. (Use my link to check it out and tell them that I sent you: https://hn266.isrefer.com/go/freetrials/susiecarder.) You can also find telesummit opportunities at conferences and events that telesummit hosts are a part of. They are often looking for guests. At live events, hosts have a chance to see and hear you in person and invite you onto their platform.

Be mindful that being a guest on telesummits is a brand awareness strategy—not a big moneymaker. It's just a lead generator and a way to capture data or capture emails for your list. When you're doing summits, you must drive the audience somewhere. You can share a free giveaway to drive traffic. If you have a mini-course or free e-book or something, you can drive them to your opt-in page. Right now, I just direct audiences to my website because I have a lead capture tool there. I don't want or need to create a bunch of products for random people. I don't want to keep track of all that. It's easier to leverage what I already have in place.

In exchange for being a guest on the show for an hour or so, I'll get the content in a recording or a video. Then I can either give that content out as a bonus to my clients or provide it as extra added value to my community, or I can use it in my social media. I can have my assistant transcribe it (or use Rev.com) and then put that on my social media sites. I transcribe my video blogs and give those to my social media team so they can do a whole month's worth of social media from that one blog. That's working smart, not hard.

Being the systems gal that I am, I have a process for filtering telesummit inquiries. When a request comes in, I reply with a standardized email that thanks them for the invitation and asks for the following information so that my team can make a decision to take on the partnership:

* What is the purpose of the event?
* What is the demographic of the clientele?
* What is your database size?
* What is your number of Facebook fans?
* What is your number of Twitter followers?
* What price point sells well with your clientele?
* What are the past successes from your programs?
* What marketing are you doing for this event?
* Are you expecting us to market this event?
* Are you video-recording the event? Can I get a copy of my presentation?

If you expect to receive more than one invitation to participate in telesummits, or if speaking on telesummits is part of your marketing strategy, you will want to have a systematic way to process the request and determine your participation. What is the break-even audience size for you to close enough sales to make your involvement worthwhile? How does the summit's audience allow you to achieve specific business and/or marketing goals? Identify these specifics to keep in your standard operating procedures so you can manage telesummits as efficiently as possible.

Additionally, you will want to pull together a summit package. So what is your summit package? It is a collection of material that you can send out that includes your bio, your topics, and your invitation of purchase (your offer). You want to gather it now so that when hosts ask for it, you're not scrambling to pull it together. Create a folder on your computer and have those things ready to go. That is how to leverage the summit. And, of course, remember your follow-up after the event.

SPONSORSHIPS

Sponsorship is a great way to grow your reach and revenues. But just like in the beer example above, not all sponsors are the right fit for your client base. And it is likely the last item on your revenue wheel. Also, if you don't have any meaningful sponsorship assets (something of value that the sponsor wants to be associated with or provide third-party endorsement for, or an audience they want to reach), a sponsor program may not be for you. Tag this action for later use. Once you have maxed out all the other revenue lines, your business has grown in influence and awareness, you have launched successful events, and you have aligned with like-minded companies, then you might consider delving into sponsorship. And when you are ready, remember that your assets can be tangible, like having their business logo on room key cards and name badges, or intangible, like official affiliation, exclusivity, or first right of refusal. An official sponsor is a company that has paid big bucks to be the top advertiser of an event, like a beer company is to a sporting event. Some sponsors will pay enough to be the only sponsor of an event, thus gaining exclusivity. And having the first right of refusal means you will be asked first before an offer is made to any other company to sponsor an event.

What I've learned the hard way about sponsors is to underpromise and overdeliver. You want to promise a lot, because you're attracting a sponsor, but if you don't deliver on that result, they can ask for their money back. So be really clear what you think you can deliver for any amount of money, because it's an investment for them. For example, if you are holding an event, sponsors may want face time alone with key clients. They will want to know the demographics and psychographics of your customers and their potential buying power (women hold a lot of buying power in today's households). If your audience doesn't live up to their expectations, or if it is much smaller than they anticipated, and the sponsor doesn't meet its objectives, you could injure a relationship.

Back when we started with our beauty network, we sold tabletops (like display tables at a business expo where they would market their business) for our events for $5,000 each. The vendor buying the tabletop couldn't be in competition with us and they had to add value to our customer base. Then vendors asked to be onstage at our event for fifteen minutes and they paid more for that. Onstage, they couldn't do a hard sales pitch, but they could do a case study or client testimonial and invite the audience to their booth or table. We were hesitant to give sponsors stage time because we didn't want to bombard the audience. You have to look at the sponsor's business model against your own and see how the relationship can add value. Sponsorship can be a great revenue stream, but remember that both you and the sponsors have to be able to get a return on investment on your company or your event or your product in that relationship.

Sponsorship is not just about having someone pay you money to put a banner up at your event or on your Web page. Sponsorship expert Ron Seaver says that sponsorship is a business relationship where you sell money at a discount. You help sponsoring organizations to better spend their marketing and advertising dollars by providing direct, prolonged, one-on-one contact to your targets. Other forms of advertising (TV, radio, internet, print) cannot guarantee this.

As an example of how sponsorship is money at a discount, consider that Company A knows that Company B will be reaching 100 of its ideal clients four times per year and their lifetime value of a client is $10,000. It would be worth it for Company A to pay Company B a five- or six-figure sponsorship fee to gain third-party endorsement in front of that audience.

If you look at the numbers, you can see why: (100 clients × 20% closing rate) × 4 events = 80 new clients per year × $10,000 lifetime value = $800,000 in revenue potential. If Company A spends $100,000 in a three-year sponsorship deal, they have just (potentially) gained $700,000 in new business for the next three-years! That is a great cost of money.

Looking at sponsorship from this perspective helps you to see why sponsorship is a multibillion-dollar industry. As you can see from the example above, you don't have to reach millions of people to gain a sponsor. You just need to be in front of the right audience for the right sponsor for the right length of time with a decent closing ratio (and note, their closing rate is up to them—you don't have to close for them). The sponsorship assets you provide to the sponsor, in addition to this discount on money, will help the sponsor to make the deal. Exposure matters (eyeballs or impressions), but the real money is in the implied endorsement from your raving fans. You can't touch your prospects through a television ad that gets muted during a program, nor can you talk to prospects through a magazine ad that costs $50,000 to run, once.

If you choose to go after sponsorship as a revenue stream in your business, you can use the tools provided in Chapter 6 on selling to hold your sponsorship sales team accountable to producing quantifiable results. They should be able to provide numbers on the leads generated, the status of those leads, the size of deal being considered, the number of deals closed, the terms, etc. Because having a sponsor is a relationship, your company will have to invest in sponsorship management to ensure that sponsors receive their assets, achieve their return on objective, provide any tangible collateral, are given an opportunity to renew in a timely fashion, honor their contractual payment terms, etc.

SPONSOR PROFILES

As you consider having sponsors involved with your business, you might create a sponsorship profile to outline the following:

* Who your audience is (psychographics),
* What you want in a sponsor,
* What their likely objectives will be, and
* What the benefits to sponsorship will be.

To take this a step further, you can research companies and create a hit list of those who match your sponsorship profile. Have an ideal client avatar for the sponsorship. Who wants to reach your audience? Who wants access to what your community has? What goals do they have that your sponsorship package could help them to achieve? What do they have that will benefit you and your community (like their reach, average customer spend, and a large database)? A good sponsor is someone who adds value to your customer base.

Armed with this information, you can go out and pursue the sponsors you want to align with.

STRATEGIC PARTNERSHIPS AND JOINT VENTURES

Most salespeople are order takers. A client asks an editor to edit a book, and they edit the book. A training company has people sign up for training, and they take that training. That is being an order taker. Our job as professionals, your job as a professional, is to ask, "What else does this client need, and what do I have in my tool kit to serve them?" What can you give them and then what else in your community do you have that will serve them while you receive a revenue share? (This is where additional "back of the head" money comes from. Serving your client with others who reward you for sharing the referral.)

To me, it's super fun to serve clients this way because I say, "Wow, what else is possible for this client?" I'm not selling; I'm serving. I know that if people take action on the coaching I provide, their lives will be transformed. If they keep doing what they're doing, then they'll keep getting what they're getting. I want to give them every opportunity to succeed, and if what they need is not something I provide, I want to connect them to a resource.

Let me clarify the difference between a joint venture and a strategic partner. A joint venture (JV) is when you share in the revenue of connecting a client to a product or service not offered by your company. In the online world, you hear it referred to as an affiliate. You love their product or service and would recommend clients anyway, so why not share in the revenue of making that referral? With JVs you are passing clients along or sending out a broadcast email for them to your community or supporting in their launch of a new product, etc.

In a strategic partnership, there is a deeper relationship where you both work with your clients or community in collaboration with one another. In this relationship, you still maintain your connection to your client, but your strategic partner may take the baton to provide certain special services to your client. Many of the same questions used in profiling a sponsor will apply to this strategic partner. You want to ensure that there is a good fit for both of you so you can build a long-term relationship for the highest good of all.

But are they really the perfect partner?

It is really important to make sure that your strategic partner's or joint venture's values are in line with yours. This reminds me of a great example from working with Lisa Nichols at Motivating the Masses (MTM). She wanted to do a JV with somebody who had a product line that emphasized eating raw foods, losing weight, and pursuing holistic wellness, but not diets. She said, "Let's do a campaign as a revenue share."

The JV sent over the email content. It looked great and was in line with MTM's brand, so I approved it. When the campaign ran, however, the subject line (which I had not seen) read, "Are you sick and tired of being fat and tired?" That was not the message we wanted our community to hear! We would never speak to our market that way.

I called the JV partner and told them what happened. I told them, "Let's not use that language again." As you can imagine, we didn't let that happen a second time.

Be mindful of your partners. Those joint venture strategies are your partners. Make sure that any joint projects are in alignment with your values.

I've had clients want to partner with me because I have a large female client base. One wanted to market feminine hygiene products to my audience. (No, I'm not selling vagina cream!) That is not in line with my brand, so no.

"Yeah, but you have all these women," said the client.

"I don't care," I responded. "No."

I see clients doing it all the time. Some of their partnerships are so random. If I was an OB/GYN, a feminine hygiene partner would be a great alignment for me, but I'm not an OB/GYN. I'm *The Profit Coach*, helping people to create profitable ventures and recognize that wealth is their birthright.

Once you have ensured alignment and found a great partnership to enter into, craft a simple memorandum of agreement so you are both on the same page about how your partnership will work, what is expected from both of you, and what your financial terms will be. It's basically a memo or letter that covers the who, what, when, and how questions of working together on a specific project and the financial obligations of doing so. It needn't be any more complicated than that (but you could have one drafted by your attorney, if you wish).

STREAMING YOUR WAY TO BIG PROFITS

I know, I know. You don't want to do video because you don't like to see yourself on camera or you don't like the sound of your voice or you're a perfectionist and you constantly critique what you did wrong versus celebrating what you did right or because it is a skill that needs to be learned even if you are a good speaker or it's just scary to put yourself out there to be judged. Does any of this sound about right?

I always tell my clients to do video because it converts. Video marketing is so important right now. I have heard that videos convert between 67 and 200 percent more above the line than text alone. Though the statistics vary, all of them recommend using video in your marketing to boost conversion and likability (the know, like, and trust factor). Video marketing expert Keri Murphy says that 80 percent of people who visit your site will watch a video and that you can see a 97 percent faster growth in revenue by using video consistently. Another significant benefit to video is that most people retain 85 percent more information shared via video than via what they read. Think about the impact you can have on your ideal client. Keri says that if you are not using video, you are giving your business to your competition.

Experts caution, however, that you not waste your time in front of your client. Since the average view length is still less than two minutes, it is best to put your meatiest content up front. Let them know why they are there, why you are unique, why they should work with you, and what you have to offer. Allow people to fall in love with you and how you make them feel. And don't forget your call to action.

Having said that, quite honestly, my highest engagements come with videos that are more spontaneous and vulnerable. So I will mix those in with those that are more polished.

"I've learned that people will forget what you said,
people will forget what you did, but people will
never forget how you made them feel."
—MAYA ANGELOU

DELIVERING YOUR MOST IMPORTANT MESSAGE

The availability of online video services means people can jump on camera at any time and share whatever they wish. That's great for consistently getting in front of your audience. The downside to this, if you are a professional in business, is it doesn't always serve you to hop on video without a point or purpose or a call to action. You don't get on a video to get on a video. You have to ask yourself if this video is leading to what you are asking people to do, whether it's to build their business or to take care of their health or to eat right and exercise. Your videos all have to be in alignment, and most people don't stop enough to think about it. They're just throwing stuff out there, hoping that it will draw people to them.

When you create a video for your clients or prospects to see, you want to give the viewing audience an opportunity to get a feel for you. You want to share stories with them that resonate and make them feel a connection. You can do this with a purpose. It doesn't have to be random feelings or stories; they can be orchestrated and still be authentic to who you are and the message you want to convey. Keep in mind that many of your viewers want to feel like they know you, in addition to having you as a source of expert information. Use video to create a relationship with your community.

In trying to be spontaneous on video, I still create a format I am comfortable with so I can be on brand. I create a list of questions from my social media that my clients are asking, and then I do video blogs around that. I do it this way versus just going on Facebook Live. The most important point about video marketing is to have a plan around it. Are you going to do video blogs? Will you do Facebook Live? If so, do them consistently at the same time and same day each week so people begin to expect it like a favorite television show.

When doing spontaneous video, still write out your bullets so you can provide consistent value; don't just chat. There is so much noise that if you just go on-air and just ramble, it's more of a distraction than a complement to what you're doing. You want to protect your brand.

Sometimes videos help more than just your customer; they can help you to leverage internal talent as well. Learn how one of my clients used video to help her team, please her clients, and give herself a little respite.

CLIENT SPOTLIGHT: VIDEOS DOING DOUBLE DUTY

I have a client who is a homeopathic doctor. Dr. Judy had a thriving practice that was doing $1.4 million in sales. But she wanted to do more for her clients. And she also wanted to do more traveling herself. The problem was, whenever she left the office for any length of time, sales dropped and her team was consistently waiting for her to tell them what to do. She felt strapped to her business and had taken the business as far as she could go.

In addition to making some price adjustments on client services, we implemented a video marketing strategy. The goal was twofold: 1) it would allow online clients to learn from Dr. Judy without her being physically present, and 2) her staff could have training videos to reference and train with so Dr. Judy's time was not required.

I suggested to Dr. Judy, "Sales are highest when you're in there making recommendations. Let's do a video series." We did fifty-two videos of fifty-two recommendations for her clients, describing what a product is, why you need it, how you use it, and how often you need to do it. We had to spend money to make the videos, but it has paid for itself fifteen times over. Online conversions increased and her passive income grew by 62 percent.

When you're in a service-based business and you're the practitioner, it feels hard to leave. In order to allow Dr. Judy to have time away, we used video to train the staff so they were better able to reproduce what she was doing with her clients. As a result, she was able to go to Costa Rica for a month with only a 10 percent dip in sales! It was so liberating for her.

So now her sales have doubled (they grew to $2.4 million), and her team can fulfill orders while she is away. The great part is that these changes did not require any more of Dr. Judy's time.

As you can see, there are many ways to use video marketing in your business. You can use it to:

* Become an icon in your industry,
* Position and introduce your company,
* Share a special promotion,
* Launch a book or new product,
* Announce personnel changes within the company, and
* Provide personality videos.

Look at the types of videos that you use in order for your business to really thrive. Establish a YouTube channel in addition to posting the videos on your website (remember, Google owns YouTube, and you want to be searchable). Put on that big, beautiful smile and connect with your ideal audience. You already have all that it takes to be successful.

Step into the Big Time: Marketing Assessment

Now it is time to take a look at where you are and where you want to go. This will help you to determine what gaps you need to close to boost your marketing strategy and positively impact your brand, positioning, exposure, and revenues. When you look at the Marketing Assessment, be honest with yourself in your responses.

As you look through each of the ten items below, rate yourself on a scale of 1 to 10, with 1 being the farthest from the truth, and 10 being "I am a marketing maven!" After you finish rating yourself in each area, add all of your points (there can be no more than 100 points).

Marketing Assessment

Rate your marketing effectiveness from 1 to 10, with 10 meaning that you are a marketing genius.

1. I have clearly written marketing goals and objectives _____
2. My organization is on brand _____
3. My website has: a) videos, b) calls to action, and c) capture tools _____
4. Social media platforms are leveraged regularly _____
5. I understand my ideal client and they can afford my fees _____
6. I am clear about my unique positioning in the marketplace _____
7. I have monthly promotions/incentives for retail and service _____
8. I understand my lead acquisition costs _____

9. I have a monthly marketing calendar   _____

10. I have a monthly marketing budget   _____

Grand total = _____

As you look at these statements, what comes up for you? Did you find that you had several low numbers? Where is your greatest weakness? Where do you need the most help? I would look closely at item #5, understanding your ideal client. Look back at your best clients—what can you learn from them and about them that can help you to attract more clients like them? Also look at item #1 and review your goals. Why are you doing social media, or speaking at events, given your goal? Generally, are your actions in line with where you say you want to go? Most of my clients score in the 20–30 point range (out of 100). No one has ever scored a 100. So if you came in around the 10–25 point range, it might be a good time to reach out for marketing support or training, read marketing books, and tap into a few how-to videos. You might think about how many leads you are tracking from your website or how many are converting into sales. And does your brand look like you did it yourself?

Take baby steps to improve one or two areas that need the most attention. Focus on the biggest need now. Then look at what the next need is, and so on. If you are already in the 26–40 point range, it may be time to invest in yourself so you can take things to the next level. What two areas can you improve in? Where could you outsource your marketing to leverage yourself, grow sales, and not spend more time yourself (like Dr. Judy)?

If you are in the top 5 percent, you are clearly ready to move ahead with growing your business. Share your ideas and success with other entrepreneurs so they can grow, too.

PAYING YOURSELF WHAT YOU
ARE WORTH—CONSISTENTLY

Many entrepreneurs don't value themselves enough. We talked about this in the mindset chapter, but once you recognize that you have to be in business to make money or you can't keep serving your client, some of that money has to come to you. There is no glory in saying "I reinvest everything back into the business." Reinvestment may be smart, to a degree, but you have to pay yourself or you cannot keep working. Would you continue to work hard, even overtime, for someone else and not ask for a paycheck? No! So why would you expect your business to be any different than any other? Pay yourself.

"The business should give us financial freedom."
—SUSIE CARDER

Your business should be providing more than just dribs and drabs after all of its expenses have been paid. It should be giving you financial freedom. To do that, it is not enough to "take owner draw" after everything else has been paid. Your salary needs to be an intentional, documented line item in the company budget. Not an afterthought. Just like you include office rent as a line item in your budget, you need to create a line item for your pay; otherwise you will never get paid. Don't just give yourself lip service. It's one thing to say that you will pay yourself; it is quite another to put $5,000 in your cash budget so you can make that direct deposit each month. Plan and do it.

Now, having said that, there may be occasions when your pay may have to be less (the team and your bills take first seat), but if you don't have your salary planned for, it will always be less. You have to be comfortable with the hiccups of the business and plan to balance the heartbeat. Business is like a heartbeat. When it's working, it's going up, down, up, down, up, down. If your heartbeat is stagnant and there's a flat line, it means you're dead.

Business is up, down, up, down, and when you're aware of that, it's not as stressful because you say, "Oh, I'm in the down, now I'm going to go up," and hopefully, over time, the downs get less steep. There won't be as big a dip. And then the upswing comes. Understanding that inside of building your business, you will have the ups and downs, you can plan for them.

My client Kady now understands this principle. She was working tirelessly around the clock in her publishing company. Everything she worked for went back into the business. Working with me, she had increased her sales more than 3,000 percent and yet she still wasn't happy.

I asked her, "Kady, what's wrong?"

She said, "I have been working so hard for so long and I never get a paycheck."

Now, I understand that feeling. I think we all have been there at some point.

So we put a plan together to pay her four thousand dollars a month and put it in the budget so she could feel the value of all the hard work and accomplishments!

Staying in a place of complacency and resignation will affect sales and morale. By putting together a strategy to reward Kady for all of her hard work, she actually worked harder. Now, the interesting thing is that all we did was reallocate the money that was already being spent on household needs, but by giving her a paycheck, she was able to measure her contribution.

WHAT TO PAY YOURSELF

If you are new to business, you just haven't been paying yourself well, or you are launching a new project, you might not know what and how to pay yourself. Part of developing your financial plan will include being fiscally responsible for your business and yourself. One way to look at your salary is: If you were to go get a job doing what you are doing, what would somebody pay you for that job? You can look at LinkedIn, job boards, local newspapers, craigslist ads, OSHA.gov reports, or whatever source will give you a dollar figure for that position. That is where you can start with your salary.

Of course, you will want to be mindful of what you need to make to support your personal expenses, but plan to keep business and personal separate. Adding a line item for your salary will help you to do this. It will also keep you accountable and fiscally responsible in both your business and home life.

Now you have to put that dollar figure into your budget. "What budget?" you ask. The one you will create by the end of this chapter. Now that we know that we are getting paid, we can feel better about creating our budget and make the math more fun!

YOUR REVENUE WHEEL

In Chapter 6, we talked about how the mix of your products and services create the multiple line items that lead to your total sales. One clear way to look at your products and services is to put them into what I call a Revenue Wheel. This wheel is like a pie with several wedges. Each wedge is a class or category of products or services that your business offers. What is so beautiful about this wheel is that you can see a variety of ways to create solutions for your clients by looking at it. This is one way that you will find opportunities to grow. For example, let's look at the Revenue Wheel (see page 250) for one of my clients who provides business and life transformations.

As you can see, the company not only provides a variety of avenues of training, but they sell products, they do speaking events, they have

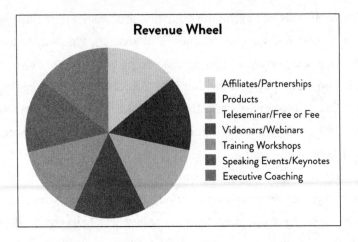

Revenue Wheel

- Affiliates/Partnerships
- Products
- Teleseminar/Free or Fee
- Videonars/Webinars
- Training Workshops
- Speaking Events/Keynotes
- Executive Coaching

joint venture partners, and they have affiliate products. So even though the core business is about transformation, they have several solutions available for their clients.

What does your Revenue Wheel look like? Are you an affiliate of other products or services that you love and believe your clients can find value in? Do you have joint venture partners who share your values? For example, if you provide quality editorial services and a publishing partner who pushes "write and publish your book in a minute" programs and wants to tap into your clients, it is probably incongruent and won't sit well with your community. Make sure the wedges in your Revenue Wheel are a good fit for your business before including them.

On the flip side, explore the opportunities that are available for you to serve your clients in another way. If you keep your client top of mind, you will constantly consider "How else can I serve?" This may cause you to expand your Revenue Wheel to include new streams of income. What actions can you take? What products can you repurpose? Do you have a training course that you can transcribe and edit into an information product or book? Do you have a book that you can add a workbook to? Do you have a webinar that you can expand into a live event? Explore your options against your business goals. Find other ways to serve your client. Be mindful, however, that the more products you have, the more noise you have, and the more succinct you have to be in sharing your value.

Let's find the money using a business that believes that it just provides one service: massage therapy. As a massage therapist, a woman has a basic massage that's $60. She may feel like all she can do is make $60 selling her basic massage and multiply that by how many massages she can do in a week, month, year, etc. But that is not all she can do. She can add essential oils to her Revenue Wheel and that might be another $15. We just found more money. Then she can add Reiki energy work and that's going to be another $25. Now instead of just her $60 service, she grew to $100 of products and services. And this doesn't even include the commission she could make off retail sales. (Back in my early days as a hairdresser, I used to pay my car note with the commissions I earned on retail products!) So now this massage therapist has expanded her Revenue Wheel by serving her clients, which helped her to find more money in her existing business.

Use the diagram below to complete your Revenue Wheel. Note that the categories in your wheel will also become line items in your cash calculator, cash budget, and income statement. We will talk about those

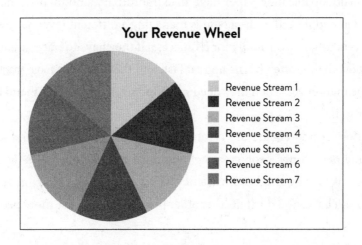

251

as we go through this chapter. Under each revenue stream, include the products, services, strategic partnerships, etc., that you will use in your business.

A WORD OF CAUTION

Many entrepreneurs try to bite off more than they can chew. Instead of launching one product and seeing it through to its success, they launch ten things at once. Keep in mind: a confused market doesn't buy. So if you are throwing fifty things at your community, they won't know which one to choose, so they won't buy anything.

We need to ask ourselves, what are we selling first? What is the low-hanging fruit? For example, right now, if you are a service provider, how can we get you booked to capacity at your highest level? Once you're booked to capacity at the highest level, then we can start looking at where else we can get money, which might be a strategic partnership. Then, the third thing we can do is create a webinar. But until we've done one and two, we're not even worried about number three. Do you see the value in that?

A lot of people want to start every revenue stream at the same time. That's not doable unless they have an extraordinary amount of money to hire ten people and each person is managing a different revenue stream and is taking responsibility for its success. If they have to raise money to support that, it often burns up real fast, and they may not have traction in the market yet. Then they need more money. I don't recommend that approach.

Most entrepreneurs are creators. They just get crazy fits and keep adding new things. Stop creating! You don't need a bunch of new programs. What you need is consistency. What you need is to maximize the level you have. You don't need another program to confuse more people.

You need to sell what you have and maximize what you have. But the entrepreneur gets bored and goes "sparkle." "I want another sparkle, sparkle, sparkle." Let's stay focused and get really clear on what you need to be doing. That is why planning and budgeting are so important. And that's why having a coach is so helpful—they can diffuse the "sparkle" and keep you on track.

WARNING: WHY LACK OF A PLAN IS THROWING MONEY AWAY

A prospect who was making $900,000 per year in her business came to me. On the surface, that sounds great. She had a nearly million-dollar business. Unfortunately, she came to me too late. She'd taken a $200,000 loan from the SBA (Small Business Administration) and she owed $120,000 to her suppliers of the retail products that she was going to sell, and she didn't have a road map. She did not have a clear financial picture or plan for her use of funds and how she would apply them.

Although she was making $900,000, she was losing hundreds of thousands every month. By the time she came to me, she needed another $86,000 just to get out of the negative and start back at zero. I looked at what the loan funds were spent on, and it was all spent on equipment. Well, you can have hundreds of thousands of dollars of equipment, but if you don't have a marketing strategy for using that equipment, then you're just wasting that money. She, unfortunately, had to close her doors because there was no plan for using her money strategically, and no plan that could turn it around at such a late stage.

It doesn't matter if you're just starting or you're a seasoned business: without a plan, things can go haywire. She had been in business for a while, and got an SBA loan, which is really hard to do, so there was some credibility in her numbers, but she didn't have the thought of *Once I spend all this money, how am I going to pay the loan back? How am I going to grow the business? How am I going to expand?*

Don't let that be you!

#MondayMotivation
"Without the numbers and a road map,
it doesn't matter how much money comes in if you
don't know where to strategically put it."
—SUSIE CARDER

PRICING—USING THE BASE PRICE WORKSHEET

One terrific tool I use with my clients to help them determine if they are leaving money on the table is the *Base Price Worksheet*. Many small businesses do not charge enough for their products or services. They may look around and see what others are doing and put themselves in the middle of the pack—not too high, not too low. If they do this without even determining what it costs them to do business, they could be doomed from the start. Every sale could be putting them closer to the business graveyard. They have to look carefully at what every client is spending with them.

The Base Price Worksheet is what we use to determine what a business should be charging. That number is usually way higher than the number they are charging right now, which freaks people out. Which is fun; I let it freak them out, but now we know that there's no way to keep charging that fee because every time they charge that fee they're losing money.

I'll give an example of that. Most of this stuff has come to me because I've learned it the hard way. I did it wrong and then went, "Holy crap, I've got to do it right now."

In one of my past businesses we had one of the top salons in the country. We were the top 1 percent in the nation and the top 10 percent in the world. We earned that right by the dollars we produced. We had a million-dollar business with only five technicians. It takes on average thirty technicians to do a million-dollar business in that industry.

I had this million-dollar business, but I was losing money every single month, and I couldn't figure it out. We had a strong average ticket, we had clients, and we were generating great income. Our compensation was in line for profitability, and I was still wondering what was happening. There was a mystery that I could not solve.

Then I broke down every single service line item and figured out what each service price had to be in order for us to make money. If a client did nothing else but get a haircut, can we still make money? And the answer was no. Every time a client came in just for a haircut and spent $45, I lost $5. So imagine if you were afraid to increase pricing—we had haircuts going from $35 up to $45. That $45 price was the highest tier around.

For every client who paid underneath that $45, I was losing more than $5. I said, "Well, we can't just do haircuts, because if we do haircuts we lose." We had a team meeting, and I showed them the insight that we were losing anywhere from $5 to $13 on just haircuts, so we can't just do haircuts. We worked on the average ticket. That's one way to do it. But it still doesn't solve the problem of losing $5 to $13 every time we do a haircut. I was so frustrated.

Then I realized that my base price had to be $50 on every haircut that walks in the door. Even if a child walked in the door they had to pay $50. If a man walked in the door he had to pay $50. That was the base price that we had to charge or we were going out of business. Now when someone said, "I can't pay $50," I said that was okay, because I'm losing money on you anyway. It doesn't make sense that I'm trying to keep you because I'm losing money when you walk in the door. If you have 100 clients per month and you're losing $13 with each one, you're losing $1,300 a month. Multiply that by twelve months; that's $15,600 a year. That money comes from your own back pocket or it goes on a credit card or comes from your savings. You can't afford to do that.

Some people say, "Oh, it's only $5 or $13." No, it's $15,600. When you multiply those 100 clients by the number of technicians we had, we lost $78,000 per year by doing 100 haircuts in a month. This is just one example of why evaluating your pricing is so important.

The Base Price Worksheet is designed to help you determine the minimum price to charge for the most commonly purchased service or product in your business. If you are an attorney, that might be a trust creation package. If you are a writer, it might be a ghostwriting project. If you are a hairstylist, it might be your basic haircut. If you are a speaker, it might be your keynote. Whatever your primary product or service is, you will identify a unit of measure for it on this worksheet (a billable hour, a written page, a client, or the engagement), and then ultimately calculate the lowest price you can charge for that unit.

See an excerpt of the worksheet below (the full, blank form is available for you in the Appendices). To exemplify the calculations on this form, we will use an attorney with trust package deals and round numbers.

Base Price Worksheet

Follow the steps below to find out your base price:

Step 1—Entering the Information:

Line 1) Total Monthly Expenses $ 20,000
(Enter ALL of your monthly expenses together on this line, in dollars. Include your salary!)

Line 2)   Projected Monthly Profit $ 2,000
(Enter the amount of profit you WANT to make each month on this line, in dollars.)

Line 3)   Number of Service Units (Clients, Packages, or Hours)   <u>20</u>
(Take the "# of technicians or sales staff" you have, multiply by the "# of units" each one can service in a month, and put the answer on this line)

Note that the monthly expenses on line 1 include your salary and all cash you expect to spend to support the regular operations of your business. It will include items like rent, supplies, employee salaries, owner salary, debt repayment, internet, utilities, etc.

For line 2, you can use the 10 percent of gross monthly sales expressed in dollars if you do not have a specific dollar figure of your own.

Line 3 is a number, not a dollar figure. It is the number of clients you typically have in a month or the number of haircuts you do or the number of cases you work on. For example, if you are a consultant and you typically see ten clients per week, this number would be forty for the month.

Now let's calculate the base price based on this information.

Step 2—Calculating the Information:

Line 4)   Total Projected Gross Sales $ 22,000
(Take the "Total Monthly Expenses" [Line 1] and ADD to the "Projected Monthly Profit" [Line 2] and put the answer on this line.)

Line 5)   Recommended Base Price $ 1,100
(Take "Total Projected Gross Sales" [Line 4] and divide by the "# of monthly client visits" [Line 3] and put the answer here.)

Line 4 above adds together lines 1 and 2 to provide the total dollar amount of sales that we need to generate to cover our expenses and profit each month.

Our recommended base price, then, takes line 4 and divides it by the number of clients (or units) that we will serve each month to give us our base price per client/unit. Note that this is just the base price that *must* be received; the actual price can be higher. This attorney cannot sell the trust packages, for example, for less than $1,100 if they are to cover their salary, their expenses, and their profit each month. If the attorney's current prices are below this dollar amount, they need to consider an immediate price increase. Otherwise, they lose money with every trust they create, their profit margins will erode, and each sale will undermine the value of the company. Keep in mind that if a price increase is required, an entire strategy should be prepared before actually doing so (for example, how to let clients know, informing staff, etc.).

Isn't this a great number to know? Doesn't that help you to know where you stand in your prices? Now you know that you are covering your costs (including your salary!) or you know what you need to do to make that happen. Juicy!

FUN WITH NUMBERS—THE CASH CALCULATOR

Now things can get really fun! We now know the products and services we are offering as defined on our Revenue Wheel. We discovered the minimum price at which to offer them. Now we can play around with our numbers to explore the possibilities of how much cash each revenue item can generate for our business, and how many leads it will take to reach that goal. This exercise is such an eye-opener.

Here is an excerpt from the cash calculator form. (A blank version is provided on page 261 for your use.)

Creating Cash Calculator, Revenue Stream 1—Online Course

Step 1: What is your gross revenue goal for the year?	$50,000
Step 2: What is the fee for your high-ticket course?	$500
Step 3: Determine the number of sales needed per year *(Step 1 / Step 2)*	100
Step 4: Determine the number of leads you need to reach goal (assume a 1 to 5 close ratio) *(Step 3 × 5 leads)*	500
Step 5: Determine how many leads you need per month (10 month year . . . rest a little) *(Step 4 / 10 months)*	50
Determine how many leads you need per week *(Step 5 / 4 weeks per month)*	13

What the results show above is that we need to have 13 leads per week or 50 leads per month (over ten months) to reach our gross revenue goal of $50,000 per year for this revenue stream. Is that a reasonable number of leads for you to acquire? That totally depends on you and your business.

Now you can follow the same process with each revenue stream that you have or want to explore. The form/spreadsheet has room for four and totals the revenue at the end. Another number to total is the number of leads per week for all of your revenue streams. If it is not feasible to generate that total number of leads, something has to shift.

What is great about this tool is that you can play with the numbers and see what works for you. You can also share the results with others on your team so that they know what the targets are. In conjunction with the Sales Member Analysis tool in Chapter 6, you have your CAT (Clarity, Accountability, and Training) covered. This tool also shows you where you are being unrealistic. For example, if you are a speaker and you are selling your book for $20, you are not likely to make enough money to cover your overhead. Books certainly provide credibility and a hook, but alone they are usually insufficient. You would have to sell 2,500 books to reach $50,000 in revenue (and most authors do not sell more than 500 copies). Those books need to be bundled with something.

HOW I MISSED OUT ON A $120,000 OPPORTUNITY

I learned this in a big way when I published my first book. I was in San Francisco to speak to a group of three hundred people. I was so excited. I'm thinking, *I'm a published author now, and I'm going to sell my book and make millions.* Being in front of the audience was awesome. They loved me. Everybody got up from their chairs and went to my book signing line—I was so excited . . . I was official. *I'm signing books. I'm an author. They love it. They're buying it.*

So, 150 people bought my book. At $20, times 150, that was $3,000 for the day. Well, with my flight and everything it took for me to get there, that's not a lot of money. Then the next speaker got up and he had a book that he held up as he was talking, but he also had a $1,200 training product. I'm thinking, *Oh, no one's going to buy that. That's just too expensive.* (This was my limiting belief around money talking.)

One hundred people went from my line over to his line and waited in line for that $1,200 product. Now, he sold $120,000. My mouth dropped open, and I finally said, "I have got to create some more expensive products," because I saw the market and the need. They literally shifted from my line and went directly to his line and paid ten times more in his line than they did in mine. My ego of "I'm a published author" went wah, wah, and fizzled down.

It was the hardest lesson for me to learn, but one of the most important. I left a lot of money on the table that day because I had nothing else to serve my audience with besides a book. Then I went back and said,

"I've got to create another package where the book is included," but if I'm only selling a book, it's going to take me a lot of book signings to get to the number that I need to achieve. That's when I strategically started putting together a plan to create other programs to offer. Why? Because his $120,000 was much more exciting than my $3,000!

Now It's Your Turn!
Complete Your Cash Calculator

Revenue Stream 1—[Insert Product or Service #1 _____]

    Step 1: What is your gross revenue goal for year? $_____

    Step 2: What is the fee for this product or service? $_____

    Step 3: Determine the number of sales needed

        per year *(Step 1 / Step 2)*   _____

    Step 4: Determine the number of leads you need

        to reach goal (assume a 1 to 5 close ratio)

        (Step 3 × 5 leads)   _____

    Step 5: Determine how many leads you need

        per month (10-month year . . . rest a little)

        (Step 4 / 10 months)   _____

    Determine how many leads you need per week

        (Step 5 / 4 weeks per month)   _____

Revenue Stream 2—[Insert Product or Service #2 _____]

    Step 1: What is your gross revenue goal for year? $_____

    Step 2: What is the fee for this product or service? $_____

    Step 3: Determine the number of sales needed

        per year *(Step 1 / Step 2)*   _____

    Step 4: Determine the number of leads you need

        to reach goal (assume a 1 to 5 close ratio)

        (Step 3 × 5 leads)   _____

Step 5: Determine how many leads you need
    per month (10-month year . . . rest a little)
    (Step 4 / 10 months)   _____
Determine how many leads you need per week
    (Step 5 / 4 weeks per month)   _____

Revenue Stream 3—[Insert Product or Service #3 _____**]**
    Step 1: What is your gross revenue goal for year? $_____
    Step 2: What is the fee for this product or service? $_____
    Step 3: Determine the number of sales needed
        per year *(Step 1 / Step 2)*   _____
    Step 4: Determine the number of leads you need
        to each goal (assume a 1 to 5 close ratio)
        (Step 3 × 5 leads)   _____
    Step 5: Determine how many leads you need
        per month (10-month year . . . rest a little)
        (Step 4 / 10 months)   _____
    Determine how many leads you need per week
        (Step 5 / 4 weeks per month)   _____

CASH VERSUS SALES VERSUS PROFIT: NUMBERS FOR THOSE WHO "DON'T DO NUMBERS"

Whether or not numbers are your thing, you will have to be friendly with them to be successful in your business. I have worked with many entrepreneurs who were earning well into the six figures, but still made financial decisions based on their income statement projections, but didn't look at their bank balance or their cash budget. They didn't understand the difference between their cash position and their profit. Or businesses will bank on a sale they have just made, but they forget that they offered their client payment terms. That means all the money hasn't been received yet. These are very common occurrences; don't feel bad if this describes you.

CASH VERSUS SALES

Cash is really king. It is important that you separate sales from cash. Cash is what actually pays the bills. Let's look at a consulting business whose revenue line items include one-on-one consulting, group coaching, and an online course. The prices for these items are as follows:

One-on-one	$25,000	Onetime or payment plan (3 payments)
Group coaching	5,000	Onetime or monthly (for 12 months)
Online course	500	Onetime

For simplicity in the example, let's assume that we sell two of each service in this one month.

The online course has a sales page and payment processor that collects payments right away before providing the course for participants to take. Your payment processor charges a 2.9 percent fee and deposits the balance in your business checking account the next day.

Sales = $500 × 2=$1,000; Cash = $971.00.

The group-coaching program uses the same payment processor at the same fee and deposits the money the next day. But some participants choose to pay monthly instead of all up front. If your sales records show that, traditionally, 50 percent pay up front and 50 percent pay monthly, your numbers for this month would be:

Sales = $10,000; Cash = $5,259.58

The one-on-one coaching uses the same payment processor at the same fee and deposits the money the next day. But some participants choose to pay in three installments instead of all up front. If your sales records show that, traditionally, 50 percent pay up front and 50 percent take the installment plan, your numbers for two sales this month would be:

Sales = $50,000; Cash = $32,366.67

Thus, if we are banking on spending the $50,000 + $10,000 + $1,000 in sales for a total of $61,000, we would be in trouble because the cash from those sales is only $38,597.25 ($32,366.67 + $5,259.58 + $971.00). Some of the cash from those sales won't come in for months, so you can't spend it right now. Do you see how that could impact you and how you time your cash expenditures? When you are building your cash flow projections, you will have to factor in the reductions in cash like the payment processing fees and payment plans. Just because a sale is made doesn't mean all of that money is available immediately for use.

This is where the road map comes in. This is where the budget and cash flow projections come in. They are so important for the management and success of your profitable business.

CASH VERSUS PROFIT

What is the difference between your cash balance and your profitability? Cash is that literal green stuff that you have on hand or in the bank. Profits are the numbers you have left after you have been paid and all the other expenses and bills have been paid. Why doesn't your cash balance on your cash budget (statement of cash flowing in and out of business) match your profit on your income statement (statement of revenues, less expenses, yielding your net profit)? One reason is that your income statement can include items that can be expensed for tax purposes that don't necessarily require cash. The easiest example is depreciation. You can expense depreciation (the using up of an asset over time), but you don't actually have to take money out of the bank to cover it. Therefore, you will have that much more cash in your bank account than shows on your net profit line of your income statement. One thing to remember is that you can pay a vendor or employee with cash, and you can show the IRS and accountants your profits, but they are two different things.

What is a reasonable percentage of profit that should be available for reinvesting in your business or using for your growth strategy or for building an additional retirement fund? That depends on your business and industry. If you have been in business for a while, you can at least see the trend of your profitability. What percentage of your gross sales is your net profit (the amount left after paying all of your bills, including your salary)? Is this percentage growing, flatlined, or declining? Can you compare that percentage to others in your same line of work? If your percentage of profit is less than the industry standard, it is time to work on your numbers.

If you don't have any idea what your profit should be, use a baseline of 10 percent for your projections. That is what an average business is generating right now. Remember, this is *after* you have been paid, so this 10 percent isn't all that you have left to pay yourself. It is what is available for future growth of the business after you have been paid. Something to keep in mind is that your salary should be funding your retirement accounts, so you don't need to eke out retirement planning funds from your 10 percent, either.

MATCHING YOUR POSSIBILITIES WITH YOUR NUMBERS: BUDGETING FOR PROFITABILITY

We now have so many great numbers to play with! It is time to put them together for our highest good—in a budget.

#MondayMotivation
"The budget gives us the GPS of where
you are going inside your business."
—SUSIE CARDER

Do not skip this section! I remember when I first started in a business. I used to get mad at my partner because he would always bring me the budget and say, "Susie, we are over budget. We agreed that we would spend $10,000 a month for all expenses but you actually spent $12,000 a month. If you continue, we'll overspend by $24,000 a year. We can certainly adjust the budget, but you said that you didn't want to go over $10,000 a month. So what do you want to do?"

When he broke it down to $24,000 a year, it hit me in the face like a baseball bat. The reality is I needed to be responsible for the strategy and for reviewing the budget every month. Seeing what I was spending or saving allowed me to accumulate or squander my wealth. Remember, profit comes from all the little things that we do, not just one thing that we do.

Reviewing and sticking to a budget would allow me to take that $24,000 and travel, invest it in my kid's education, or put a down payment on a dream home. What would you do with the extra $24,000 or even the $2,000 per year? If you have the goal, or if you have a big why that you want, along with the budget and the funds, it becomes extremely fun and satisfying to review.

When we plan our profits, or more specifically our cash, we can have more fun creating it. Didn't I tell you that *Math Is Money and Money Is Fun*? This is where we get to roll all of that fun into one place.

In excerpts below, I share a version of a cash budget that I use with my clients to help them to put their dollars where their ideas are. We now know what products and services we are offering (from our Revenue Wheel), we know how much money we need to make with each unit of sale (from our Base Price Worksheet), and we have explored our opportunities for how many of each item we need to sell to generate our revenue goals for the year (cash calculator), and we understand the difference between our sales figures and our actual cash position, so now we can put it all together in our cash budget.

The spreadsheet opens with the unit projections for each of the products we are going to sell in each month. In the example below, we are only including two months, but your spreadsheet will include all twelve months in your fiscal calendar year.

Unit Projections	January	February
Training Workshop: One-hour Gratis	1	5
Products: Books, CDs, Apps	10	12
Home Study Course		
Intro Course: Half-Day Training		1
Advanced Course: Full-Day Training		
Webinar Series	80	90
Consulting/Coaching	10	12
Speaking Engagements		1
Sponsorship		

Remember, we will have strategies in place to help us to achieve these sales projections, so it is not just pulling numbers out of the air and throwing them on the spreadsheet. We are using our CAT—Clarity, Accountability, and Training—to ensure that each of our team members has every opportunity to be successful in achieving our goals.

The next section of the spreadsheet combines the sales projections in units and multiplies it by its price to create the sales revenues per line item. For example, above we noted that we would sell ten products (books, CDs, apps) in January. Below, given the price for those items at $50, our January sales equal $500 (10 × $50 = $500).

Income	Price	January	February
Training Workshop: One-hour Gratis	$0	$–	$–
Products: Books, CDs, Apps	$50	$500	$600
Home Study Course	$149	$–	$–
Intro Course: Half-Day Training	$299	$–	$299
Advanced Course: Full-Day Training	$497	$–	$–
Webinar Series	$597	$47,760	$53,730
Consulting/Coaching	$4,999	$49,990	$59,988
Speaking Engagements	$5,000	$–	$5,000
Sponsorship	$0	$–	$–
TOTAL INCOME		**$98,250**	**$119,617**

The next section of the spreadsheet provides the variable costs for each of the products or services that are sold. Variable costs are those that vary in direct relation to the sale of that product or service. They are called "cost of goods sold" for that reason. For example, if you sell a physical product like a book, there is an acquisition or production cost of that actual book that will be incurred when a book is sold. If no books are sold, none are acquired nor produced, thus no cost will be incurred. The variable cost is directly related to the sales activity of that line item.

Subtracting the variable costs from the gross sales revenue of each line item equals our gross profit. This is the money we have available to cover all of our other expenses of running the business, whether we sell anything or not. Gross profit is what we will use to pay our office rent, employee salaries, other expenses, and our owner's salary. The more profit the merrier here.

Variable Costs		January	February
Training Workshop: One-hour Gratis	$1.50	$2	$8
Products: Books, CDs, Apps	25%	$125	$150
Home Study Course	10%	$0	$0
Intro Course: Half-Day Training	33%	$0	$99
Advanced Course: Full-Day Training	33%	$0	$0
Webinar Series	20%	$9,552	$10,746
Consulting/Coaching	25%	$12,498	$14,997
Speaking Engagements	$800	$0	$800
Sponsorship		$0	$0
Total Cost of Goods Sold		$22,176	$26,799
GROSS PROFIT		**$76,074**	**$92,818**

The final section includes all of the fixed costs associated with running the business. Fixed costs are those that remain relatively constant regardless of changes in sales activity. These are things like membership dues, office rent, postage/shipping, licensing and permits, office supplies, and utilities. These are expenses that you will incur whether you sell 100 products or none (so it is better to be selling!). See below for an example of the expense portion of the spreadsheet. You may have more expense categories to add to this list. Only include what your business needs. Again, this only shows two months, but you will expand your spreadsheet to include all twelve months (January–December) plus add a "total" column at the end.

Expenses	@	January	February
Automobile Expense		$	$
Bank Service Charges			
Cash over/short			
Content Development			
Contributions			
Currency Conversion			

Expenses	@	January	February
Dues and Subscriptions			
Education			
Meals and Entertainment			
Handouts/Materials			
Insurance—Health			
Insurance—Liability			
Interest Expense			
Internet Service			
Legal			
Licenses and Permits			
Marketing and Advertising	10%		
Networking			
Office Expenses			
Office Supplies			
Outside Services			
Payroll Fees			
Postage and Delivery			
Printing and Reproduction			
Professional Development			
Professional Fees (NSA)			
Promotion/Gifts			
Publishing			
Recruiting			
Rent			
Repairs			
Shipping			
Signage			
Taxes	14%		
Telephone			
Travel			
Utilities			
CEO			
Operations/Finance			

Expenses	@	January	February
Website Management, Development, and Hosting			
VP of Sales / Sales Promotion	5%		
Social Media Manager			
Customer and Administrative Service Manager			
Payroll Taxes			
Business Coach			
Miscellaneous			
Other			
TOTAL EXPENSES		$	$

Note that to see how important cash flow is here, your expenses should be included where the actual cash expense will be incurred. For example, if you pay your insurance premiums quarterly, you can put the quarterly payment amount (for example, $150) in January, April, July, and October, instead of spreading the total annual premium of $600 into every month (@$50). When you put the money where it will actually be spent, you will be able to see where you may have cash shortfalls or overages. And just like in our discussion of cash versus sales, this can be very important to your bank balance.

ANALYZING YOUR NUMBERS: FINANCIAL INDICATORS AND INDUSTRY STANDARDS

Ideally, you should have three team members working with you to help ensure your numbers are in line. They are: a tax strategist, an insurance strategist, and a financial manager. You might meet with your tax person quarterly, your insurance person annually, and your financial manager or accountant monthly. This financial team should always be looking for ways to ensure your financial freedom. That's one of the reasons you started your business, isn't it? You want and deserve financial freedom. Well, that freedom has to be planned for.

I recommend scheduling these meetings in advance as standing appointments on your calendar so that the *busyness* of life doesn't get in the way of minding your financial freedom. The last thing that you want to *not* do is not have time for your financial freedom. That is the bigger plan than the day-to-day work; the business should give you financial freedom.

There are several items that I review with my clients that your coach or financial team may review with you. They are:

1. Gross sales
2. Profits (gross and net)
3. Percentage growth
4. Debt ratio

I won't go into a deep dive here, but I will share a brief note about each. If you really want to delve into this deeper and have a more detailed financial analysis, be sure to connect with your CPA or bookkeeper. (If you don't have one, find a qualified professional who understands your industry. Ask colleagues for a referral or find one through local networking groups.)

1. Gross sales—What are the total sales (total revenues) that have been created from each of the revenue line items in the business? This is at the top of your income statement and tells us the amount of value you are creating for your clients. Remember, even if you provide what you perceive to be just one service whose capacity is capped by time (how many clients you can see in a month), there are still opportunities for you to grow your sales. Anticipate the needs of your clients and ask yourself what else they would enjoy, what else you can offer them, and what other service you can provide that would lead to them wanting more. Also remember, it is your job to educate your clients, and it is their job to choose.

2. Profits—With gross profits, we want to know if there is enough money, cash, after spending money on variable costs (tied directly to sales, like inventory or sales commissions). Is there enough money to pay for everything else? Can you cover the cost of all other expenses with the gross profit?

The net profit tells me if after I've paid for everything, is there any money left over? Now, in business, we don't want a lot of money left over, but what that net profit tells me is that there is money to reinvest in the company or to pay the owners a dividend to put in their retirement accounts (if they haven't been doing that all year long).

3. Percentage growth—The percentage of growth is really my measuring stick of whether we are on target so that we are working to grow every single day. If I'm looking at it every single day or having a weekly meeting, it won't feel like we're going anywhere, but there's still a sense of validation. So when we measure, over time we see it and say, "Oh, look at my percentage of increase."

I always look at the percentage of growth quarter over quarter because month by month might not seem exciting. Looking at numbers quarter over quarter is very exciting when you see your percentages rise. You want your business to be growing, not staying stagnant and not falling behind. And if your exit strategy is to sell the business at some point, you are going to need this percentage to look strong.

At Motivating the Masses, we've grown double digits year over year. That's exciting, but it's also exhausting. If you don't look at the indicator and say, "Wow, even from the previous year we grew double digits," it is hard to see and celebrate that exponential growth; we need to be paying attention to it.

Percentage growth is our scorecard. It's your scorecard. You can ask, "How am I doing? Oh, I'm doing good." Or "I'm not doing good." Either way, I'd rather know how I am doing, month to month and quarter over quarter versus waiting until the end of the year when filing taxes.

4. Debt ratio—My debt ratio to sales tells me how long will it take me to pay off any debt. What I love about all my businesses is we're debt-free. In my business, if I can't afford to do something, I don't do it, or if I need to borrow a small loan, then I immediately have a payback strategy. Debt will sink a business if it's not careful and not paying attention to it by just swiping a credit card—just like it sinks a person, it sinks the business to where you just can't get out of it. Just like that "Warning" case study earlier in the chapter. They got into debt and couldn't get out. Note, however, that there is good debt, as I describe below in the "Leveraging Your Resources" section.

As you are reviewing your numbers, you always want to look for the indicators for your business and industry. Different businesses have different ratios, so you have to work with the right indicators. For example, the company that purchased one of my consulting businesses years ago was a publishing company. The publishing industry had very high profit margins, but the consulting industry didn't have the same margins. That acquisition eventually failed because they were looking at the wrong indicators in trying to manage the new company.

Since you will have a financial manager or bookkeeper or accountant working with you to stay current with your numbers, you will be able to provide information to your tax strategist to make sure you are in the best position, tax-wise, to take advantage of taxable opportunities. It is important that you not wait until the end of the tax year to look at your tax liabilities and impacts. Plan your tax planning meetings into your calendar to ensure that you are best positioned at tax time.

LEVERAGING YOUR RESOURCES: BOOTSTRAPPING AND RAISING MONEY

As I have said previously, you don't want to carry debt that you rack up on a credit card or for day-to-day activities. It is not a strategic approach to leveraging your resources. There are times, however, when you can benefit from taking on what I call good debt. See how in the next client spotlight.

CLIENT SPOTLIGHT: GOOD DEBT

I have a client who is a plastic surgeon, and there is no debt right now in the organization. Now he needs to buy equipment to grow. So if we sign an agreement with this one company, and we buy $400,000 worth, they are willing to strike a deal. What they're willing to do for us is finance $200,000 worth of equipment and they'll give us the other $200,000. Basically, we're getting $400,000 worth of equipment value for $200,000.

If we do this deal, our payment is $3,000 a month. We figured we would have to sell one additional service to pay that $3,000 for that machine. So we have to ask, "Are we comfortable with this debt? Do we think we can sell one extra service to cover $400,000 of equipment?" Remember, we're only paying $200,000, but we're essentially getting another $200,000 free.

In this case, it makes sense to go into debt. We thought about just paying cash as we go, but then they threw this big carrot and said, "If you buy it all at once . . ."

There's a lot of markup in that equipment, but I'm going to take it because if we paid along the way, we would spend more than $400,000, so it didn't make sense to pay cash. It makes sense to finance it. Now we can pay the loan off quicker and faster at only $200,000 with no ramifications. It doesn't make any business sense to not go into debt in this particular situation.

Not every opportunity is going to be as beautiful as the one in the spotlight above. Sometimes you will have big goals that cannot be financed internally. Sometimes you will have big opportunities arise that you haven't budgeted for. These are times to consider leveraging yourself with someone else's money.

By now, you know that I will encourage you to plan out these opportunities. Meaning, if you are going to consider going into debt, or you want to capitalize on a great opportunity that you cannot internally afford, you have to plan it out before you act on it. The time you take planning your payback or doing a cash flow analysis will pay for itself many times over. If you need help with this evaluation, call on your coach (me), your accountant, and your tax advisor.

One of the tools that will be helpful in planning your use of funds is that cash budget worksheet. This is where you will add the increased sales that will result from the opportunity, and its resulting financial impact. On your cash budget, both the principal amount of the debt and its interest expenses will appear. (On your income statement, only the interest expense will appear—another difference between your cash balance and your profitability.)

If you cannot show a measurable benefit for the debt or you cannot regain profitability after acquiring and paying down the debt, you have to question whether the debt is a worthwhile acquisition. As we learned in the "Warning" spotlight earlier, just because a loan helps you to buy equipment doesn't mean you can recoup your investment of that equipment to make it a worthwhile, strategic investment. If your business doesn't grow from it, what is the point of acquiring it?

There are a myriad of other factors to consider when leveraging your resources with those of others. These are just a few thoughts to keep in mind. My first approach is to devise a plan, a road map, to generate the funds internally before seeking outside resources. By revisiting your Revenue Wheel, using the cash calculator, double-checking your base price calculations, and monitoring success with the Sales Member Analysis Worksheet (from Chapter 6), you may be able to generate alternative streams of revenue within your own team, products, and services that would make creating debt or seeking investors unnecessary.

Step into the Big Time: **Cash Budget Worksheet and Profit Business Assessment**

Now it is your turn. It is time to create a full cash budget for your business. A blank, two-month cash budget is provided here for your use in gathering the numbers you need. It will be best, however, to use a spreadsheet version to actually enter your numbers so you can include all twelve months and have it calculate the numbers for you. Your bookkeeper or CPA can provide additional guidance in setting this up.

CASH BUDGET

Unit Projections		January	February
Product/Service (P/S) #1			
P/S #2			
P/S #3			
P/S #4			
P/S #5			

Income	Price	January	February
Product/Service (P/S) #1	$	$	$
P/S #2	$	$	$
P/S #3	$	$	$
P/S #4	$	$	$
P/S #5	$	$	$
TOTAL INCOME		$	$
Variable Costs (VC)	*	January	February
Product/Service (P/S) #1	$1.50	$	$
P/S #2	25%	$	$
P/S #3	10%	$	$
P/S #4	33%	$	$
P/S #5	33%	$	$
Total Cost of Goods Sold		$	$
* Change $/% to reflect your VC			
GROSS PROFIT (Income—VC)		$	$
Expenses	@	January	February
Automobile Expense		$	$
Bank Service Charges			
Cash over/short			
Content Development			
Contributions			
Currency Conversion			
Dues and Subscriptions			
Education			
Meals and Entertainment			
Handouts/Materials			
Insurance—Health			
Insurance—Liability			
Interest Expense			
Internet Service			
Legal			
Licenses and Permits			
Marketing and Advertising	10%		
Networking			
Office Expense			
Office Supplies			

Expenses	@	January	February
Outside Services			
Payroll Fees			
Postage and Delivery			
Printing and Reproduction			
Professional Development			
Professional Fees (NSA)			
Promotion/Gifts			
Publishing			
Recruiting			
Rent			
Repairs			
Shipping			
Signage			
Taxes	14%		
Telephone			
Travel			
Utilities			
CEO			
Operations/Finance			
Website Management, Development, and Hosting			
VP of Sales / Sales Promotion	5%		
Social Media Manager			
Customer and Administrative Service Manager			
Payroll Taxes			
Business Coach			
Miscellaneous			
Other			
TOTAL EXPENSES		$	$

If you want to expand your thinking on the opportunities to increase your profit potential, review the Profit Points Business Assessment below. This form not only helps you to gauge your success in leveraging various profit drivers, it will also help you to see where you are leaving money on the table. Working with your coach, you can turn low numbers (or blank spaces) into profitable areas in your business.

Once again, when you look at the Profit Points Business Assessment below, be honest with yourself in your responses. As you look through each of the ten items below, rate yourself on a scale of 1 to 10, with 1 being the farthest from the truth, and 10 being "Whoa, I am on it." To help you to understand what you are rating in each area, use the explanation listed with each rating item below.

After you finish rating yourself in each area, add all of your points (there can be no more than 100 points).

Profit Points Business Assessment

Rate your profitability from 1 to 10, with 10 meaning that you are rocking profits.

Your Rating

1. Pyramid profit—You have tiered pricing (low, mid, and high) to catch more sales.   _____

2. Multiple income profit—You leverage multiple income streams like affiliates, and various products/services   _____

3. Time profit versus base profit—Are we selling time (trading time for money) versus adding additional products/services to the mix?   _____

4. WOW profit—How are you WOWing people to get five-star reviews? If you use Yelp or customer evaluations, are they giving your business a WOW response? Do we continually try to impress our clients (provide excellent customer service as expected)?   _____

5. Entrepreneurial profit—You are actually planning for profit (because there is never any money left over!). Profit must be planned. _____

6. Specialist profit—Declaring yourself as a specialist (I am a money magnet) versus trying to be everything to everyone. _____

7. Salesperson profit—You determined what each salesperson needs to produce to create profit. No slackers allowed! They know what that number is. _____

8. Transaction and turn profit—How many transactions do we need to do to create profit? For products, how many turns do we have to have to leverage profit? (When do we tip the scale to profit?) _____

9. After-sale profit—What are we doing to add additional or follow-up revenue after the service is completed? We have follow-up campaigns for additional services. _____

10. Digital profit—What are the online products you can incorporate into your business? Can you offer a webinar or downloadable product? Can you offer retail products online? Are you using technology to leverage your product or services? _____

Grand total = _____

Did you find that you had several low numbers or some with zero points? I wouldn't be worried or surprised if that were true. Remember, no one has ever scored a 100 on any of these assessments. If you scored low on item #1 because you only sell one product or service, that's okay. It just means that it is time to think of new ways to serve your client and at varying price points. For example, an editor who normally just edits a manuscript (one basic service at a set rate) could offer a self-editing guide and sample edit for free, a book jacket review for a couple of hundred dollars, a manuscript evaluation for a few hundred more, and a substantive or developmental edit for significantly more than her standard copyedit. Now, instead of one service at one price, she has multiple levels on both counts.

If you came in around the 10–30 point range overall, it might be a good time to:

1. Research other opportunities for generating revenue within your market niche.
2. Survey your customers to ask what other products or services they would love you to offer, ask for their level of satisfaction with existing products, or seek testimonials from highly satisfied customers.
3. Look at past profit trends and factor them into your budget for the upcoming fiscal year. If you don't have trends, build in 10 percent profit into your budget.
4. Refine your product mix and stop trying to be the Jack or Jill of all trades. Focus your energies on serving one market well, and then expand.
5. Consider adding a onetime offer (OTO) after a successful sale. If they have their card out to buy one item, they may be likely to buy another that can help them.

If you are in the 31–60 point range, you are more self-aware, so it may be time to invest in yourself so you can take things to the next level. Look at where you are stuck the most. What areas can you improve in? Pick one or two that could stand the most improvement, and of those, focus on the area that is the biggest priority for you or that would generate the highest level of additional profit with the least amount of effort.

If you are in the 60–90 point range, congratulations on where you stand. Make sure you have documentation in place that shows how you are able to achieve such good results. Improve from here with additional action plans, especially in your two lowest-scoring areas.

If you are in the top 5 percent, you are clearly ready to move ahead with your intention to create a powerful, profitable business. Maximize your profitability and it will help position your business for future sale or acquisition. Be open to keeping your pulse on the results of this assessment in case they change over time. You don't want to fall behind.

If you need ideas, support, and guidance to meet your goals, reach out for help. Your accountant, your bookkeeper, your coach, or colleagues in your network may be able to help.

Chapter Nine

YOU GOT THIS!

LIVE IN THE NOW, WHILE BUILDING A BUSINESS FOR THE FUTURE

It is easy to allow yourself to get frustrated that you are not there yet. When you spend time planning your future business direction, you have this cognitive dissonance that says, "That's what I want, but this is where I am. I am not there yet. Why not?" On the one hand, that is good tension to have. It means that you recognize that you have not become all that you intend to be, so step into action and you can make it your reality.

You have to be careful with that tension, though. If you allow the negative emotion of that tension to well up, and you focus on that lack of being there instead of where you are headed, you may allow yourself to get stuck. Be mindful of this possibility so you can recognize it if it happens, but create a game plan for moving around the obstacle if it appears.

T. Harv Eker, author of *Secrets of the Millionaire Mind*,[1] has a funny example he shares about how poor people think versus how rich people think that can be likened to this cognitive dissonance. Rich people, he says, have their cake and eat it, too; poor people have a donut and focus on the hole! I encourage you to think of your plan versus where you are as having your cake and eating it, too, rather than the donut hole.

285

Before you is this beautiful, scrumptious cake of an awesome business. See yourself enjoying every last morsel! Neville Goddard reminds us that where we go in our imagination, and feel it real with all the sensory vividness of reality, there we will go physically. It will become very real indeed.

In the opening chapter of the book I shared with you how past hurts and limiting beliefs can impact your current reality because we internalize them. It is through those lenses that we see, or miss, opportunities and perceive them as good, bad, or indifferent. If your first read through this book was with those old lenses, you might not be quite ready to step into powerful profits with your business. Or, if you start, you may cave in at the first obstacle. I promise you, however, that if you work on your mindset, release your old money stories and limitations, and reread this book, you will be able to see opportunities all around you. They are already there. I have just illuminated them for you so you can take action on them now.

YOUR MONEY RELATIONSHIP

Throughout this book and particularly in Chapter 8, "Math Is Money and Money Is Fun," you have learned many new ways to create more money in your business. There have been times when I have met with a client for an hour's consultation, and within the first twenty minutes I identified where their floodgates were and how to open them. Many clients leave our conversations with an additional six figures laid before them. I am not kidding!

Given this, you would think that everyone I speak to is six figures richer, right? Not necessarily. If they do not have the right money mindset, they may squander the riches I have opened them to. Will you allow that to happen to you?

Consider your answers to these questions:

* What is your current relationship to money?
* What does money mean to you?
* Do you deserve money?
* Is money a burden to you?
* Is it hard for you to keep money?
* Are you of the mindset that you are prosperous? Or are you poor?

It is imperative that you uncover what money means to you. Because if you don't, that underlying belief you have about money might sabotage your efforts to apply your learning from this book.

As a child, my dad used to say that money comes and money goes. He was right . . . when it came to *his* life. It was hard to keep up with all his monthly expenses. What he didn't realize was that he was creating his own reality, one that he inadvertently passed to his offspring. I grew up able to make money, but I sure had a hard time holding on to it! I spent it as fast as I got it. The crazy part is that my dad raised nine kids and there were two adults to feed and clothe, too. What was my problem? I just had me! Here's a hint. It was my mindset.

My dad also gave me these pearls of wisdom, for which I am eternally grateful. He said, "You can earn whatever you want; work hard and do the job better than the next guy and you won't have any problems." All true. I work hard, really hard, and money flows in from my efforts. Plus, I am better than the next guy. Here is the surprising part. I had to learn balance. I knew how to work hard but had a hard time balancing work and play. All I knew how to do was work hard, and this is a mindset that leads to burnout if you don't learn to balance your work with other things in life.

Can it be that easy? In the book of Proverbs it says that as a man "thinketh in his heart, so is he." I have also heard it said that what you think about, you talk about; what you talk about, you bring about. So, what are you thinking about?

James Allen published the book *As a Man Thinketh*[2] in 1902. Below are excerpts from the book, which I hope you will take to heart. (A colleague of mine reproduced this public domain book in a beautifully designed downloadable PDF. Request a free copy at http://TanyaLoves.me /Thinketh.)

> **"A man is literally what he thinks, his character being the complete sum of all his thoughts."**

This means that your thoughts create your reality, both positive and negative. If you think about it, when we try to diet, we usually don't succeed because the first thing we think about is what we can't have. If you don't believe me, pay attention this week to the chatter in your head. You will notice that most of those conversations are self-defeating. Garbage in, garbage out!

> **"Cherish your visions. Cherish your ideals. Cherish the music that stirs in your heart, the beauty that forms in your mind, the loveliness that drapes your purest thoughts, for out of them will grow all delightful conditions, all heavenly environment; of these, if you but remain true to them, your world will at last be built."**

> **"The soul attracts that which it secretly harbors, that which it loves, and also that which it fears. It reaches the height of its cherished aspirations. It falls to the level of its unchastened desires—and circumstances are the means by which the soul receives its own."**

What do you have to lose except your negative baggage? Tell yourself that you have lived too long with that baggage and it's time to upgrade the thinking, which will upgrade the action, which upgrades the result.

I have lived my life from this premise of putting powerful thoughts in my mind and manifesting those thoughts. Unfortunately, that can work against you if you aren't careful. Test it yourself: pay attention to your thought process regarding money, wealth, and abundance. Do your thoughts run along the lines of *you'll never be rich, your family holds you back,* or *you don't have the right education, the right look, the right husband, the right wife, the right friends, the right job,* etc.? If these thoughts are constantly running in your mind, you are on the wrong thought path, my friend. You need to change course and start thinking more positively. This isn't Pollyanna; this is quantum physics.

Until you come to grips with what you are putting into your mind, you won't have access to the financial freedom you desire or deserve. You can make money or you can make excuses, but you can't make both. We have to retrain our childhood conditioning and break free from our mental chains that keep us down and keep us small. You are far more powerful than you think! I'm living proof of this theory. I had to change my childhood conditioning and the way I thought about money. I now believe I can earn as much as I want and be happy doing it. Guess what? My beliefs are my reality. So, too, can yours be.

TURN YOUR THOUGHTS INTO ACTION

To really change your conditioning, you must also change your habits. For example, if you tend to overspend your paycheck every month, then even with a change in your mindset you still can't create abundance. You have to change your *habits.* In coaching businesses over the past twenty years, I have witnessed this firsthand through clients who live by their budget and put a plan together to pay off their debts to start reaping the financial rewards.

Credit cards have gotten more businesses in trouble than I can count. The credit card culture in our country has also created lazy businesses. The business can just put the expenses on a credit card and not worry about it if sales are slow. They believe that it is a short-term fix. But what happens in this scenario when following this pattern is you end up getting in a big financial mess.

Don't get me wrong. I use credit, but I use it wisely and I pay off the debt when the credit card bill comes in every month. In the past, I ran into trouble with credit cards. They were like free money to me. Once I finally wriggled free of credit card debt, I swore I'd never go back. Now I use credit cards that give me miles so I can travel and see my family, or I can give them the miles. I use credit cards like American Express for my business, because it makes me think about my purchases. Can I pay this off when the bill comes in? If I can't, I don't buy it. That's my mantra. I put the money in savings and save for the expense versus having that instant gratification and charging it. It seems incredibly silly, but if you have a propensity to spend more than you earn, you have to put structure in place that forces you to follow the system.

When you learn to use a budget as a tool versus a budget as a penalty, you start to discover financial freedom. If you don't track your income and expenses, how will you ever know if you're successful? You can't manage what you don't measure. If you are not watching where your money is going, you may not see it come back!

I had one client who was a successful auto mechanic. He decided to open a second location closer to his home to reduce his commuting time. Once established, he would close the first shop. Unfortunately, during all of his long hours, he wasn't keeping track of his finances. To make matters worse, he didn't put a personal budget or a business budget together. Instead, he stuck his head in the sand and decided that ignorance is bliss.

When I met with him, we sat down and went through every receipt and every expense, and it was easy to see that he was in a financial bind. His wife had also been running up the credit card balances. It was now likely that his wife needed to get a job to help pay them off. It was a mess, but he wasn't alone in his misery. I read an article online that said about 43 percent of American families spend more than they earn each year, and that the average household carries about $8,000 in credit card debt. Further, personal bankruptcies have doubled in the past decade. With statistics like these, it's clear that we need to dig out of debt and stay on top. Accepting that responsibility is essential to making it happen. As is working on our mindset: the same thinking that gets us into debt is not the thinking that will get us out.

YOU ARE THE DESIGNER OF YOUR SUCCESSFUL BUSINESS FUTURE

Do you remember the equation in Chapter 1 of $E + R = O$? It shows that how you respond (R) to the events (E) in your life will determine your outcomes (O). So I ask you: Now that you know that you can *Power Your Profits* by assessing your current state, charting a new, systematic path, and measuring your results, what are you going to do?

> *"Once you make a decision,*
> *the universe conspires to make it happen."*
> —RALPH WALDO EMERSON

Everyone else who reads this book will either decide to take responsibility and put their learning into action, or they will put the book down and continue down their road to mediocrity. What will you decide to do? You know, it is a beautiful thing that when we make a decision, the universe conspires to open new opportunities to act on it. Once you make that decision to stop allowing your business to bleed out or stop stifling your financial growth, the doors will open to the people, resources, and tools you need to stand by that decision.

Test this out by taking action. Review each of your assessments from each chapter and identify one thing you can do today to make a difference in your business and your life. You don't have to lay out your next ten years; just focus on the next step you can take to move in the right direction for you.

#MondayMotivation
"Passion fuels the persistence required to persevere."
—SUSIE CARDER

THERE ARE NO LIMITS EXCEPT THOSE YOU CREATE

What you think about with emotion you can bring about in your business and in your life. Can you see your business reaching new heights? If not, I encourage you to go back to Chapter 8, the money chapter, and revisit the cash calculator tool. I love using this tool with clients because it helps them to see what is possible. You can plug in revenue goals, and play with prices to see the number of units that need to be sold to make certain amounts of money. Then you can easily calculate the number of leads you need per month or week to make that happen. It is so fun to explore the possibilities!

Most of my clients love discovering what is possible using this spreadsheet tool. I hope you will enjoy it as well. If you like seeing how your efforts translate in dollars, this tool will provide that. If you think easier in number of units, this tool can provide that as well. No matter how you look at it, there is money there for you to make. If you want to grow exponentially, you can do it.

> *"Whether you think you can or think you can't, you're right."*
> —HENRY FORD

You have likely heard this quote or something similar. I totally believe it is true. If you tell yourself you will have a successful business and you believe it in your heart, you will have it. Why not make that true for you? Who would you have to become to have a profitable business? What negative thinking or bad habits would you have to let go of? Could you do that (let them go)? Would you? When?

One personal development resource that has a long chapter dedicated to eliminating counter-intentions and limiting beliefs is Joe Vitale's book *The Miracle*[3] (see http://amzn.to/2kWYo9h). There are several clearing techniques discussed in the book, so you can choose a path that resonates with you. Whatever approach you use to clear your limiting beliefs, I encourage you do so. It will help to expedite your business journey.

CONTINUOUS LEARNING = CONTINUOUS SUCCESS

I have been a student all of my life. Whenever I experienced something negative in my business, I set out to learn how to avoid it in the future. I have read hundreds of books on business topics, attended many a workshop or conference, and hired coaches for every aspect of my business and personal development. I am a perpetual learner.

Earlier in my business career, I would sometimes have to remind myself that many of the business skill sets I was learning were always in development. Even today, I am continually improving upon my leadership abilities. Once I get to one level, I am challenged to go to the next level. I invite you to do the same. Mastery of leadership and other business skills is a continual process—a journey, not a destination. Recognize that you will always be learning and discovering new and better ways to lead and inspire your team to higher levels of business success.

As I work with Lisa at Motivating the Masses, I see many business leaders return for one program after another. They may use one event to focus on one particular aspect of their development, and a second of the same program to work on another growth area. There is this hunger to learn more, to do more, and to be more. If you are not growing, you are contracting. Don't allow yourself to shrink back to where you were when you started this journey with me. Keep pressing forward, keep learning, and keep growing.

FOLLOW THE LEADER

There is always someone who has been there before you. When you struggle and climb to get to the top of the cliff, someone is standing there waiting for you. So is that true for creating a profitable business. I have been there, several times, creating my own multimillion-dollar businesses, and helping my clients to grow theirs. You do not have to do this alone. Allow yourself to learn from those before you so you can shorten your learning curve. Let go of the ego and allow yourself to indulge in the wisdom of others.

You can tap into our community whenever you need support by visiting SusieCarder.com. You can review resources I may have mentioned throughout this book to reinforce your own learning. You can use the handouts in the Appendices as resources. Be open to learning to use new tools and exploring how they can open blind spots for you in your business ventures.

"Take the coins from your purse, invest them in your mind,
and your mind will fill your purse to overflowing."
—BENJAMIN FRANKLIN (PARAPHRASED)

Step into the Big Time: Coachability Assessment

Now it is time to take a look at how ready you are to move forward with support from others. This will help you to determine whether you are willing to let go so you can grow. When you look at the Coachability Assessment, be honest with yourself in your responses. If you can release your ego's grip on your mind, you may not be a good candidate for receiving the help and support you need to take your business to the next level. Allow yourself to open up to new ideas, input, and wisdom from others.

As you look through each of the ten items below, rate yourself on a scale of 1 to 10, with 1 being the farthest from the truth and 10 being "I am so ready for your help!" After you finish rating yourself in each area, add all of your points (there can be no more than 100 points).

Coachability Assessment

Rate your coachability from 1 to 10, with 10 meaning that you are open to the wisdom of others and are ready to grow.

1. Willing to let go of being a lone ranger   _____
2. Ready to hear a different perspective   _____
3. Willing to be responsible   _____
4. Committed to my growth and development   _____
5. Know my blind spots   _____
6. Have a community that calls me out   _____
7. Am ready to hire a coach   _____
8. Willing to take radical action   _____

9. Understand the difference between right and righteous _____

10. Coachable—willing to see what I can't see _____

Grand total = _____

As you look at these statements, what comes up for you? Do you feel resistance when you think of sharing your current status with others so they can help you? Are you ready to stand up authentically and review your practices transparently?

This is your last assessment on your journey to *Power Your Profits*! Are you excited? Are you ready to take all of the assessments and start working on growing your best business ever? I stand ready to help you when you need it. Just reach out and my hand will be there.

As always, if you need ideas, resources, and guidance to enhance your experience as you grow, join us in our online community so we can support you. Find us at SusieCarder.com.

YOU'VE COME SO FAR AND YOUR FUTURE IS BRIGHT

We have traveled far to reach this part of the book. You have learned how creating systems leads to predictable success. When you put systems in place in your business, you have every reason to believe that you will reach the top. Let's reminisce a moment and glance back to review the nuggets of wisdom found on these pages. Then you can look forward to the bright future that awaits you.

In "Mastering Your Mindset," we explored the mental fortitude required to step into your greatness and take on the mindset of success. You learned that we often have baggage that we need to release in order to grab hold of the business of our dreams. Knowing that we can joyfully release all that no longer serves us, we can face new events with a new response that will lead to more successful outcomes (E + R + O). This opens us to new possibilities so we can visualize our ideal businesses and step into that vision.

In "Leading Your Business with Power," we looked at who we have to become to lead our businesses. We learned principles of effective leadership, and how our roles as leaders will change throughout the life cycle of our business. Here I introduced you to the gold standard in assessment tools: the Harrison Assessment. This tool helps us to recognize how we flip when we are under pressure and the impact our actions likely have on others. Reviewing attributes like self-control and continuous improvement provided guidance to our leadership journeys.

We learned the importance of planning for our success in "Planning Your Profitable Business." We traveled through the seven stages of business and how business planning becomes the manifestation of our highest business intentions. When you know what you want and why you want it, you will apply the perseverance to make it real. Developing a solid business plan with the seven major sections that addresses strategic and operational plans will significantly increase your business survival and success rate. We now know that SWOT analysis is a more useful tool than originally thought, because we can use it for our product launches and projects and not just our initial positioning. And now we recognize that having a way out of our business can help us to take the right action when we get into business.

In "Selecting and Building Your Team," we paved the way for changing our lonely-preneur status. We discovered our guiding principles, which allows us to hire employees that fit our culture. We learned that we can first grow with independent contractors, but we must be careful that they are not deemed employees for tax purposes if that is not our intention. We addressed performance measures, plans and reviews, and external sources of support.

It is exciting to look at the "Operations Infrastructure" of the business to learn how it creates the fertile ground for our business growth. When we build a functional operational plan, we actually create freedom within the structure. With systems in place, we can scale our business much more effectively, and with documentation to back those systems up, we can bring on new team members to operate those systems. Systems help us to stay focused and intentional in our daily business operations.

In "Selling Your Products and Services" we clearly saw the difference between selling and marketing. We know that loving a product doesn't mean money for the business if we don't ask for the sale. Thankfully, we were shown how to evaluate each sales member's effectiveness with an analysis tool. We found multiple income streams and how small increases in the average ticket can significantly leverage our sales potential. For entrepreneurs who just want to be of service and don't like to sell, the stair-step questions help us to connect with our prospects deeply, and authentically provide a solution to their problems or needs. Momentum is built by connecting with people online and providing them with nurturing information until they are ready to take action, and we found the map in this chapter.

We recognized the importance of identifying and marketing to our ideal client avatar in "Marketing and Sharing Your Message." We discussed results-based and branded marketing and how systems can positively impact the messages we share. We reviewed marketing strategies like public relations and telesummits and how we can leverage them to grow our community and share our expertise. We also found another way to collaborate with others through strategic partnerships and joint ventures. Putting on your best smile and getting in front of the camera boosts our conversions by a minimum of 67 percent, so we recognize we need our faces out there on a consistent basis to grow our reach and our bottom lines.

Money and finding it is nothing to fear from what we learned in "Math Is Money and Money Is Fun." Discovering what our numbers say about us, how to pay ourselves what we are worth, and how to use the Revenue Wheel to increase our revenue streams will make it easier to finance our business dreams. The base price and cash calculator worksheets made it fun to explore different scenarios before taking risks. And getting a handle on the difference between cash and sales will help keep us in the black. Understanding key financial indicators will allow us to leverage our resources better.

That all led us back here to "You Got This!" Now we can really feel like we do. All of the assessments and tools throughout the book help us to put concepts into action and grab hold of the "it." Our mind is a powerful tool, and used in the right direction, we can do anything— including growing a profitable business. When we turn our thoughts into right action, there is no stopping us because there is no limit to what we can create.

REMEMBER, WEALTH IS YOUR BIRTHRIGHT

Ah, the journey is complete. But we've only just begun. I want to acknowledge you for your bravery and your courage. Look at where you are and what you've accomplished.

Now grab a three-ring binder and put in these sections:

* Sales
* Marketing
* Operations
* Finance
* Leadership
* Personal

You have created the foundation that continues to work on your business, not in your business. I want to celebrate you for being willing to go there, to look at it, and dive in. I want to celebrate you for completion. I want to acknowledge you for the leader that you are.

You see, I, like you, was a lonely-preneur doing it by myself until I could afford to hire a coach. My mentors have been books, audio programs, and online courses. I invite you to always be hungry for more and always be willing to look at how you can improve, whether you are just starting your business or your business now generates millions. Know that I'm your sister in your journey and I'm here for you.

ACKNOWLEDGMENTS

This book has been a journey, and as with all journeys, it would not have been possible without the support and help of my community. Every great business starts with an idea and a dream; this is no different. It's really been ten years in the making. All the stories and client successes and failures gave texture to the book, and for that I say thank you. Thank you for your commitment to excel and succeed. I am proud to be called your coach, mentor, and friend. Your stories are what make this book special.

I want to thank God for giving me the courage, the strength, and the assignment on my life so big that it scares me and pushes me to greatness.

There are some amazing rock stars who have supported this journey from the beginning. Each of you has made a profound difference in my life. Of course, I thank my boos, Amanda Fields Schular and Megan Fields Van Slyke, for being my source of accomplishment. Learning to provide for you and be an example helped shape me as a businesswoman; I am humbled to be your mom and honored to be Gigi to Hayden and Harlow.

Tanya Brockett and Randy Peyser, my secret weapons, thank you for helping me make my stories SING.

Chris Winfield and Jenn Gottlieb, you are truly angels sent from GOD. Without you, I wouldn't have met Michelle Herrera Mulligan from Simon & Schuster—a match made in heaven. Michelle, thank you for seeing the gift inside me and for believing in me.

Iza Socha, thank you for supporting me in getting the word out. You are an amazing publicist and ride-or-die kinda girl. Angela, Nick, I appreciate you and your wisdom.

Lisha Barnes, thank you for doing whatever I needed, whenever I needed, to support the content and serve my clients. You are an amazing friend and Shesha.

Sam Stone, thank you for taking care of me on the road—I need you and you got me. Dr. Ali, I appreciate your commitment to serve. Kim and Lionel Grimes, you guys are a force to be reckoned with. Bert Wright, thank you for being my brother and having my back. Kay Suthar, thank you for trusting me and taking care of the community. Josie Martinez, you are a blessing; I love your mind and your spirit. Amber Ludwig Vilhauer, thank you for making me raise my prices and for supporting me with structure and playing BIG in the world. You make me want to play with giants. Patti Zorr, your leadership and commitment to systems is very sexy.

Megan Meketa, thank you for being my voice, editor, right arm, left arm, and friend. I would be lost without you.

Pat Senecal—my mother from another—your belief in me, your love for me, and your commitment to family is breathtaking. I am so lucky that we found each other. Thank you for being the mom I never had.

Lisa Nichols, we have been on this wild ride for many years. You picked me up when I was at my lowest point, and you gave me purpose again. Thank you for SEEING me; thank you for reminding me of who I am; and thank you for playing full-out and risking with me!

ACKNOWLEDGMENTS

Sometimes the greatest gifts are wrapped in sandpaper—such is my family. They didn't believe in me, and they didn't support me, but it caused me to fight—fight for recognition, fight to prove them wrong, and fight to be something bigger than I knew myself to be. So, Gerald Koshak, thank you. You taught me to be MORE. Unknowingly, you taught me grit and work ethic, and for that I am grateful. I am the woman I am because of our family dysfunction. I love you and miss you.

Finally, Daniel Paul, thank you for your love, friendship, and belief in me, and for not quitting when I tried to sabotage us. Thank you for being an amazing GPA and providing fun and play and possibility.

Most important, my clients, the reason for and the source of everything I do! You give my life purpose and meaning! I am grateful and honored you choose me!

ASSESSMENTS, READER RESOURCES, TOOLS, AND BONUSES

HOW TO IMPROVE LISTENING SKILLS

1. *Limit your own chatter.* You can't talk and listen at the same time.

2. *Be interested and show it.* You must convey a genuine concern and a lively curiosity. You want to encourage your prospects or customers to speak freely so you can better understand their needs, wants, and viewpoints.

3. *Tune in to the other person.* Are you giving your full attention to the person with whom you are conversing or is your mind wandering? Concentrate by practicing to shut out outside distractions.

4. *Think like prospective customers.* They have problems, needs, and wants that are important. You can understand and retain these problems, needs, and wants better if you clearly understand their point of view.

5. *Ask questions.* If you don't understand something, or feel you may have missed a point, clear it up *before* it embarrasses you.

6. *Hold your fire.* Plan your responses only after you are certain you have a complete picture of your prospect/customer's point

of view. Prejudgments are dangerous. A pause, even a long one, doesn't always mean they've finished saying everything they want to say.

7. *Look and listen for buying signals.* Focus on key, hot-button comments. In our dealings with others, we must be cognizant of their prime motivating factors. Once we have identified these factors, we can gently "push" their "buttons" to get the response we desire.

8. *Listen for ideas, not just words.* You want to get the whole picture, not just isolated bits and pieces.

9. *Use interjections.* An occasional "Yes," "I see," or "Is that so" shows the prospective customer you're still listening and interested, but don't overdo or use these words as a meaningless comment.

10. *Turn off your own worries.* This isn't always easy, but personal fears, worries, and problems not connected with the customer form a kind of "static" that can blank out the speaker's message.

11. *Prepare in advance.* Remarks and questions prepared in advance, when possible, free your mind for listening. Prepare a checklist of items you want to discuss and clarify.

12. *React to ideas, not to the person.* Don't be distracted by what people say or the manner in which they say it. Chat about their ideas instead.

13. *Notice nonverbal language.* A shrug, smile, laugh, gesture, facial expressions, and other body movements often speak louder than words. Start to "read" them.

14. *Don't jump to conclusions.* Avoid making unwarranted assumptions about what the prospect or customer may say, guessing about what they might say next, or mentally trying to complete sentences for them.

15. *Take notes.* This practice will help you remember important points. However, be selective. Trying to write down everything that is said can result in being left far behind or retaining irrelevant details. A short pencil can be more effective than a long memory.

16. *Get feedback.* Make sure you're really listening by asking questions to confirm with the speaker what you understood. In sales work, effective listening is extremely essential in the critical area of handling objections. These objections are not always clearly stated; hence effective listening can help identify "sincere" and "insincere" objections. Listen to the prospect/customer's objections and use them to help you close the sale.

The rewards your team, clients, and you receive from learning these skills are many. You can use these skills to create the optimal working conditions that can create amazing results and rapport in your business.

PLAN AND REVIEW FORM

(Monthly)

This form is designed to help you achieve great success while working here. It will help you stay clear about what your goals are and what areas of your business you are intending to improve upon. It will help you to distinguish your strengths and weaknesses, thus allowing you to accelerate your success.

This form needs to be completed and returned to your team leader at the end of each month of employment. It will be used at your plan-and-review meeting with the team leader.

Team Member: _____

Date: _____/_____/_____

Please list three (3) things that you like about working here (be specific)

1) _____

_____

2) _____

_____

3) _____

_____

Please list one (1) thing that you would like to see improved upon (be specific)

_____

_____

Please list three (3) things that you feel you are doing well (be specific)

1) _____

_____

2) _____

_____

3) _____

_____

Please list one (1) thing that you are going to work on improving in the next month (be specific) _____

_____

BASE PRICE WORKSHEET

This worksheet is designed to help you calculate your "base price." The "base price" is the price you charge for the most commonly purchased service in your business. If you are a salon, it's what you charge for your basic haircut. If you are a spa, it's what you charge for your basic facial or massage.

The "Base Price" calculation tells you what you need to charge each client, in order to stay in business.

Follow the steps below to find out your base price:

Step 1) ENTERING THE INFORMATION:		
Line 1)	**TOTAL MONTHLY EXPENSES** (Enter ALL of your monthly expenses together on this line)	$_____

Line 2:	**PROJECTED MONTHLY PROFIT** (Enter the amount of profit you WANT to make each month on this line)	$
Line 3:	**# OF MONTHLY CLIENT VISITS** (Take the "# of technicians" you have, multiply by the "# of clients" each one can service in a month, and put the answer on this line)	$
Step 2) CALCULATING THE INFORMATION:		
Line 4:	**TOTAL PROJECTED GROSS SALES** (Take the "Total Monthly Expenses" [Line 1] and ADD to the "Projected Monthly Profit" [Line 2] and put the answer on this line)	$
Line 5:	**RECOMMENDED BASE PRICE** (Take "Total Projected Gross Sales" [Line 4] and divide by the "# of monthly client visits" [Line 3] and put the answer here.)	$
STEP 3: UNDERSTAND THE INFORMATION		

The formula above allows you to determine a pricing strategy that is right for *your* business. If your current prices are below your "Recommended Base Price" shown above, you should consider an immediate price increase. Remember to prepare an entire strategy before raising your prices (that is, how will you let the clients know, how will you let the staff know, etc.)

An article in the May 2000 issue of *Inc.* magazine, titled "The Case for Higher Prices," states that *raising your prices is a sound business practice, and it's important to raise prices regularly*. Otherwise you'll let your profit margins erode and it will undermine the value of your company!

NOTES

CHAPTER ONE: MASTERING YOUR MINDSET

1. Neville Goddard, "The Secret of Imagining," audio, AudioEnlightenment .com.
2. Richard Bolles, *What Color Is Your Parachute* (New York: Ten Speed Press, 2019), http://www.parachutebook.com/.
3. Janet Atwood and Chris Atwood. *The Passion Test: The Effortless Path to Discovering Your Life Purpose* (New York: Plume, 2008), https://thepassion test.com/.
4. Sue Ascioti-Plange and Tanya Brockett, "Contrast to Clarity Exercise," Live Your Best Life Now course, 2017, http://liveyourbestlifenowcourses.com.

CHAPTER TWO: LEADING YOUR BUSINESS WITH POWER

1. Steven Rush, *Leadership Cake: A Recipe for Success in Leadership* (Vale of Glamorgan, England: Improov, 2013).

CHAPTER THREE: PLANNING YOUR PROFITABLE BUSINESS

1. Denise Lee Yohn, "Ban These 5 Words from Your Corporate Values Statement," *Harvard Business Review* online, www.HBR.org, February 5, 2018, https://hbr.org/2018/02/ban-these-5-words-from-your-corporate-values -statement%EF%BB%BF.
2. Suzanne Meehle, "Take Your Best SWOT!" Blog post, Solo Practice Univer-

sity, February 2, 2012, http://solopracticeuniversity.com/2012/02/09/take
-your-best-swot/.

3. Michael Gerber, *The E-Myth: Why Most Businesses Don't Work and What to Do About It* (Pensacola, FL: Ballinger Publishing, 1985).

CHAPTER FOUR: SELECTING AND BUILDING YOUR TEAM

1. Publication 15-A: Employer's Supplemental Tax Guide, Internal Revenue Service, PDF, www.irs.gov.

CHAPTER SEVEN: MARKETING AND SHARING YOUR MESSAGE

1. Jill Lublin, Jay Conrad Levinson, and Rick Frishman et al., *Guerrilla Publicity: Hundreds of Sure-Fire Tactics to Get Maximum Sales for Minimum Dollars* (Avon, MA: Adams Media, Chapter Nine: You Got This! 2002).

CHAPTER NINE: YOU GOT THIS!

1. T. Harv Eker, *Secrets of the Millionaire Mind* (New York: HarperBusiness, 2005), p. 134.
2. James Allen, *As a Man Thinketh* (1902), pp. 3, 36.
3. Joe Vitale, *The Miracle: Six Steps to Enlightenment*, Hypnotic Marketing, 2016, pp. 109–54.

INDEX

A

accountability, 50, 96, 131, 136–38, 187
  leadership and, 48
  standard operating procedures (SOPs)
    and, 158–59
accountability coach, 175
accounting system, 31, 49, 75, 133–34,
    150, 274
acknowledgment and praise, leadership
    and, 51–52
ACT, 159
active listening, leadership and, 47, 305–7
Agile CRM, 186
agreement pacing, 200
Allen, James, 288
Allen, Robert G., 20
Angelou, Maya, 237
anger, 45
As a Man Thinketh (Allen), 288
Ascioti-Plange, Sue, 30
assessments, 292
  Business Planning Assessment,
    116–18
  Coachability Assessment, 295–96
  Harrison Assessment, 46, 59–62,
    126–28, 297
  Leadership Assessment, 64–66
  Marketing Assessment, 240–41
  Profit Points Business Assessment,
    279–83
  Selling Success Assessment (SSA),
    210–13
  Systems Self-Assessment, 170–72
  Team Assessment, 140–42
  value of, 60–61
Atwood, Chris, 24
Atwood, Janet, 24
authenticity, 108
Average Ticket Worksheet, 192–95

B

Baer, Jay, 218
Baez, Joan, 170
balance sheet, 49
banking industry, 58
bankruptcy, 70, 291
Base Price Worksheet, 84, 254–58, 267,
    299, 309–11
beauty industry, 4–6, 9, 23, 25, 34, 56,
    73–74, 110, 114, 148–49, 159, 251,
    255–56
belief statements, 41
beliefs versus action, 16–17
blame game, 14
Blanchard, Ken, 148
bold statements, 121–23, 130
Bolles, Richard, 24
bookkeeper, 75, 272, 274, 277
BPlans.com, 105
brainstorming, 72
Brand Integrity Guide, 220–23
Brockett, Tanya, 30
budgets, 243, 244, 249, 266–68
Bureau of Labor Statistics, 135

business concept section of business plan, 98, 101, 111
business plan, 5, 15, 21, 28, 35, 49, 57, 219
    business concept section, 98, 101, 111
    Business Planning Assessment, 116–18
    current business position section, 99–100
    excuses against, 96–97
    exit strategy, 114–16
    financial features section, 98–99
    financial requirements section, 99
    goals, milestones, and targets, 113
    major achievements section, 100
    market definition section, 101–2
    mission statement, 87, 104–5
    motivation and, 87–88
    profitability section, 101
    sections of, 97–102
    setting intentions for success, 81–83, 85
    SWOT analysis and, 107–13, 297
    value statement, 106
    vision statement, 102–4
    writing, 89, 97
Business Planning Assessment, 116–18
business spotlight, 124, 153, 177
business success
    beliefs versus action, 16–17
    clarity and, 85–87
    client spotlights, 7, 14–15, 26–27, 60–61, 84, 90–91, 128, 180–81, 194–95, 202–3, 238–39, 244–45, 275–76
    coaches and, 34–37, 52, 65, 175
    feasibility study and, 28–29
    goals of (see goals)
    ideal business exercise, 21–22
    identifying ideal client, 25–26, 35, 101
    mindset and, 10–15, 38–42, 103, 246, 286, 287, 289, 291, 296–97
    opening mind to new possibilities, 17–18
    planning (see business plan)
    Seven Stages of Business and, 71–80
    Step into the Big Time, 7, 34, 37–40, 63–66, 116–18, 140–42, 168–72, 210–13, 240–41, 277–83, 295–96
    stirring up rebel child, 18–19
    visualization and, 19–21, 32, 34
BusinessPowerTools, 89, 117
by-when date, 155–56

C
capital, 99
Carder, Susie
    in beauty industry, 4–6, 9, 23, 25, 34, 56, 73–74, 110, 114, 148–49, 159, 251, 255–56
    childhood of, 2–4, 10–11, 18, 37, 289
    Microsoft Innovative Business Award and, 6
    mother of, 10–11
    Profit Coach brand and, 78
    quoted, 13, 19, 92, 124, 144, 247, 254, 266, 292
    research by, 1–2, 4, 23
    speaking engagements of, 25–26
CareerOneStop.org, 135
Carter, R. Douglas, 198–99
cash budget worksheet, 276–79
cash calculator, 84, 258–59, 261–62, 267, 292, 299
cash flow statement, 49, 98
CAT (Clarity, Accountability, Training) system, 187, 259, 267
certified public accountant (CPA), 140, 272, 277
Chamber of Commerce, 94
Chrysler, Walter, 157
clarity, 29–31, 85–87, 187, 259, 267
client management system, 159–61
client spotlights, 7, 14–15, 26–27, 60–61, 84, 90–91, 128, 180–81, 194–95, 202–3, 238–39, 244–45, 275–76
Coachability Assessment, 295–96
cognitive dissonance, 285
Cold Stone Creamery, 103
commissions, 135
compensation, 133, 135–36, 147, 247–49
competitive advantage, 92
concept/establish stage of business, 71–72
conditions of fulfillment, 138–39
consistency, 82, 222, 252
continuous improvement, leadership and, 45, 293–94, 297
Contrast to Clarity exercise, 29–31
core values of owner, 102
credit cards, 290–91
current business position section of business plan, 99–100
customer relationship management (CRM), 150, 151
customer retention, 96

INDEX

D

Dale Carnegie, 148
Davis, Craig, 215
De Angelis, Barbara, 23
debt, 274–76
debt ratio, 274
decision-making process, 111–12
demographics, 224, 231
depreciation, 265
design services, 90–91
develop/prepare stage of business, 71, 72–74
DISC, 59
discernment, leadership and, 46
dissatisfaction, listening to, 29–31
distribution channels, 101–2
dream and goal boards, 7
Dyer, Wayne, 41

E

E + R = O (events plus response = outcome), 17, 291, 296–97
E-Myth, The: Why Most Businesses Don't Work and What to Do About It (Gerber), 114
earned media, 225
ego, 51, 52, 54, 57, 80
Eker, T. Harv, 235
Emerson, Ralph Waldo, 291
emotional empathy, leadership and, 47–48
Emotional Freedom Technique (Tapping), 41
emotional life, 24
empathy
   distinguished from sympathy, 47–48
   leadership and emotional, 47–48
engage/release stage of business, 71, 79–80
enrich/increase stage of business, 71, 76–77
Evernote, 151
exit strategy, 114–16
expectations, 50–51
expenses, 269–71

F

Facebook, 151, 210, 225
Facebook Live, 108, 238
faith, 24, 32
fear, 174, 202, 244, 245
feasibility study, 28–29
feedback, 112

financial features section of business plan, 98–99
financial literacy, leadership and, 49–50
financial manager, 271, 274
financial plan, 15, 88, 97, 249, 253–54
financial projections, 15
financial requirements section of business plan, 99
financial spreadsheet, 35–36
Findlaw.com, 134
first-time managers, 54, 56
Fiverr.com, 136, 223
fixed costs, 269
flex time, 135
follow-up systems, 70, 109
Ford, Henry, 293
forecast/expect stage of business, 71, 75–76
Franklin, Benjamin, 67, 295
fund-raising process, 68

G

Gallup StrengthsFinder, 59
Gerber, Michael, 114
goals, 21, 39, 69, 113
   marketing, 219–20
   milestones and actions for, 32–34
   must and stretch goal, 90
   posting, 34
   priorities, 32
Goddard, Neville, 21, 286
good debt, 275–76
Google, 105, 239
Gray, John, 24
gross profit, 273
gross sales, 272–73
Guerrilla Publicity: Hundreds of Sure-Fire Tactics to Get Maximum Sales for Minimum Dollars (Lublin et al.), 226

H

HARO (Help a Reporter Out), 226
Harrison Assessment, 46, 59–62, 126–28, 297
Harvard Business Review, 106
Hay, Louise, 41
hiring (*see* team)
hit list, 69, 70
holistic approach, 24, 27
holistic learning, leadership and, 48
Honest Tea, 105
Ho'oponopono, 41
Hootsuite, 151

I

ideal business exercise, 21–22
image (branded) marketing, 218
Inc. magazine, 311
income statement, 49, 178–81, 264–65, 272, 276
independent contractors, 130–34
individual contributors, 54, 56
influence/capitalize stage of business, 71, 77–79
Infusionsoft, 159
Instagram, 151
insurance industry, 58
insurance strategist, 271
intellectual life, 24
Internal Revenue Service (IRS), 126, 133, 134, 265
internships, 134–35
Intuit, 103
investment strategy, 69–70

J

job descriptions, 52–53, 152, 161–65
job interview, 122, 127
joint ventures (JVs), 223, 234–35
journaling, 41, 82–83

K

Keap, 159

L

Landry, Tom, 36, 37, 52
Lao Tzu, 61
Lapin, Jackie, 228
lawyers, 140
leadership, 43–66, 94, 174, 297
  accountability and, 48
  active listening and, 47, 305–7
  continuous improvement and, 45, 293–94, 297
  discernment and, 46
  emotional empathy and, 47–48
  failed, 57–58
  financial literacy and, 49–50
  genuine acknowledgment and, 51–52
  great, 45–52, 57–58
  guidance for and attributes of authentic, 44–45
  Harrison Assessment, 46, 59–62
  holistic learning and, 48
  job description and, 52–53
  Leadership Assessment, 64–66
  levels of, 54–56
  organization and, 46, 65–66
  quantifiable expectations and, 50–51
  relationship-building and, 46–47
  results-based management and, 48–49, 66
  self-control and, 45–46
  surrounding with other leaders, 58–59
Leadership Cake: A Recipe for Success in Leadership (Rush), 47–48
leads funnel, 205–7
life purpose, 23–24, 26–28
listening skills, 47, 305–7
Live Your Best Life Now course, 29
LivePlan, 84, 89, 117
loss leader, 190
love relationships, 24
Lublin, Jill, 226

M

maintenance services, 90–91
major achievements section of business plan, 100
Management Tools Binder, 144–45, 150, 166–67, 172
manager managing others, 56, 554
mantras, 41
market analysis, 101–2
market definition section of business plan, 101–2
marketing, 215–41
  Brand Integrity Guide, 220–23
  essential types of, 218–20
  goals, 219–20
  ideal client/avatar and, 216–18, 225, 298
  Marketing Assessment, 240–41
  public relations (PR) and, 225–27
  sponsorships, 230–33
  strategies, 223–25
  telesummits, 227–30
  video, 236–39
marketing plan, 15, 101, 145, 158, 174
McDonald's, 105
meditation, 38, 82
Meehle, Suzanne, 107
memorandum of understanding (agreement), 130, 235–36
Microsoft Innovative Business Award, 6
mindset, 10–15, 38, 103, 246, 286, 287, 289, 291, 296–97
Mindset Assessment, 39–42
mini-business plan, 28–29
minimum wage, 134
Miracle, The: Six Steps to Enlightenment (Vitale), 293

mission, 69
mission statement, 87, 104–5
Momentum Map, 191, 204–10
money, 243–83, 286–87, 298
　budgets, 243, 244, 249, 266–68, 290–91
　cash budget worksheet, 276–79
　cash calculator, 84, 258–59, 261–62, 267, 292, 299
　cash versus profit, 264–65
　cash versus sales, 263–64, 271
　credit cards, 290–91
　financial plan, 15, 88, 97, 249, 253–54
　leveraging resources, 275–77
　paying yourself, 247–49
　pricing (see pricing)
　Profit Points Business Assessment, 279–83
　revenue streams, 250–52, 259, 261–62
　Revenue Wheel, 197, 249–52, 258, 267, 277, 299
Motivating the Masses Inc., 57, 68, 120, 143, 220, 234–35, 273, 294
motivation, 87–88, 97
Murphy, Keri, 236
must goal, 90
Myers-Briggs Type Indicator (MBTI), 59

N
needs analysis, 196–97
net profit, 273
networking, 15
New York Times, 24, 34
Nichols, Lisa, 57, 62–64, 79, 120, 143, 220, 234–35, 294
99designs, 223
nondisclosure agreement, 70
numbers (see money)

O
OneNote, 151
online businesses, 71
online freelance communities, 136
operating procedures, 75
operations infrastructure (see organizational systems)
organizational chart, 154
organizational systems, 143–72, 297–98
　basic systems, 150–51
　building functional plan, 148–50
　client management system, 159–61
　evaluating, 166–72
　job descriptions, 161–65
　leadership and, 46, 65–66

Management Tools Binder, 144–45, 150, 166–67, 172
　reliance on others, 146–48
　scalable systems, 152–53
　SOPs and (see standard operating procedures)
　Systems Self-Assessment, 170–72
overtime, 134

P
parenting, 24
passion, 23, 24, 27, 29, 45, 72
Passion Test, The: The Effortless Path to Discovering Your Life Purpose (Atwood and Atwood), 24
payroll account, 133
percentage growth, 273–74
performance management, 93, 97
perseverance and persistence, 23
personal development coaching, 12, 13, 15, 24–25, 41, 216–17
personnel systems, 152
pharmaceutical industry, 57–58
physical location, 71
pitch (summary document), 89
pitch deck, 69, 70
Plan and Review Form, 139–40, 308–9
planning (see business plan)
poverty mentality, 246
prayer, 82
press/media release, 226–27
pricing, 76, 101, 176, 180, 201
　Base Price Worksheet, 254–58, 267, 299, 309–11
profit and loss statement (P&L), 178–81
Profit Coach brand, 78
Profit Points Business Assessment, 279–83
profitability section of business plan, 101
profits, 273
project description, 152
promotional strategies, 102
psychographics, 224–25, 231, 233
public relations (PR), 225–27, 298

Q
quantifiable expectations, leadership and, 50–51

R
reality, creating, 19
reciprocity, law of, 78
reinforce/improve stage of business, 71, 74–75

relationship-building, leadership and, 46–47
relationship coaching, 217
reporting system, 49
responsibility, 17, 18
results-based management, leadership and, 48–49, 66
results-based marketing, 218
résumés, 127
retirement planning, 265
return on investment (ROI), 69, 70, 98
Rev.com, 228
Revenue Wheel, 197, 249–52, 258, 267, 277, 299
Ring, Joanie, 18
Ritz-Carlton, 124
Rush, Steve, 47–48

S
sales, 49, 75, 135, 145, 148, 150, 173–213, 186, 216, 298
    Average Ticket Worksheet, 192–95
    calls, 95, 186
    closing, 186
    developing strategy, 197–98
    fear and, 174, 202
    Momentum Map, 191, 204–10
    needs analysis, 196–97
    pricing (see pricing)
    profit and loss statement (P&L) and, 178–81
    revenue streams, 189–92
    Sales Member Analysis Worksheet, 151, 181–89, 259, 277
    Selling Success Assessment (SSA), 210–13
    stair-step question process and, 198–202, 298
    start-up system, 151
Salon Training International, 114
Saville Assessment, 59
SBA (Small Business Administration), 253, 254
SCORE (Service Corps of Retired Executives), 94, 118
Seaver, Ron, 231
Secrets of the Millionaire Mind (Eker), 235
Securities and Exchange Commission (SEC), 63, 68, 69
Sedona Method, 41
self-assessment, 37–42
self-control, leadership and, 45–46, 297
self-worth, 11
Selling Success Assessment (SSA), 210–13

Seven Stages of Business, 71–80
"shoulds," 27
skip management, 154
slow bleeder, 180
Small Business Development Center, 118
soap operas, 37
social media, 150, 151, 218, 228
SOPs (see standard operating procedures)
Speakertunity, 228
speed to market, 96
Spin Selling Questions, 198
spiritual life, 24
sponsorships, 230–33
stair-step question process, 198–202, 298
standard operating procedures (SOPs), 115
    accountability and, 158–59
    benefits of, 156–57
    creating, 154–56
Starbucks, 153
Step into the Big Time sections, 7, 34, 37–40, 63–66, 116–18, 140–42, 168–72, 210–13, 240–41, 277–83, 295–96
strategic partnerships, 223, 234, 252
strategic plan, 88
    core elements in, 91
    developing, 93–96
    perspective and, 92–93
stretch goal, 90
subconscious self-sabotage, 38–39
Susie Snacks (newsletter), 207
SusieCarder.com, 63, 140, 205, 294, 296
SWOT analysis, 107–13, 297
sympathy, distinguished from empathy, 47–48
Systems Self-Assessment, 170–72

T
Tao Te Ching, 61
target customer, 69
tax strategist, 271, 274–75
team, 95, 119–42 (see also organizational systems)
    accountability and, 136–38
    average business, 122–23
    best practices for new hires, 121–22
    compensation, 133, 135–36
    conditions of fulfillment and, 138–39
    family members, 127–29
    guiding principles for, 119–23, 130, 297
    Harrison Assessment and, 126–28
    hiring, 68–69, 75, 100
    independent contractors, 130–34, 297

internships, 134–35
  meetings, 137–38
  Plan and Review Form and, 139–40,
    308–9
  tax implications, 132–34
  Team Assessment, 140–42
telesummits, 227–30, 298
test anxiety, 168–69
therapist, working with, 41
360 Feedback, 59
Time magazine, 24
training programs, 95, 147–49, 187, 196
transparency, 108
Twitter, 151

U
Upwork, 223

V
value statement, 106
variable costs, 268–69

verbal acknowledgment, 51
video marketing, 236–39
visions, 57, 58
  business, 95–96
  cultural, 95, 96
  vision board, 18, 81, 82
  vision statement, 102–4
visualization, 19–21, 32, 34, 81, 82, 85
Vitale, Joe, 17, 215, 293

W
Warby Parker, 105
Wealth Dynamics, 59
Welch, Jack, 57
What Color Is Your Parachute? (Bolles),
    24, 25

Y
Yohn, Denise Lee, 106
Your Beauty Network, 85
YouTube, 239

ABOUT THE AUTH

Susie Carder is *The Profit Coach*. Her company, SC thousands of businesses to establish a solid business i develop systems to achieve exponential growth usin; tainable business strategies. She does this through pr ing, training, and coaching on an international level.

Susie believes that business should be fun, that ow: to pay themselves first, and that having a solid infra: freedom and predictable success.

Susie is the former president and COO of Motiva Inc., and the author of several books, including the h salon industry standard, *Passion: A Salon Professional Building a Successful Business* (1995; Salon Training Inte

Susie is a twenty-year business veteran who has bui lion companies and sold her businesses for millions. Sk distributor of the Harrison Assessment and helps client: results in their leadership positions. Susie has worked business leaders, including John Assaraf, Lisa Nichols,

via Andrews, Keri Murphy, Doug Carter, Redken, Paul Mitchell, mpson Learning, Dell, and more.

Connect with Susie Carder:
Website: SusieCarder.com
Facebook: Facebook.com/SusieCarder
Twitter: Twitter.com/SusieCarder
LinkedIn: Susie Carder
Instagram: SusieCarder